101 Crossword Puzzles For Dummies, Volume 2

Cheat Sheet

W9-AAI-172

Top Ten Three-Letter Women's Names

1. EVE Arden
2. EVA Gabor
3. AVA Gardner
4. IDA Lupino
5. UNA Merkel
6. INA Balin
7. ALI MacGraw
8. AYN Rand
9. ANN Blyth
10. MIA Farrow

Top Ten Three-Letter Men's Names

1. ELI Wallach
2. RIP Torn
3. ART Carney
4. IRA Gershwin
5. LEN Deighton
6. LEE Majors
7. NAT King Cole
8. DAN Rather
9. IAN Fleming
10. ROD Steiger

Top Ten Four-Letter Women's Names

1. ELLA Fitzgerald
2. ANNA Sten
3. RENE Russo
4. EDIE Adams
5. ETTA James
6. ELKE Sommer
7. LENA Horne
8. OONA O'Neill Chaplin
9. ELLE McPherson
10. RITA Hayworth

Top Ten Four-Letter Men's Names

1. ERLE Gardner
2. EERO Saarinen
3. ARLO Guthrie
4. OMAR Sharif
5. ALEC Baldwin
6. ELIA Lamb
7. ELIE Wiesel
8. OTTO Preminger
9. ERIC Ambler
10. ENOS Slaughter

Characters Found in the Clues

- **2 wds or 3 wds:** One of these tags simply means that the entry is comprised of more than one word. For example, you may see a clue like "Garbage, 2 wds," that corresponds to the entry ASH CAN.

- **?:** A clue that ends in a question mark is up to something sneaky. The entry for such a clue is either related to the theme, a play on words, or both. For example, the clue "Day follower?" could be asking for either LIGHT or NIGHT.

- **abbr.:** The entry is some sort of an abbreviation. For example, the clue "Post office abbr." yields the entry SASE.

- **e.g.:** The clue is an example of the person or thing alluded to in the entry. For example, the clue "Dan and Walter, e.g." corresponds to the entry ANCHOR.

- **var.:** The spelling of the entry varies from the typical spelling.

Hungry Minds™

For Dummies™: Bestselling Book Series for Beginners

101 Crossword Puzzles For Dummies, Volume 2

Cheat Sheet

Top Ten Birds in the Grid

1. EMU = "Ratite"
2. ANI = "Blackbird"
3. ARA = "Macaw"
4. ERNE = "Sea eagle"
5. MOA = "Flightless bird"
6. SORA = "Rail"
7. LOON = "Diving bird"
8. TERN = "Gull"
9. DODO = "Extinct bird"
10. RHEA = "Ostrich"

Top Ten Crossword Menagerie

1. ANT = "Emmet"
2. EEL = "Moray"
3. EWE = "Lamb's mom"
4. RAM = "Lamb's dad"
5. SOW = "Farm animal"
6. ROAN = "Type of horse"
7. ANOA = "Celebes ox"
8. ASP = "Poisonous snake"
9. IBEX = "Mountain goat"
10. GNU = "Wildebeest"

Top Ten Mythic Figures

1. ARES = "God of war"
2. MARS = "God of war"
3. AMOR = "God of love"
4. EROS = "God of love"
5. IRIS = "Rainbow goddess"
6. LEDA = "Mother of Castor"
7. ERIS = "Goddess of discord"
8. EOS = "Goddess of the dawn"
9. HERA = "Wife of Zeus"
10. RHEA = "Mother of the gods"

Top Ten Abbreviations in the Grid

1. ETC = "Common catchall"
2. ET AL = "List ender"
3. EPA = "Govt. agency"
4. ETA = "Airport abbreviation"
5. FCC = "Govt. watchdog"
6. PTA = "School org."
7. RNA = "Genetic material, for short"
8. DNA = "Genetic material, for short"
9. REM = "Sleep cycle"
10. UAR = "OPEC member"

Praise for Michelle Arnot and Crossword Puzzles For Dummies

"Crosswords! Cryptograms! Acrostics! No need to be puzzled any longer. This addition to the Hungry Minds library deciphers and reveals the secrets behind the grid. You find out how puzzles are constructed, plus you get insiders' steps and hints, puzzle makers' techniques, along with sample puzzles from the top constructors. Beginners and pros alike will enjoy Michelle Arnot's insight into the world's greatest pastime. She will have you quickly join the millions of puzzlers who delight in word game addiction."
— Marilynn Huret, Editor, *At The Crossroads,*
www.atthecrossroads.com

"It is a pleasure to endorse Michelle Arnot's sprightly written book, which opens the door to the adventure and joy that is puzzle solving."
— Trude Michel Jaffe, Editor, *Los Angeles Times* Syndicate
Daily Puzzle

"Michelle Arnot is one of the clearest, liveliest, most entertaining writers in the world of puzzles. Here is an excellent beginner's guide to mastering the secrets of crosswords."
— Will Shortz, Crossword Editor, *The New York Times*

"If you're a committed puzzlehead, this book is a MUST. You've got to buy it. If you're not a puzzlehead, give your brain a break — an enchanting workout. Develop your vocabulary, impress your friends, and live happily forevermore!!"
— Thomas H. Middleton, Double Acrostics Constructor,
The New York Times and *Harper's* magazine

"Michelle Arnot's *Crossword Puzzles For Dummies* seduces newcomers into working puzzles and entertains acrossionados with a clear but comprehensive approach to the subject. She writes with authority about the culture and history of crossword puzzles from their origins to where you can find them today on the Web, gives helpful advice for solving various styles of American and British puzzles, and tests your skills with quizzes and sample puzzles. This is a great book!"
— John J. Chew, III, Chairman, National SCRABBLE® Association
Dictionary Committee, www.math.utoronto.ca/jjchew

"I give a hearty bravo to *Crossword Puzzles For Dummies*. I especially enjoyed Chapter 13, "Deciphering the Cryptic Crossword," and encourage everyone of all ages to check it out."
— Frank W. Lewis, "Setter" for the *Nation* Cryptic Crossword

101 CROSSWORD PUZZLES FOR DUMMIES.®
VOLUME 2

Edited by Michelle Arnot

Hungry Minds™

HUNGRY MINDS, INC.

New York, NY ◆ Cleveland, OH ◆ Indianapolis, IN

101 Crossword Puzzles for Dummies® Volume 2

Published by
Hungry Minds, Inc.
909 Third Avenue
New York, NY 10022
www.hungryminds.com

Library of Congress Catalog Card No.: 97-81243

ISBN: 0-7645-5110-8

Printed in the United States of America

10 9 8 7 6 5

1B/SR/QT/QR/IN

Distributed in the United States by Hungry Minds, Inc.

Distributed by CDG Books Canada Inc. for Canada; by Transworld Publishers Limited in the United Kingdom; by IDG Norge Books for Norway; by IDG Sweden Books for Sweden; by IDG Books Australia Publishing Corporation Pty. Ltd. for Australia and New Zealand; by TransQuest Publishers Pte Ltd. for Singapore, Malaysia, Thailand, Indonesia, and Hong Kong; by Gotop Information Inc. for Taiwan; by ICG Muse, Inc. for Japan; by Intersoft for South Africa; by Eyrolles for France; by International Thomson Publishing for Germany, Austria and Switzerland; by Distribuidora Cuspide for Argentina; by LR International for Brazil; by Galileo Libros for Chile; by Ediciones ZETA S.C.R. Ltda. for Peru; by WS Computer Publishing Corporation, Inc., for the Philippines; by Contemporanea de Ediciones for Venezuela; by Express Computer Distributors for the Caribbean and West Indies; by Micronesia Media Distributor, Inc. for Micronesia; by Chips Computadoras S.A. de C.V. for Mexico; by Editorial Norma de Panama S.A. for Panama; by American Bookshops for Finland.

For general information on Hungry Minds' products and services please contact our Customer Care Department within the U.S. at 800-762-2974, outside the U.S. at 317-572-3993 or fax 317-572-4002.

For sales inquiries and reseller information, including discounts, premium and bulk quantity sales, and foreign-language translations, please contact our Customer Care Department at 800-434-3422, fax 317-572-4002, or write to Hungry Minds, Inc., Attn: Customer Care Department, 10475 Crosspoint Boulevard, Indianapolis, IN 46256.

For information on licensing foreign or domestic rights, please contact our Sub-Rights Customer Care Department at 650-653-7098.

For information on using Hungry Minds' products and services in the classroom or for ordering examination copies, please contact our Educational Sales Department at 800-434-2086 or fax 317-572-4005.

Please contact our Public Relations Department at 212-884-5163 for press review copies or 212-884-5000 for author interviews and other publicity information or fax 212-884-5400.

For authorization to photocopy items for corporate, personal, or educational use, please contact Copyright Clearance Center, 222 Rosewood Drive, Danvers, MA 01923, or fax 978-750-4470.

About the Author

A funny thing happened to **Michelle Arnot** on her way to a Master's degree in 18th century French literature at Columbia University: She ended up making a career of her hobby in crosswords. Instead of writing a thesis, Michelle constructed a crossword. When the puzzle was accepted for publication, she switched gears immediately.

Michelle has been omnipresent in the world of puzzles since the publication of her book *What's Gnu: A History of the Crossword Puzzle* (Vintage Books, 1981). She has served as Editor and Publisher of dozens of national puzzle magazines, most notably for *The Herald Tribune* and the Kappa Publishing Group. Additionally, she taught seminars on solving for the New School For Social Research and the Learning Annex. Her editorial career gradually extended into the marketing of puzzle magazines in the direct mail arena. Michelle edited *101 Crossword Puzzles For Dummies,* Volume 1, and she is also the author of *Crossword Puzzles For Dummies,* both published by Hungry Minds, Inc.

In her other life, Michelle is a health writer who specializes in subjects of interest to women. She's written books on topics as diverse as infertility and foot care.

When she's not at the word processor, Michelle is often found exploring London, where she currently lives with her husband and daughter. You can easily identify Michelle in warm weather by her T-shirt adorned with a crossword grid.

Dedication

To my husband Roger with love at our 20th anniversary. Time flies when you're solving puzzles!

Author's Acknowledgments

The author extends sincere thanks to Mark Reiter of IMG for coming up with the great idea that became this series, and to all the good people at Hungry Minds, Inc., and Dummies Press for creating this unique opportunity. Hats off to Mark Butler for taking the project off the shelf, and to Allison Solomon for her marketing efforts on my behalf. Above all, thanks to my editor, the serene and supremely talented Mary Goodwin. Her insight, patience, direction, good humor, and genuine interest created a productive working relationship that has extended over three books and one ocean. And to think there's another great lady just like her in the world — she's got a twin!

A stellar group of talented constructors provided the puzzles that fill the pages of this fine collection. Thanks go to Florence Adler, Janet Bender, Mary Brindamour, Theresa Curry, Gayle Dean, John Greenman, Randall Hartman, Geri Harris, Betty Jorgensen, Alfio Micci, Gregory Paul, Fred Piscop, Scott Schilling, and Jay Sullivan. Special thanks to Marilynn Huret of At The Crossroads (www.atthecrossroads.com) for her contribution and valuable input, and to my technical editor Nancy Schuster for infusing the material with her wit and wisdom.

As I've journeyed in the land of puzzles I have been fortunate to meet scores of puzzle people. These people have influenced me and generously shared their knowledge. Among these many talented editorial people, too numerous to fully list here, special thanks to Will Shortz, Stan Newman, and Trude Jaffe. All the best to Mary Lou Tobias on her retirement after a long, productive career with Official Publications. Also thank you to the Kappa Publishing Group, which I've had the pleasure of being affiliated with for over a decade.

Publisher's Acknowledgments

We're proud of this book; please send us your comments through our Hungry Minds Online Registration Form located at: www.dummies.com.

Some of the people who helped bring this book to market include the following:

Acquisitions, Editorial, and Media Development

Project Editor: Mary Goodwin

Acquisitions Editor: Mark Butler

Copy Editors: Joe Jansen, Rowena Rappaport

Technical Editor: Nancy Schuster

Editorial Manager: Elaine Brush

Editorial Assistant: Paul Kuzmic

Reprint Editor: Bethany André

Production

Project Coordinator: E. Shawn Aylsworth

Layout and Graphics: Lou Boudreau, Matt Coleman, J. Tyler Connor, Angela F. Hunckler, Brent Savage, Janet Seib, Deirdre Smith

Special Graphics: Lou Boudreau

Proofreaders: Christine Berman, Rachel Garvey, Henry Lazarek, Nancy Price, Janet M. Withers

Indexer: Sharon Hilgenberg

General and Administrative

Hungry Minds, Inc.: John Kilcullen, CEO; Bill Barry, President and COO; John Ball, Executive VP, Operations & Administration; John Harris, CFO

Hungry Minds Consumer Reference Group

Business: Kathleen A. Welton, Vice President and Publisher; Kevin Thornton, Acquisitions Manager

Cooking/Gardening: Jennifer Feldman, Associate Vice President and Publisher

Education/Reference: Diane Graves Steele, Vice President and Publisher

Lifestyles: Kathleen Nebenhaus, Vice President and Publisher; Tracy Boggier, Managing Editor

Pets: Dominique De Vito, Associate Vice President and Publisher; Tracy Boggier, Managing Editor

Travel: Michael Spring, Vice President and Publisher; Suzanne Jannetta, Editorial Director; Brice Gosnell, Managing Editor

Hungry Minds Consumer Editorial Services: Kathleen Nebenhaus, Vice President and Publisher; Kristin A. Cocks, Editorial Director; Cindy Kitchel, Editorial Director

Hungry Minds Consumer Production: Debbie Stailey, Production Director

Hungry Minds Packaging: Marc J. Mikulich, Vice President, Brand Strategy and Research

Contents at a Glance

Cartoons at a Glance

By Rich Tennant

page 3

page 125

page 135

page 111

page 69

Fax: 978-546-7747
E-mail: richtennant@the5thwave.com
World Wide Web: www.the5thwave.com

Table of Contents

· ·

Introduction

●●

Happy 85th birthday to the crossword puzzle! Unlike some octogenarians, the hardy crossword shows no sign of slowing down. In fact, every day more than 2,000 newspapers include a puzzle in their pages, to the delight of 40 million avid American solvers (and counting).

In *101 Crossword Puzzles For Dummies,* Volume 2, you're guaranteed to find hours of puzzle amusement. These puzzles are especially geared to suit every taste or, if you're on the fence, to develop a special favorite. Go for it! Compulsive solving is the one compulsion that comes guilt-free.

If puzzles make you think of dictionaries, think again. The crosswords in this book are chockablock with puns, rhymes, jokes, song lyrics, and other up-to-the-minute references to pop culture. Puzzles are designed to amuse and relax, rather than send you back to the books.

If you are new to the world of the Across and Down clues, a copy of my other book, *Crossword Puzzles For Dummies,* published by IDG Books Worldwide, Inc., might be the ticket to set you on the road. Filled with tips and strategies, you find some techniques that jump-start the fun.

Why a ...For Dummies Crossword Puzzle Book?

Yes, this book is different from those other puzzle books you see on the shelf or in the bins at the supermarket (you know, right next to the *National Enquirer*). *101 Crosswords Puzzles For Dummies,* Volume 2, delivers puzzles, puzzles, puzzles in a way that makes them easier and more fun to work:

- ✔ You get 101 of the puzzles that people actually like to work, including daily-size crosswords, Sunday-size crosswords, acrostics, diagramlesses, and cryptograms.

- ✔ The puzzles make use of today's most common *repeaters,* or words that frequently appear in crossword puzzles.

- ✔ The puzzles vary in theme and difficulty, but none of the puzzles is insurmountable. I provide solving tips and hints when I think that you may appreciate a boost.

- ✔ The clues are easy to read, and the grid blocks allow you plenty of room to pencil in your answer.

- ✔ You have room in the margins and around the page to doodle with possible entries before you enter them in the grid.

- ✔ You always find the grid located close to the outside of the page, making it easy to write in your answers.

- ✔ Each puzzle has a number (and most of the time a name, too), making it easy for you to find the answers to your puzzle in Appendix A.

- ✔ I make the answer grids large enough so that you can actually read them. Go ahead and put away that magnifying glass.

How to Use This Book

I divide this book into five parts:

Part I: Working Daily Puzzles

Every puzzle in this part is no larger than 15 x 15 squares, which should be the perfect size puzzle to conquer during your lunch break or over breakfast.

Part II: Sunday Puzzle Fun

The puzzles in this part are generally 21 x 21 squares, which means that you may need to set aside some time to enjoy these puzzles. Most of the puzzles offer a theme to add to your solving pleasure.

Part III: Stepping Away from the Crossword

What does it take to be a "non-crossword" puzzle? In Part III, you find cryptograms, acrostics, and diagramlesses waiting for your amusement. Visit this part of the book for a little variety in your puzzle life.

Part IV: The Part of Tens

Part IV offers quick answers about some of the most frequently asked questions I hear about creating crossword puzzles. I also provide you with some tips to help give you a leg up into the grid.

Part V: Appendixes

You get to satisfy your curiosity in this part. In Appendix A, you can find the answers to all the puzzles in the book. Appendix B offers a guiding hand to working the non-crossword puzzles you find in Part III.

Icons Used in This Book

I use icons periodically throughout this book to point out important tips and topics that I want you to know.

As in any game, puzzles have rules, both written and unwritten. Just to make sure that you're on your toes, this icon reminds you of these important rules.

Next to this icon you find advice and information that can make you a savvier solver.

Sometimes I offer hints on how to solve particular puzzles in the book. If you'd rather take a crack at the puzzle without my help, this icon steers you clear of any information that may spoil the challenge for you.

Part I
Working Daily Puzzles

The 5th Wave   By Rich Tennant

"I'm going to conduct a little word association exam with you. Just tell me what 7-letter word pops into your head when I say, 'Metallurgical waste product.'"

Puzzle 1-1: Giant Steps

The title of a puzzle applies only to the theme entries. For example, in this puzzle, the title helps you with solving 17 and 64 Across and 10 and 35 Down.

Across

1 Boxer's moves
5 Composer of "Over There"
10 Crooked
14 Director Kazan
15 Rancho rope
16 Light bulb, in a cartoon
17 Charlie Chan's creator
20 Additions, to Johnnie Cochran
21 Wild ducks
22 Isinglass
24 Abound
25 KLM rival
28 Gourd fruit
30 Platforms
34 Word with apple or grass
36 1995 NL Rookie of the Year
38 Cable network
39 Prefix with freeze
40 Hobo
42 Forbidden fragrance?
43 Wear the crown
45 Bangkok native
46 Went over 55
47 Freshmen at West Point
49 Once more
51 Campus org. of yore
52 ". . . happily — after"

54 Long-legged example of 3 Down
56 — *Graffiti*
60 Eternally
64 1994 baseball film
66 HS requirement
67 Cut up
68 One of the Three Bears
69 Yachting
70 Barbara and Anthony
71 Stroller in London

Down

1 Make fun of
2 Jai —
3 Category for 54 Across
4 Capital of Oregon
5 Lunar shape
6 Poetic word
7 Damage
8 No longer on deck
9 Sewed up, with "down"
10 Marital enthusiasts?
11 German river
12 Dork
13 Soviet news agency
18 Party pooper
19 Shine, as in one's eye
23 Nautical direction
25 Steep slope
26 Synthetic fiber
27 Composer Erik
29 Nebraska city
31 Ginger — (cookies)
32 Receded
33 Desert Storm missiles
35 WW I cannon
37 Man from Muscat
41 Spotted horses
44 Novelist Shute
48 Withdraw
50 Sly trick
53 Fanatical
55 Overwhelm with work
56 — mater
57 Mamma and Farrow
58 Suffix with major
59 City on the Riviera
61 Culture medium
62 Arizona city
63 Stitches in a row
65 Four-star off.

Puzzle 1-2: Have You Read . . .

Across

1 "Tea for —"
4 PC key
8 First edition, perhaps
12 Capt. Kirk's record
13 Have —! (Give me a break!)
16 Skillfully
17 Miler Sebastian
18 Account book
19 Told a whopper
20 Hugo's tale of woe
23 Turner or Danson
24 Gambits
25 Went too far
29 Sports org.
30 Creators of *Sesame Street,* for short
33 Milanese money
34 Ump's call
36 City on the Missouri
38 Hemingway collection that includes "The Killers"
42 Jesse of Olympics fame
43 — Wednesday
44 Experiment
45 Draft org.
46 HS classroom
49 Gets cozy
51 Sault Ste. — Canals
53 — Aviv
54 D.H. Lawrence tale of domination
59 Derogatory remark
60 Medium-priced fur
61 Thumbs up
63 Gander's remark
64 Footless
65 Python, for one
66 Wound up
67 Mates
68 Big Dipper setting

Down

1 Nurse's asset, for short
2 Sheep's clothing, perhaps
3 Arched molding
4 Soothed
5 Dostoyevsky's story of Prince Myshkin
6 Warren Beatty film of 1981
7 Aged beer
8 Galas
9 NY theater award
10 Corrida cheers
11 *The Spanish Tragedy* playwright
14 Summer TV fare
15 Worthless stuff
21 Scattered
22 Under
25 Actor Edward James —
26 Watches
27 Sea eagles
28 "Oh, I was so stupid"
30 Abdul's mount
31 "— are the good old days"
32 Desires
35 Fit — T
37 Blotch
39 Mecca religion
40 Where to find Annapolis alums: abbr.
41 Kafka's courtroom chronicle
47 Sphere of activity
48 Raise the price, at Sotheby's
50 Calyxes
51 Vague
52 Prevent, legally
54 Trudge
55 Respiratory organ
56 Wagner's earth goddess
57 Arrests
58 Resembled, with "after"
59 — *Stoops to Conquer*
62 "Wheel of Fortune" Starr

Puzzle 1-3: Seeing Double

55 Tune by The Playmates, 1958
60 College refrain (circa 1920)
63 Type of duck?
64 Ordered
65 "There's no fool like — . . ."
66 Its root is money
67 River through Hesse
68 Heads, to Héloïse
69 Go soft

Down

1 Stinger
2 Turkish title
3 Actor McClure
4 Pay no heed
5 Dam site in the Mideast
6 Type of carpet
7 Farm fixture
8 — *the President's Men*
9 Extinct bird
10 Regional languages
11 Sandwich, for one
12 The inner you
13 Miami hoopsters
19 "— pleasure!"
21 Long arm of the Amazon
24 Robin's truelove
25 Namesakes of Nora's pooch
26 "Glory — in the highest"
27 Intention, in law
28 Title for José or Mateo
29 African scourge
30 Psychologist May
31 Full speed direction
32 "I — hug"
33 Coupe relative
36 Oodles
39 One with a visa . . .
44 . . . and what he takes
47 One of the Simpsons
49 Insignia
51 Peruses
52 French cleric
53 *Abbey* — (Beatles album)
54 Style
55 Shape of Italy
56 Model Macpherson
57 Icicle hangout
58 Actor Jannings
59 Attack with snowballs
61 Face Guidry
62 *A Chorus Line* hit

Across

1 Dry gully in the Sahara
5 State of Northern India
10 Spoon's partner, in rhyme
14 Wide-eyed
15 Neil Diamond classic
16 Words of understanding
17 Avoid
18 Produce center in Washington
20 Pacific island
22 "— my heart in San Francisco . . ."
23 Campaigned
24 Word with soul or stale
26 Spud
29 Grouch's homes on *Sesame Street*
34 Lennon's love
35 File by category
37 "My country 'tis of —"
38 Meaning
40 *As You Like It* role
41 *The Bad* —
42 Actor Sharif
43 Finally
45 Nabokov heroine
46 Sam the newsman
48 Fortification
50 Workbench adjunct
51 Edge
52 Weapons, to Pierre

Puzzle 1-4: Seaside Sights

In a clue, the word "opener" means prefix, as in 22 Down.

Across

1 1994 NL MVP Bagwell
5 Gloomy atmosphere
9 Small hat
14 Jump for Tara
15 *The Time Machine* people
16 Three-time Wimbledon champ
17 El — (weather phenomenon)
18 Milieu for 14 Across
19 Gets on a horse
20 Dept. of Transportation division
23 Camper's cooking fuel
24 Genetic ID
25 The Altar constellation
28 Mideast peninsula
31 Woodcutter's warning
33 Brawl
36 One of the Queen's residences
38 Old Testament book
40 Chinese philosophy
41 Apple pie à la —
42 Antonia Fraser's fictional sleuth
47 Wings or Sox color
48 Playing marbles
49 *Golden Boy* playwright
51 Solo of *Star Wars*
52 Ernesto Guevara
54 Shrimp dish
58 "Good Vibrations" guys
61 Iris color
64 Part of Indonesia
65 Egg or bed follower
66 Porcelain variety
67 — Steven
68 Lotion ingredient
69 Short putt
70 Owner's document
71 — souci (carefree)

Down

1 Two-faced god
2 Walk the earth
3 Stolen goods dealer
4 Puts the pedal to the metal
5 One's public image
6 Dismounted
7 Yearn
8 Israeli political party
9 Land, to a strategist
10 *Metamorphosis* poet
11 Letters after a geometry proof
12 English actress Mary
13 SAT administrator: abbr.
21 Black cuckoos
22 Opener for thesis
25 Loathe
26 English novelist Charles
27 Ready for battle
29 Picnic pests
30 Sun Valley's state
32 Movie studio letters
33 Indian prince
34 Last Greek letter
35 *The — in White* (Wilkie Collins novel)
37 Crucifix
39 Command to Fido
43 Fine Flemish lace
44 Arthur of tennis fame
45 Cancel
46 Engrave with acid
50 Native-born Israelis
53 Receded
55 Dough
56 Pilot's marker
57 Capri and Man
58 Actress Garr
59 Roof overhang
60 Away from the wind
61 Single or double
62 Org. for Dr. Spock
63 Use a microwave

Puzzle 1-5: Masterful Mix

Where a clue mentions Caesar, the entry is in Latin (see 58 Down).

Across

1 Just misses the basket
5 9th grader, for example
9 Sailor
13 Land in the news, 1998
14 Practice rhetoric
15 "Un bel di" is one
16 Word from Mork
17 Posh accommodations on the *Titanic*
19 Little Ricky's dad
20 Aficionado
21 Some freight vessels
22 *Family Matters* nerd
24 Actor Wallach
25 It may follow a quake
27 Foretell
31 Drivel
32 He created Rosemary's baby
34 Schemes
36 Bird of Paradise constellation
38 Nostalgic film of '82 set in Baltimore
40 Airline to Tel Aviv
41 *ER* extra
43 Comparatively nasty
45 Title for Jeanne or Thérèse
46 Colorful mementos of Mexico
48 Packed
50 — Vegas
51 Take care of

52 Island of giant statues in the Pacific
56 Mythical goat-man god
57 Eye part
60 Show-offy
62 Producer Preminger
63 Buster Brown's dog
64 Typesetter's removals
65 Noah's son
66 Kenton or Getz
67 Belgian river
68 Brontë's *Jane* —

Down

1 Orange throwaway
2 "Dies —" (Latin hymn)
3 Gentleness
4 Wriggle from guilt
5 Kafka subject
6 Merit
7 Creatures from outer space
8 Curl up
9 Part of la casa
10 Composer Khachaturian
11 Thpeak like thith
12 News agency in Russia
14 Bid
18 Like some cereals
23 — Nidre (Hebrew prayer)
24 Sea eagles
25 Trolley
26 Boxing ring enclosure
27 Hawaiian exports: Span.
28 Stout
29 *Forsyte Saga* author
30 Related on Mom's side
33 Psychic emanations
35 Rosebud, for one
37 Letter opener
39 Feels insulted about
42 Biblical spy
44 66, for one: abbr.
47 Do a take-off on
49 Lazy
51 More together upstairs
52 Lizards
53 Landed
54 It's a long story
55 Fed. agents
56 Ashen
58 Road, to Caesar
59 Undetermined amount
61 —, *I Can* (Sammy Davis bio)

Puzzle 1-6: Use Your Noodle

Across

1 "It — Be You"
6 Invitation letters
10 Stereo knob
14 "You — a roll!"
15 Director Kazan
16 Actress Chase
17 Snake in the grass
19 In the doldrums
20 Krazy and others
21 Want-ad letters
22 Sleuth Vance
23 Madly in love
27 Harris or Boss
29 Actress — Knight Pulliam
30 Turkish decrees
32 "— gratias" (thanks to the Lord)
33 Type of race
37 *The Karate —*
38 Distress signal
40 Vitamin stat
42 Lennon's lady
43 "— small world after all . . ."
45 Jackie's sister
47 Teem
49 He played Tortelli on "Cheers"
52 Sea eagles
53 Runs amok
57 Silkworms
58 AFL- —
59 Goddess, in Greece
62 *On Golden —*
63 Abbot's role
66 Within: prefix
67 Grimm character
68 Clink glasses
69 Canine remark
70 Tribulations
71 — a happy note

Down

1 Cabbie
2 Venezuelan mining town
3 Middle managers: abbr.
4 Tournament favorite
5 Somebody
6 Attach again
7 Like a sweater
8 — Veneto
9 Doctor, as an expense account
10 Braggart's feature?
11 *Kate and —*

12 Part of a Jolly Roger
13 Greek isle
18 Like a beet
22 — Beta Kappa
24 Summer coolers
25 Danish weight
26 Valerie Harper sitcom
27 Kon — (Heyerdahl's craft)
28 Habeas corpus, e.g.
31 Old Italian coin
34 Foe of England's Charles I
35 Actress Archer
36 Twilight of the —
39 John, in Ireland
41 Have — in one's bonnet
44 Leading
46 Ophthalmologist's forte
48 Speech
50 Double curve
51 Stage whispers
53 Pepe — of WB cartoons
54 Maine college town
55 "It's a — tell a lie"
56 Bobby-soxer's dance
60 Exxon predecessor
61 Notation on an env.
63 "— do I love thee?"
64 Self
65 Hwy. sign

Puzzle 1-7: Family Affair

Across

1 Skater Lipinski
5 1993 Tom Cruise film, with *The*
9 Capital of Guam
14 Excited
15 Gallimaufry
16 Like a beaver?
17 Durable sitcom of the 1950s
20 Trick alternative
21 Black fly
22 Slalom curve
23 Sean Connery, e.g.
26 H. Rider Haggard title
28 Nacre
34 Free (of)
35 *Rendezvous With* — (Arthur C. Clarke)
36 Wabash Cannonball
38 Finish
41 Capitol party, for short
42 Cream of the crop
43 Palimony lawyer
44 Freudian topics
46 Copy Betsy Ross
47 1970 David Lean film
51 Denial in Dundee
52 Tuck away
53 *The Twilight Zone* creator Serling
56 Go with the —
59 Sign at Woodstock, perhaps

63 John Irving novel about an Indian surgeon
67 Step on the pedal
68 Former Yugoslavian leader
69 Hide
70 Rich dessert
71 Middle East sultanate
72 Mex. miss

Down

1 27th President
2 Seaweed extract
3 Repetitious procedure
4 Shocked
5 "Go — the gold!"
6 Type
7 Place to pick a fight
8 *Dark Side of the* — (Pink Floyd)
9 Lover of art
10 Prattle
11 *Night of the Hunter* screenwriter
12 Costner role of 1987
13 Carney and namesakes
18 Do aquatints
19 Stinger
24 "— the ramparts . . ."
25 Swapped
27 James — Jones
28 A man in a lode of trouble
29 In a strange way
30 Alpha's opposite
31 *The Lifestyles of the Rich and* —
32 Increase
33 Metric measure
34 Confederate soldier, for short
37 In mint condition
39 — Bator, Mongolia
40 *H.M.S.* — (G&S operetta)
45 — *Pepper's Lonely Hearts Club Band*
48 One's inner person
49 Pueblo Indian
50 Punks
53 Huck Finn vessel
54 Frogner Park city
55 Jim Morrison, for a while
57 Preminger of filmdom
58 Fancy
60 Pete Sampras, for one
61 Fanatical group
62 "Como — usted?"
64 *Wayne's World* refrain
65 LAX info
66 Not pro

Puzzle 1-8: Dessert Menu

Common crosswordese includes many non-English words, even words for letters of the alphabet in other languages (see 28 Down).

Across

1 Grammy category for Puff Daddy
4 Nora's pooch
8 Charges
12 Manhattan follower?
13 Grand — home run
14 Endure
15 Ballerina's prop
16 Sarajevo native
17 Play opener
18 Dessert chef?
21 Louvre display
22 Annoy
23 Exhausted
26 — in a million
27 Place for Salinger's catcher
30 Frog's milieu
31 Dessert fruit
32 Country in Southeast Asia
33 Give a hand
34 — in the Family
35 Tears
36 Paternity test material
37 Motorists' org.
38 Dessert selection
45 Norse god
46 Hydrocarbon suffixes
47 "— another thing . . ."
48 Farm fixture
49 "And then there were —"
50 Freshwater fish of Europe
51 Young trailer
52 "— you could make it!"
53 Heavy weight

Down

1 Actress Moreno
2 Perched on
3 Sneak a look
4 Put forth
5 Napped
6 Starchy root
7 Taking a stroll
8 Wine container
9 Per
10 Villa d' — (Italian estate)
11 Awaken
19 Arrive on the airstrip
20 Dublin's location: abbr.
23 Watering hole
24 Dish made from 6 Down
25 Terminus
26 Lubricate
27 Kurasawa film classic
28 Hebrew letter
29 Sigmoid shape
31 Setting alight
32 What Mrs. Sprat couldn't eat
34 Columnist Landers
35 Born and —
36 Generous soul
37 Sports venue
38 At a — (speechless)
39 Fix a text
40 Measure for a marathoner
41 Chemical compound
42 Step
43 Take apart
44 Steinbeck's *East of* —

Puzzle 1-9: Rhyme Scheme

Across

1 Looks at the small print
6 SALT, e.g.
10 UPC units
14 Misbehave
15 Bread, in Bari
16 — Bator
17 Edith Wharton hero Ethan
18 Thor's lord
19 Parcel (out)
20 "— Connection" (Elton John)
22 Soft cheese
23 Auto pioneer Ransom Eli —
24 He has lots and homes
26 Org. for Johnny Cochran
29 London district
31 Before JFK
32 "A Boy Named Sue" singer
34 Atlas pages
36 Receded
40 Book before Philemon
42 Actor Fernando
43 Impoverished
44 *Ghostbusters* goo
45 Agatha's contemporary
47 Border lake
48 Ovine cry
50 "—, poor Yorick!"

52 Nancy Drew's beau
53 Conked out, as a car
57 *La Traviata* tune
59 Pirates' number
60 Novel for young readers by S.E. Hinton
65 Perching on
66 Kind of exam
67 *Platoon* director Oliver
68 Notorious Colombian city
69 Make cookies
70 Mortise insert
71 Place for a patella
72 Eve's grandson
73 Yemen natives

Down

1 *Kon-tiki,* for one
2 Hose shade
3 Tiny amount
4 Disney flier
5 Incantations
6 Part of a farm machine
7 Adjutant
8 Town —
9 Took care of
10 "Flight of the —"
11 Foghorn, for one
12 Math proportion
13 Dirty look
21 Dead Sea kingdom
25 Gulf in the Mideast
26 Book after John
27 Way out of jail
28 Italian vino center
30 *Faust* is one
33 Meal for a humiliated one?
35 Word parts
37 Swiss capital
38 Chanteuse Adams
39 Decorated Easter eggs
41 Member of an elite Navy group
46 Chief Justice Warren
49 Type of microorganism
51 Nap in Tijuana
53 Bite
54 Satellite of Saturn
55 Chameleon's cousin
56 Heavyweight Roberto
58 Following
61 Type of shark
62 New Rochelle college
63 Uppity one
64 Biddies

Puzzle 1-10: Comedy Teams

Korbut is another Olympian with the same given name as 54 Across.

Across

1 Takes advantage of
5 Urged, with "on"
10 Shakespeare's river
14 — -a- Wreck
15 Baby bug
16 Look sad
17 Lhasa — (Tibetan dog)
18 Nom de plume
19 Suffix for a rich person
20 *Babes in Toyland* comedy team
23 Like a tabby
24 John — (tractor brand)
25 Flow slowly
28 Mary Lou of gymnastics
32 Newsman Donaldson
35 Take five
38 Rubberneck
39 *Sing a Song of Six Pants* comedy team
43 Dean Martin theme song
44 *Bridge on the River* —
45 Tippler
46 Tape deck button
48 Smell bad
51 Autos in Asti
54 Olympian Comaneci
58 *Up in Smoke* comedy team
62 — the Red (Viking name)
63 Clarinetist Shaw
64 — Bator
65 "— we forget . . ."
66 Two-fingered greeting
67 "— of your beeswax!"
68 Tableland
69 Proprietor
70 Another name for Mars

Down

1 Europe-Asia boundary range
2 Flower part
3 Come after
4 Mall units
5 Airline to Tel Aviv
6 Lavish affair
7 Prepare the coffee beans
8 Give the slip
9 One of Santa's team
10 Almond-flavored liqueur
11 Partner of null
12 Nashville attraction
13 Wedding announcement word

21 — out a living
22 "You — Beautiful" (Joe Cocker)
26 Drop the ball
27 Slip off the blindfold
29 Touches with the ball
30 Nabisco perennial
31 Hornet's home
32 Play the lead
33 "Alas!"
34 Felix's cry
36 Suture
37 Ivan is one
40 Race track bet
41 Ice star Sonja
42 Draw
47 From the beginning, in music
49 Business letter abbr.
50 Big — (Hawaiian VIP)
52 Hurled
53 Beelzebub
55 Sorrow: poetic
56 Nonsensical
57 Actress Moorehead
58 Manitoba tribesman
59 Snake's sound
60 "No more Mr. — Guy!"
61 Roebuck, e.g.
62 Shade tree

Puzzle 1-11: Plain Geometry

Across

1 Western evergreen
6 Not very exciting
10 Seance sounds
14 Author Rogers St. Johns
15 *Damn Yankees* siren
16 Israeli airline
17 Mogul ruler
18 Colorado tribe
19 '60s hairstyle
20 Solzhenitsyn novel
23 Impresario Hurok
24 Neighborhood in downtown NYC
25 Excessive fondness
27 David Sarnoff's co.
28 Snap
29 "We are — amused" (Queen Victoria)
30 Arizona athlete
35 Actress Joanne
36 Flightless birds
37 — pro nobis
38 Having no cards in a suit
39 *Dateline* network
40 Hoedown event
44 NYC subway line
45 Leo's month: abbr.
46 Stimpy's pal
47 Well-groomed

49 Teen follower
51 Police announcement: abbr.
54 Where Myanmar meets Laos and Thailand
57 Forearm bone
58 Roman fiddler
59 Musical composition
60 Ludwig — van der Rohe
61 Hipbones
62 Diving bird
63 Pea holders
64 Vigor
65 Artist's prop

Down

1 Suit part
2 Sun Valley state
3 Stairway post
4 Norwegian king
5 Cracker and cookie maker
6 Turn red
7 Gambling game
8 Actor Guinness
9 Jewish sect
10 Respond to stimuli
11 FDR's opponent in 1936
12 Pain reliever
13 Super —-mo
21 Dappled horse
22 Type of music
26 Piece by Chopin
27 Real estate abbr.
28 Carson's predecessor
30 French patron saint
31 Complicated, difficult situation
32 Sold at Sotheby's
33 Magician Henning
34 Bikini top
38 Family vehicle
40 Chopin's patron
41 Michael Korda novel: 1985
42 ". . . — saw Elba"
43 Confuse
48 "Heart of —" (Blondie)
49 Courtyards, to Caesar
50 Unhappy sound
51 Choreographer de Mille
52 Freshman at West Point
53 Nut or palm
55 Jodie Foster flick
56 Novelist Ephron
57 Masked man at home?

Puzzle 1-12: Weekend To-Do List

Across

1 — Vista
5 Reduce to liquid
9 Indian princes
14 Actress Cannon of *Ally McBeal*
15 Hautboy
16 *Nana* author Zola
17 Repulsive, informally
18 Red Cross leader Elizabeth
19 Helen Reddy says she's this
20 Gift for Dad
21 To do: Saturday afternoon
23 Adjective for a manor
25 Podiatrist's concern
26 Editorial mark
27 Highlander
32 Republican, for one
34 Sharon of Hollywood
35 Pay follower
36 One of HOMES
37 Reduces, with "down"
38 Hoofer Verdon
39 Part of SASE: abbr.
40 Actress Dern
41 Guitar's ancestors
42 Apple skins
44 Sale terms, perhaps
45 Put on an — (fake it)
46 Bow and arrow event
49 To do: Saturday evening
54 Fabrication
55 Came to
56 Type of school, for short
57 Broad bean
58 Recipient
59 Telegram
60 Mad as — hen
61 Iditarod vehicles
62 Tipsy ones
63 Picnic crashers

Down

1 Mine entrances
2 Legitimate
3 To do: Sunday afternoon
4 *Knock on — Door* (1949 film)
5 Space unit
6 Dark wood
7 "Whatever — wants . . ."
8 High-schooler
9 Fixed a text
10 Italian sweethearts
11 Iwo — (WW II battleground)
12 Economist Greenspan
13 Fax
21 Depend, with "on"
22 Some collars
24 Place for a chapeau
27 Moves
28 Robin Cook book
29 To do: Saturday morning
30 Away from the wind, at sea
31 Kempner and namesakes
32 Chick sound
33 "Rule, Britannia" composer
34 Fake token
37 — Fe
38 Spew
40 Nuts at the Chinese restaurant
41 Place for an aglet
43 Needed
44 *Law and Order* plot lines
46 Forestall
47 Metal bolt
48 Irish poet
49 Crumples, with "up"
50 MP's quarry
51 Set the —
52 Kittenish sounds
53 Mishmash
57 Pilot's org.

Puzzle 1-13: Take the Day Off

Some puzzle titles must be taken literally when solving.

Across

1 Part of MIT: abbr.
5 Danson and Turner
9 Separated
14 Mover and shaker
15 Caspian Sea feeder
16 Type of bear
17 Scat singer Fitzgerald
18 Meter maid of song
19 Cheer up
20 1962 Lemmon film?
23 Young man
24 Mai —
25 Not her
28 Carol
31 Impassive
36 In the thick of
38 Legal serving
40 Idiotic
41 1977 Travolta film?
44 Actress Ryan
45 1987 Best Actress winner
46 Belgrade native
47 Emulate Scorsese
49 Type of duck
51 Piggery
52 *The Plastic — Band*
54 Marker
56 1967 Moody Blues album?

65 1979 Sigourney Weaver thriller
66 Makes doilies
67 Patriot Nathan
68 Sound of a fallen egg
69 Mr. Rochester's hired governess
70 Lamb with a sister Mary
71 Soothsayers
72 Film critic Rex
73 Great Barrier —

Down

1 Bad time for Caesar
2 — contendere
3 — -composed (calm)
4 Fish for bass
5 Just say no
6 Empire State canal
7 Facts and figures
8 Bias
9 Before-dinner drink
10 Prince Charles's sport
11 "Woe is me!"
12 Evaluate
13 Uno y dos
21 007 creator Fleming
22 — *Boot*
25 Member of a Jewish sect
26 Japanese porcelain
27 Picture frame joint
29 Guitarist Clapton
30 *The Charge of the — Brigade*
32 Change for a fiver
33 Washes
34 Like the noble gases
35 Kentucky —
37 Frank Herbert classic sci-fi novel
39 Biblical pronoun
42 Spins a tale
43 Hiked
48 Cable channel
50 Mauna —
53 Peripheral
55 Seating aide
56 Lip
57 Old Greek flask
58 Rank companion
59 Have no —!
60 Funnylady Martha
61 Raison d' —
62 Reason to riot at Macy's?
63 Nobelist Wiesel
64 Unheeding

Puzzle 1-14: Duffer's Course

Across

1 Tiger's cry?
5 Freudian phenomena
10 Male hog
14 Tucked in
15 Gin and —
16 Stake
17 Watering hole?
19 British gun
20 Studies in grammar
21 Comforted
23 "For sale," and others
24 Curved molding
25 Gets one's goat
29 "Satin —"
31 Sal of song
34 Crochet creations
35 Indian princess
36 Baseball stat
37 Role for Caron
38 Quoted
39 Turns right
40 Canine comment
41 Sidney who played Charlie Chan
42 Lobster claw
43 By all means!
44 Hebrew measure
45 Straightens out
46 Chick's home
48 Org. relating to this puzzle theme
49 Dave of fairway fame
52 Turn water into club soda
56 Steak order
57 Pebble Beach event, e.g.
60 "— the Rainbow"
61 "Weird" Al Yankovic take-off
62 British boys' school
63 Tableland
64 Mini, for one
65 — egg account

Down

1 Groupie
2 Newspaper item
3 Philosopher Descartes
4 First garden
5 Spirited horses
6 Fine soil
7 Public house
8 Grape eater's problem
9 Educated
10 Sew loosely

11 Ready to putt
12 Suit to —
13 Tear
18 Ivan and Nicholas
22 Eye rudely
25 Calm
26 Bête — (fearsome thing)
27 Caddy's measures?
28 Prefix with gram
29 Postal equipment
30 Unique person
32 Poplar
33 Bonet and namesakes
35 Irritate
38 Participated in the Masters
39 4, on a phone button
41 Take a spin, with "around"
42 Bow or Barton
45 Ten-percenters
47 La Scala offering
48 Setting of *Les Misérables*
49 Sr. year event
50 Roof part
51 Fly high
53 Last word
54 Head, to Pierre
55 Son of Seth
58 Shoshonean
59 Explosive initials

Puzzle 1-15: Biography

48 Metric area measure
49 Remits up front
52 Parish officer
56 Rush hour rarity
57 Subject of this puzzle
60 Suffix with utter
61 Mature
62 BBs, perhaps
63 — the line (obeyed)
64 Indian princess
65 Affirmative votes

Down

1 Fed. watchdog
2 Co. officer
3 Opera set in Egypt
4 Musial of baseball
5 Tastes
6 Treating fine wine
7 Under the weather
8 Laze
9 Most cloying
10 Musical Lopez
11 57 Across's role in Hull House
12 Totals
13 Beet or carrot, essentially
18 — *Hope* (one-time soap)
22 Film critic James
25 Summoned to court
26 Idolize
27 Prize for 57 Across
28 Corrida cheer
29 Worries
30 Regrets
32 Type of trap
33 Kick out
35 One of the Three Bears
38 Place for goodies
39 Summer cooler
41 Lake in Ethiopia
42 In the lead
45 Make up
47 Chose, with "for"
48 Poplar
49 HS juniors' exam
50 Janet of Justice
51 Thompson of soaps
53 June 6, 1944
54 Glamorous material
55 Poet Lazarus
58 Whoopi role, in two films
59 "Please send help!"

Across

1 There are seven in an atlas
5 Navigates
10 Ski lift
14 Way out
15 Radiant
16 Alter, as the decor
17 Illinois birthplace of 57 Across
19 Prefix with China
20 The Grand —
21 Most trim
23 Neighbor of Brazil: abbr.
24 Weekend-lover's cry
25 Rules
29 Algonquin Indian
31 Playwright Burrows
34 Matinee — (heartthrobs)
35 Hesitate
36 Courteney of *Friends*
37 Soliloquy start
38 Proofreader's mark
39 Sitting on
40 Poetic preposition
41 Records, in a way
42 Building material out West
43 Neighbor of N.J.
44 Literary collections
45 Ladd of TV
46 *On Golden —*

Puzzle 1-16: Sightseeing

Across

1 Emulate Toni Morrison
6 — fu
10 Sense
14 Burr in history
15 Type of hygienist
16 Peruvian capital
17 Centennial State landmark
20 Capitol VIP
21 Misfortunes
22 Napa sight
23 Sports org.
24 Screech and tawny
25 Like Holland in spring
28 Cookie man Famous
29 Actor Ayres
32 Influence
33 Carrey role
34 Actress Lollobrigida
35 Coyote State landmark
38 Diner sign
39 Earthenware jar
40 Ambiguous
41 Wall and Main: abbr.
42 Cabbage's cousin
43 Make a new lawn
44 Ties the knot
45 Opens a window
46 Aspen visitors
49 Cinder follower
50 TV's Charlotte
53 Keystone State landmark
56 Put — on it! (pipe down!)
57 Workers' advocate: abbr.
58 Wrinkled
59 Lyricist Hart
60 — and file
61 Gets a free ride, with "away"

Down

1 Gossips
2 "What is so — . . ."
3 Persia, today
4 Heavy load
5 Groton School founder Peabody
6 Australian native
7 Garden pots
8 Vote against
9 Firefly
10 Sweets in Sevilla
11 Emerald Isle
12 Arab prince

13 — Susan
18 Happy as a —
19 Zeros
23 Parts of speech
24 WW II password
25 High points
26 Swell
27 Clodhoppers
28 Usher's beat
29 Vassal's lord
30 Follow
31 Crossed, as a stream
33 Down times
34 Mower's focus
36 Car for recreational driving
37 Farmer in the dell outfit
42 *The King and I* costar
43 Streamlet
44 Gardener's bane
45 Smart one?
46 Word before dunk or bang
47 Metric weight
48 Sacred bird
49 Black, to Byron
50 Nevada city
51 Once more
52 Football positions
54 Capitol Hill vote
55 Stop for an auto racer

Puzzle 1-17: Plays on Words

HINT   Another clue for 21 Down is "Type of terrier."

Across

1 Nigerian seaport
6 Mixed bag
10 Closes, as jeans
14 — in the bucket (not much)
15 Tear
16 Caspian feeder
17 Trump hotel property
18 Bedazzled
19 — parker (snoop)
20 Shady office supply store?
23 Snooze, in San Jose
24 Organ lever
25 Ready-fire connection
27 Grand — (offshore Florida island)
32 Sheltered, at sea
36 Defeat decisively
39 Fell for
40 Honest accountant?
43 Shaped like Humpty
44 Horse color
45 Rams' ma'ams
46 Mickey of diamond fame
48 "— a bird . . . " (Superman intro)
50 Foot unit
53 Theater name of yore
58 Really rare sirloin?
62 Vacillate

63 Hay bundle
64 Circus worker
65 Back up a burglar
66 Tells a whopper
67 Piano key material
68 Makes one
69 Heels of bread
70 — *Macabre* (Saint-Saens)

Down

1 Reindeer herders
2 Ike's opponent
3 Type of juice
4 Seeps
5 Victor in the Peloponnesian Wars
6 Type of thermometer
7 — and Clark
8 Maladroit
9 *Goldfinger* henchman
10 Pueblo tribe
11 Old Age?
12 One of the tenses
13 Stallone, to pals
21 Trail marker made of stones
22 Iridescent stones
26 Othello was one
28 Sewing machine inventor
29 Maintain
30 Monique's mother
31 Totals
32 Teensy particle
33 Hot issue?
34 Chromosome segment
35 Give forth
37 ET's ride home, perhaps
38 Bangkok native
41 Unscripted insert
42 Preamble, briefly
47 Permit
49 Winnowed
51 *State Fair* star Jeanne
52 — up (concealed)
54 Addis —
55 Dud
56 High-schoolers
57 "A pocket full — . . . "
58 Housecoat
59 Gave the once-over to
60 Pixels
61 Capone captor
62 Swerve, as a ship

Puzzle 1-18: Letter Scrambling

HINT

Each of the longer entries in this puzzle contains an anagram, which is a word formed by scrambling the letters of another word.

Across

1 Nickname for Ms. Walters, maybe
5 Mattress rating
9 Neglect, as responsibility
14 French fancy
15 Diamond Head locale
16 Cliff dwelling
17 At hand
18 Foreboding
19 — Dixon line
20 Dressed-up Wisconsin native?
23 Adage
24 Fleming of fiction
25 Hitter's stat
28 Interpret
31 Thin layer of wood
33 Utah state flower
37 Cool carnivore?
39 City famous for its cheese
41 FBI guy: abbr.
42 Don Carlos's country
43 Primate plaint?
46 *A Death in the Family* author
47 Weak
48 Novgorod negative
50 WW II landing boat
51 Relish, with "up"
53 Find one's bearings
58 Insectivore institute?
61 Native of New Zealand
64 Word with head or heart
65 Cult leader
66 One more time
67 Film detective
68 Probability
69 Muddle
70 Overindulge
71 Tracy's truelove

Down

1 Right on!
2 *Let's Make* —
3 Longfellow had a long one
4 Some Slavs
5 Darwinian hierarchy
6 Metrical foot
7 Mother of Zeus
8 Sic transit gloria —
9 Uniformity
10 Pay attention to
11 April org.
12 Copacabana town
13 Barbie's beau
21 Corn unit
22 Chipped in
25 Wrap again
26 Refute
27 Rich or Ryan
29 Winged, in botany
30 Philistine god
32 California wine county
33 Pamper
34 Merits
35 City Hall scam
36 Former Atlanta arena
38 Command, to Toto
40 Coming to terms
44 41 Across, e.g.
45 Geological epoch
49 Uno e due
52 Expanse
54 Gold bar
55 Chopin study
56 Dorks
57 Support of a sort
58 Tom, Dick, and Harry
59 Reverberate
60 Grow rough with cold
61 Fairy queen
62 "— cannot wither her. . ."
63 Bumbler

Puzzle 1-19: Crossing the Grid

47 Buttons, e.g.
48 Media event
55 H.H. Munro's pen name
56 Pen name
57 Word with elbow or guest
58 British gun
59 Slowly, in music
60 — Brith
61 Little ones
62 Added lace
63 Bellow

Down

1 Praise, in a way
2 Singer Tennille
3 Tel —
4 Biblical transgressions
5 Hostess Perle
6 Oily corrosives
7 Greeting, in Dublin
8 Considers
9 Show feeling
10 Car contest
11 Norwegian ruler
12 Lemon alternative
13 Nicholas, e.g.
21 1040 people
22 Roofer, at times
25 Molts
26 Water vehicle
27 Star in Perseus
28 "What kind of fool — . . ."
30 Touch
31 Bias
32 Type of surgery
34 No — of roses
35 H'way
37 Laughing and others
38 Refusal, in Dublin
43 — one's heels (waited)
44 Sun. talk
46 Bathroom fixture
47 Plant a new lawn
48 Hey you!
49 Pro —
50 Got by
51 Kismet
52 Nary a soul
53 Anthracite
54 Oscar winner Jannings

Across

1 Elem. school groups
5 Type of bike
10 Blockhead
14 Nothing, to Navratilova
15 Marry without the trimmings
16 New Haven types
17 Part of LSU: abbr.
18 Old-time photo color
19 Michele Phillips, once
20 Eyeball
23 Gun lobby: abbr.
24 Curled-up, like an unborn child
25 Oodles
28 — a Wonderful Life
29 Like some statistics
33 Barbara who played Della
34 Humbug intro
35 Eye part
36 Solitaires, perhaps
39 Gizmo
40 West of Hollywood
41 Flirt with
42 Convinces
43 Bashful
44 Turn up one's nose
45 — no? (choice words)

Puzzle 1-20: Hodgepodge

Another clue for 61 Across is "Daughter of Prince Andrew."

Across

1 Harp on
8 Crib toys
15 Learned
16 Seafood dish
17 Takes back
18 — to donuts
19 Woolly one
20 Definite
22 Where pins are made
23 Drive — (fast-food lane)
25 Dirty tricks
26 Buster Brown's dog
27 2,000 pounds, in Paris
29 *Der Spiegel* article?
30 Short companion?
31 Low on iron
33 Heavenly drinks
35 Centuries and centuries: var.
37 Twosome
38 Hyenas and dingos
41 Pandemonium
45 Yo-Yo Ma's instrument
46 Hesitant sounds
48 Camel's South American cousin
49 Word in CD-ROM
50 Race place
52 Abba — of Israel
53 Put away
54 Cheery
56 Verb suffix
57 Atlantic game fish
59 Mazatlan market
61 Empress of France (1853–1871)
62 Kingdom of biological classification
63 Measure of wit
64 Guile

Down

1 Chevy coupe
2 Samuel Butler's utopian novel
3 Alpine lake
4 Nabokov heroine
5 Tough spot
6 Web-footed mammal
7 Bail out
8 Caused a tantrum
9 Wind instruments
10 Bare-faced

11 Poorly
12 Richer, as soil
13 Provokes
14 Sonnet section
21 "The doctor —"
24 Far from macho
26 Poppycock
28 Farmer's refrain?
30 Romanticist Mme. de —
32 Play for a sucker
34 Den denizen
36 Material for Woody Allen
38 Horse-man of myth
39 Cause of a sneeze, maybe
40 Gig's cousin
42 Lip-shaped
43 Pays and Plummer
44 Tropical fruits
45 Wearing a chesterfield
47 Little rascals
50 Port on the Barbary Coast
51 Mournful sound
54 Fido's cache
55 Place for a TV dinner
58 Big house
60 Cable channel

Puzzle 1-21: Speaking of Sports Stars

Across

1 Endow with power
5 Florida five
10 Island near Corsica
14 Apiece
15 Deca-doubled
16 Before you know it
17 Godunov, for one
18 Complete
19 Caber tosser
20 Persistent Aikman?
23 Over 12
24 Baby in blue
25 Lounger's robe
28 Snarl
30 Grate stuff
33 Way off base?
34 Magnetic induction unit
35 Cry of discovery
36 Elite Abdul-Jabbar?
40 Heart lines?
41 Turns pages
42 Backboard attachment
43 Get the picture
44 Take out
45 Hardly a mansion
47 Gymnast's goal

48 Water vessel
49 Rebellious Borg?
55 Overcharge
56 Lop- — (like some dogs)
57 Take wing
59 Assault from Moe
60 Look in wonder
61 Minotaur's home
62 Grace period?
63 Adds zest to
64 Wall Street acronym

Down

1 Bull doser?
2 Right on the map
3 Vaccination memento
4 Choke
5 Boxing glove, e.g.
6 Type of squash
7 — hell in a handbasket
8 "Do as —, . . ."
9 Durante's Mrs. —
10 Op-ed offering
11 Places
12 Timely benefit
13 Picnic spoiler
21 Vote in Congress
22 Prickly shrub
25 Bakery display
26 Come to
27 Valley —
28 Social blunder
29 Enthusiastic
30 Round-tripper king
31 Film session
32 Holiday word
34 Capricorn, e.g.
37 Senior
38 Ignobility
39 Politician's asset
45 Engstrom and Celsius
46 Take an ax to
47 Keepsake
48 Half a reviewing team
49 Baby —
50 Fine, slangily
51 "So long, luv!"
52 Thermometer type
53 Good earth
54 Stupefy
55 Fitness center
58 A Harrison

Puzzle 1-22: Awards Time

 The names of entertainment awards are echoed in the given names of celebrities that answer to the theme clues. (See 20, 25, 42, and 47 Across.)

Across

1 Russian ballet company
6 — Lanka
9 Remove the skin of
13 Dwarflike fellow
14 Contented kitty sound
16 Emcee Trebek
17 Nail- — (tense situation)
18 Succulent plant
19 Mr. Kotter's first name
20 *The Pleasure Seekers* actor
23 Auction offering
24 Corn-eater's throwaway
25 *The Gold Bug* author
32 Motionless
33 Wolf down
34 Ultimatum ender, perhaps
36 Burma's U —
37 Half a diam.
38 Boorish
39 Prefix with nuke or freeze
40 Not "agin"
41 Oil-producing fruits
42 The Odd Couple
45 Central: prefix
46 Hearst-napping org.
47 Country hit-maker
54 — bargain
55 Moon goddess
56 Violins' big brothers
58 Whopper producer?
59 Use a swizzle stick
60 Dark
61 Ruth or Mantle, for short
62 Oil-treatment letters
63 Multiple-choice, et al.

Down

1 Soviet security agcy.
2 "I'm only — for the money"
3 Tiller starter?
4 Foreshadowing
5 Absolute final
6 Militaristic city-state
7 Ms. Lenska
8 Like the *Monitor* or the *Merrimac*
9 When doubled, American Samoa's capital
10 "How sad!"
11 Singer McEntire
12 English river
15 Paint over
21 Sumter or McHenry
22 — Saud
25 Race: prefix
26 Mild oaths
27 Photo finish?
28 Live's partner
29 Serious risk
30 Norwegian king, 995–1000
31 Antique auto
32 — loss for words
35 Tricky turn
37 Computer reports
38 Sharply defined
40 Brand X's lack
41 *Man — Mancha*
43 Actress Madigan
44 Black piano key
47 *Essays of —* (Lamb work)
48 Downright nasty
49 Olympic hero Spitz
50 Yard or pound
51 Philosopher Descartes
52 Woes
53 Gill opening
54 Two- — (like some paper towels)
57 "— the economy, stupid"

Puzzle 1-23: Container Collection

59 "Rule, Britannia" writer
60 Bradley of the 1st Army
61 "The Wreck of the Mary —"
62 Garrison of tennis
63 Perennial batting champ Gwynn
64 Millie and Jemima
65 Mimic

Down

1 G-men
2 Director Kazan
3 He played Obi-Wan
4 Kind of force
5 "Enough!"
6 Dumbbell
7 Med. school subject
8 Revolutionary hero Warner
9 Compass dir.
10 Lassie, for one
11 Diminish
12 Kind of face
13 House of Lords members
19 Public demonstration
21 Trendy
24 Lab dish
25 Depraved
26 Zhivago's love
27 School founded by Henry VI
28 *Winter of Artifice* writer
29 Boston suburb
30 Carpe —
32 Quickly
33 Fictional Wolfe
34 Wife of Jacob
35 *Picnic* playwright
36 Scarlett's home
39 Dr. Dentons, e.g.
41 1993 Jackson album
42 Colorful horse
43 Number system
45 Wooden shoe
46 Car rental name
47 Boston's airport
48 Put into action
49 Workbench attachments
51 Kind of cheese
52 Pearl Buck heroine
53 Mideast strip
54 Plumbing problem
55 Actress Archer
56 Five— Plan
58 Author LeShan

Across

1 Tour de force
5 1996 Final Four sch.
10 Sadie Hawkins Day inventor
14 "— Cinders" (old comic strip)
15 March 7, e.g.
16 Organ stop
17 — laughing (cracks up)
18 Oregon national park
20 Goat's-hair fabric
22 Do a vet's job
23 Barnyard creature
24 Dentist's need, at times
25 Kate Nelligan movie
29 Fred's sister
31 Swiss Guard's state
34 Put a match to
37 Word with curling or shooting
38 Falk of *Columbo*
39 Federico of the Clinton Cabinet
40 Multi-PC hookup
41 Hockey's 1995 Art Ross Trophy winner
43 Strips in the supermarket
44 Milo of theater fame
45 Like the Caspian
48 One of the Gabors
50 Solo
51 Post-Christmas celebration
57 Trifles

Puzzle 1-24: On the Stump

Across

1 Cleanliness eschewer
5 Emulates James or Floyd
9 Woman's shoe
13 Pillow filling
15 — Disney (French theme park)
16 Where Columbus is
17 *One Day at* —
18 Anna of *Nana*
19 Mandolin cousin
20 D.C. insiders are inside it
22 Ticks off
23 Jewish holiday
24 Like a Vincent Price movie
25 — Kong
29 Hood's heater
30 "Psst!"
31 — about
32 *The Berlin Stories* author
37 Land of cedars
40 *Look Back in Anger* playwright
41 Relaxing rubbers
43 Make out at the drive-in
44 — Lanka
45 Chat
47 Big name in abstract art
48 Pack animal
51 Thelonious and Art
53 Aoki of golf
54 Popular with most
59 Late-evening Jay
60 Astronomical bear
61 Bizarre
62 Mend, as bone
63 Stone, in combinations
64 Napa Valley wares
65 Ben Cartwright's three
66 Diet-food label word
67 Canaveral gp.

Down

1 Three-player card game
2 Carpenter's strip
3 Mayberry boy
4 Fail big-time
5 Keeps in check
6 Gets the best of
7 Minnow family member
8 Betamax introducer
9 Influential D.C. type
10 *Star Trek* lieutenant
11 Bishop's topper
12 Keats's forte
14 "— on truckin'"
21 Oaf
24 Slobodan Milosevic, for one
25 Actress Celeste
26 Draft status
27 Wealthy ones
28 Like some campaigns
30 "I'm Dickens, — Fenster"
33 Shouts of praise
34 Hurler Hershiser
35 Children's-story starter
36 Astronaut Slayton
38 Pianist Peter
39 Yes, to Pierre
42 Self-absorbed ones
46 Vols.
48 Sells a bill of goods to
49 — hooks (carton warning)
50 Put the collar on
51 An Osmond
52 Pack in a footlocker
54 Martin of *Mary Hartman, Mary Hartman*
55 On the road to —
56 Sicilian spewer
57 Bellicose god
58 Tableland

Puzzle 1-25: Sound Judgment

 The title tells you that the theme involves sound, as in words that sound the same but are spelled differently.

Across

1 "Now!" in the ER
5 Plaza Hotel minx
11 Predicament
14 Carnegie Hall section
15 Ancient military unit
16 Grounded bird
17 1966 James Coburn film
19 Major record label
20 Pencil filler
21 Ditty bag item
23 Unspecified number
24 Act the gadabout
26 Smooth, to Ozawa
30 Unproven
34 Matinee —
35 One of The Chipmunks
36 — Tin Tin
37 Half a work day?
41 Big name in dye
42 Cabaret singer Karen
43 Baltic feeder
44 Uses makeup, perhaps
46 In good spirits
48 Singer Celine
49 Fidel's friend
50 Part of EEOC
53 Make hostile
58 *House of the Rising —*

59 Jascha Heifetz's teacher
62 Give an assist to
63 Kind of skiing
64 Act the blowhard
65 Words for 31 Down
66 Takeover attempts
67 Lip

Down

1 Wade through the surf
2 Promote a book, in a way
3 Taj Mahal site
4 Fill-in worker
5 Pacific current
6 Grove or Gomez of the mound
7 Make eyes at
8 Sundial numeral
9 Favorite —
10 Hops on the el
11 "— Louise!"
12 Magazine articles?
13 *The Ghost and Mrs. —*
18 Pull a rabbit out of —
22 G.P.'s gp.
24 Literary Uncle
25 — about (circa)
26 Petrol measure
27 Former Attorney General Meese
28 Bible verb
29 Everything
30 Stylish dresses
31 Wedding-cake figurine
32 Big house denizen
33 Contest mail-in
35 Charlie of *Platoon*
38 Flavorful seedpods
39 Housewares name
40 Clod chopper
45 Palindromic OK city
46 Hot peppers
47 Pay attention to
49 Make a copy of
50 Actor Morales
51 Pound sterling, slangily
52 Loosen
53 — in a poke
54 Arrests
55 Distinctive quality
56 Earl Grey wares
57 Work units
60 Connecticut collegian
61 Unlock, poetically

Puzzle 1-26: Berg-men

The title offers a common element from the theme entries.

Across

1 1040 preparers
5 Pack tightly
9 Disconcert
14 Humdinger
15 River to the Caspian
16 Frank of The Mothers of Invention
17 Love, Spanish style
18 *Death on the* — (Christie mystery)
19 Hoopster Shaquille
20 "Leader of the Band" singer
23 Crystal-ball users
24 Golfer Ballesteros
25 Disposable diaper brand
28 High-tech recording mediums
30 Stately property
32 CIA precursor
35 Conduct the class
38 State firmly
39 *Amistad* director
43 Composer Khachaturian
44 Branch of Islam
45 Bambi's mom
46 More shocking, as horror movies go
49 On the — (accepting bribes)
51 Some 45s
52 Costa —
55 Father
58 Creator of intricate contraptions
61 Composers' gp.
64 Devil-may- — attitude
65 Part of HOMES
66 "Hare Krishna," e.g.
67 — -Tass (Russian news agency)
68 Saudi simoleon
69 Jamboree structures
70 Word with contact or zoom
71 Koppel and Kennedy

Down

1 Dressed
2 Cougars
3 Like a soliloquist, perhaps
4 Browsed the Web
5 Light bulb metal
6 1990 Indy champ Luyendyk
7 Modern-day agoras
8 West Point freshman
9 Islands west of Portugal
10 — *the Drum Slowly*
11 Kong, for one
12 Mineral spring
13 *2001: A Space Odyssey* computer
21 Indulge in bombast
22 Cain raiser
25 Washed
26 In — (unborn)
27 Brink
29 Talk back to
31 Indent maker
32 Midwestern Amerind
33 Barber's sharpener
34 Chicago's — Tower
36 PC's "brain"
37 Solver's aid
40 Keydets' sch.
41 They make things possible
42 Cottoned to
47 Emulates Etna
48 Pick on
50 "Pretty Baby" composer van Alstyne
53 Designer Beaton
54 Banded gem
56 Really strange
57 Major chord
58 Rave's partner
59 North African port
60 Hairstylists' substances
61 Play part
62 "Thar — blows!"
63 Soup buy

Puzzle 1-27: Metallic Mischief

Across

1 T. Rex, for one
6 Up
11 Devitalize
14 United
15 Seckel et al.
16 Chamberlain's org.
17 Stained-glass artist's need
19 — -up (infielder's chance)
20 Boys' wear, once
21 French — (abrupt departure)
23 Last gasp
24 Circle occupier
25 Set
29 Valerie Harper spinoff
30 Dakota
31 Astronaut's outfit
33 Former Cabinet member Aspin
36 Lodging houses
37 Out-of-order condition
38 Criticism
39 Reagan was its pres.
40 *Spenser: For Hire* star
41 Excitable
42 Russia's adversary in 1904–1905
44 Anklet pattern
45 *Get* — (1995 film)
47 Composer Bartok
49 Christine of *The Doctor*

50 Chop-shop wares
55 Hookah part
56 "Step on it!"
58 Spring attraction?
59 Elegant
60 Put on cloud nine
61 Biker's bike
62 It has eyes but can't see
63 Log Cabin, e.g.

Down

1 Take great satisfaction
2 "Time — My Side"
3 Kind of lamp
4 *The Never Ending Story* author
5 Throw out
6 Imitating
7 X, to a king
8 They're often punched
9 Comic-strip bark
10 Ezra Pound protégé
11 Pop music district
12 Upstairs
13 Word with Manila or India
18 Bugs' bane
22 Finish
24 Superskillful one
25 Egyptian goddess
26 Singer Simone
27 *Treasure Island* character
28 Ger. neighbor
29 Justice Ginsburg
31 It may go from ear to ear
32 "That's how *he* spelled it!"
34 Grid Hall-of-Famer Campbell
35 Ione of film
37 Unravel
38 Statue leaf
40 Tense
41 Cool desserts
43 — Deco
44 Succulent plant
45 Kind of fund
46 Chico's brother
47 Montana mining town
48 Old-time anesthetic
50 ". . . three men in —"
51 With skill
52 Laugh heartily
53 Met garb
54 Plan part
57 — de Cologne

Puzzle 1-28: Nothing Special

Across

1 Rental sign
6 He raised Cain
10 Worshiper's distance?
14 Novelist Calvino
15 Vigor
16 It's often converted
17 Vitamin C target, to Pauling
19 Burrows and Saperstein
20 Takes care of
21 Psychic phenomenon, for short
22 Tops
23 Deli offering
25 Square partner
27 Tax-return figure
34 Strike down
35 Thrived on
36 Class favorite
37 Crones
38 Medellin moola
39 Galley mark
40 *Bambi* doe
41 Senator Hatch
42 Bump, in poker
43 "My dog has fleas," e.g.
46 Son of Zeus
47 A lo-o-ong time
48 Principal copper producer
50 Alley trailer?
53 Richard's successor
58 Noted doorbell-ringer
59 Everyman
61 Heap
62 Author — Douglas Wiggin
63 Represent on stage
64 Keg contents
65 Coaster
66 Hart of tennis fame

Down

1 Nervous contractions
2 Nebraska native
3 Ineffectual
4 *Desire Under the —*
5 Transvestite of film
6 *NYPD Blue* network
7 Knock down
8 Has a bug
9 Does some stock-car work
10 Kind of numeral
11 Like modern transmissions wire

12 "Dead man's hand" pair
13 Observe the Sabbath
18 "Cat" or "dog"
24 They may "cotton" to their work
26 Furthermore
27 Muscat native
28 Song and dance
29 Wino's bane
30 "Sweet — O'Grady"
31 DeCarlo of *The Munsters*
32 Reagan Cabinet member
33 Major suffix
34 The Beatles' "— Leaving Home"
38 Washing-machine cycles
39 — Martin (Argentine revolutionary)
41 "— Buttermilk Sky"
42 Made a bridge booboo
44 Thins out
45 Old Roman raiment
48 John Phillips or Dennis Doherty
49 Infamous
51 Shaped like nothing?
52 Rival of Andre
54 She succeeded Barr
55 Unshut
56 Points in math
57 Hammer and Spade: Abbr.
60 Part of Roy G. Biv

Puzzle 1-29: The Forest Floor

Across

1 Kind of race
5 Finish an "i"
8 Dutch cheese
12 Variable stars
14 Vein contents
15 Yucky stuff
16 Enjoyed immensely
17 Nada
18 Pine nut
19 Social parasite
22 Wall St. deg.
25 Mary — (cosmetics name)
26 Catch some busses
27 Legal matter
28 Belle Starr, e.g.
30 Overhangs
32 Detach, in a way
33 Penny- — (small-time)
34 Tried partner
38 Treacherous one
41 Jane of fiction
42 Not one
43 Pear-shaped instruments
44 Got up
46 *Gulliver's Travels,* for one
47 Draft org.
50 Toronto's prov.
51 Firing-squad command

52 CIA forerunner
53 Enjoy a children's game
57 Competitor
58 Salon job
59 Canceled
63 Adored ones
64 Indignation
65 Collect
66 *Breathless* star
67 — Lingus
68 Kind of board

Down

1 *Jurassic Park* letters
2 Degenerate
3 NYC's Park is one
4 Modern-day France and Belgium, roughly
5 An Osmond
6 Not a dup.
7 It's mental
8 Of the yrs. 1558–1603
9 Kuwait currency
10 Con — (lovingly, in music)
11 Darns
13 Expo '74 site
15 Malice
20 Woodcock's org.
21 Mississippi River sight
22 PC accessory
23 Bugs, e.g.
24 Stock-purchase phrase
29 Madonna's "— Virgin"
30 — nous
31 — one's stuff (show off)
33 Oscar-winning role for Bergman
35 Price-earnings —
36 Cyberspace frequenters
37 Snaky shapes
39 3- — (household oil)
40 Compelling charm
45 Restaurant freebies
46 Round Table title
47 Unit of mistletoe
48 Pool accessory
49 Really enjoy
51 Chasing
54 New Haven university
55 "Le — Goriot"
56 Annoying insect
60 Rock vocalist Ronnie James —
61 Follower's suffix
62 Pee — River

Puzzle 1-30: Apt Adjectives

The country of origin of 26 Down is Australia.

Across

1 Quest
5 E-5
8 Kind of symbol
14 Pureeing gadget
16 She played Jo in 1994
17 Stylish actor?
19 It may be hot or dead
20 Picnic visitor
21 Huron-Superior canals
22 Supporters of a sort
27 Ollie's partner
28 You love: Lat.
29 Not at home
30 Runners carry them
31 Tibetan beast
32 "For pity's sake!"
34 Animal that killed Adonis
35 Sunburned comedian?
39 Rastafarianism, for one
40 Othello's tricker
41 — populi
43 Make smithereens
45 Biddy
46 Parcel (out)
47 Kind of top
48 Checked
51 Actor Byrnes
52 Arthur Conan Doyle title
53 Word before Antiqua or Nova
54 Sincere director?
61 Of a son
62 Election times, usually
63 Be imaginative
64 Close
65 Batik needs

Down

1 It'll get you to JFK PDQ
2 DDE's command
3 East ender?
4 Rapid transports?
5 Breathe hard
6 OT starter
7 Take a stab at
8 Trumpeters
9 Shade
10 Burns-Allen link
11 Bagel browner
12 Do a roadie's task
13 Permanent locations?
15 The Beatles' "Yes —"

18 Spellbound
22 Mr. Leno
23 *Rubaiyat* poet
24 Maugham satire
25 Fork site
26 Swagmen and jackeroos
27 Louver component
30 Aria, e.g.
32 Eero Saarinen's Gateway —
33 Pig tail?
34 Pass the hat
36 Kind of dictionary
37 *Critique of Pure Reason* author
38 It's found in scores
42 Crossed out
43 Martina foe
44 Prado locale
45 Mannheim mister
46 Don't carry well?
48 Garand, for one
49 Took care of the leaves
50 Current discharges
52 32-card game
55 Long or Peeples
56 Patronized the greasy spoon
57 Wimple wearer
58 Suffer retribution
59 Pumpernickel alternative
60 Mule's dad

Puzzle 1-31: Window Boxes

Across

1 Star in Cygnus
6 Loses firmness
10 Many Wall St. types
14 "— song go . . ."
15 Coagulate
16 Whodunit game
17 Mandrake, e.g.
19 March 17 garb
20 Kowtows
21 They should be dressed
23 Miranda v. — (1966 case)
27 Had no use for
28 Neiman and Anderson
29 Kind of artery
32 They may be clicked on
33 *Lady Windermere's Fan* playwright
34 Word before off or out
35 Descend
36 Actress Phoebe
37 Rats' milieus, often
38 Nonprescription: abbr.
39 Emulates De Niro's "Bull"
40 Helicons
41 Gelded
43 Gourmet's asset
44 More cloddish
45 Ruffles and flourishes may accompany them

46 Major-city areas
48 Psychiatrist Jung
49 Spirited steed
50 Tourist, at times
56 Thalia's sister
57 Republic proclaimed in 1949
58 Confusion acronym
59 Layers
60 Precipitated
61 It may depict vice or virtue

Down

1 Hubbub
2 Ransom — Olds
3 Like some elec. charges
4 Biblical suffix
5 Sluggers' luggers
6 Inverted "e"
7 Br. Columbia neighbor
8 Word on a dollar
9 Takes charge of
10 Composer Rod
11 Like a stereotypical umpire?
12 Burns title starter
13 Venn-diagram areas
18 — *of the Desert*
22 Oklahoma tribesman
23 Novelist Lurie
24 Enumerate
25 Post-World War II barrier
26 Monty Hall booby prize
27 Wiffle Ball features
29 Summoned to court
30 Give back
31 Sycophant's replies
33 Stake
36 Pets
37 Humdinger
39 Second draft
40 Sears Tower adjective
42 Some superchargers
43 Tonsorial touch
45 Ready to burst
46 Speed-of-sound word
47 Perry's creator
48 Use the smokehouse
51 Wise
52 Genetic code letters
53 Kind of car or cart
54 Craft in the tabloids
55 Reaction locale?

Puzzle 1-32: Who Are These Guys?

A question mark at the end of a clue indicates wordplay.

Across

1 High school class
5 Costa —
10 — and lot (municipal tax)
14 Mystery writer John Dickson —
15 Disneyland attractions
16 George or Victoria
17 Graphic intro?
18 Turn away
19 Populous place
20 He's in the National Anthem?
23 Avenger Emma
24 Unknown ordinal
25 Tack on
28 Symbol of thinness
30 Trains on trestles
33 Sorrowful drop
34 Wound up
35 Big shot
36 He's in the Lord's Prayer?
40 Cal. page
41 Strike from the record
42 Frigg's mate
43 Short
44 River to the Rhine
45 "Dixie" composer
47 Distinctive doctrine
48 Protesting
49 He's in the Pledge of Allegiance?
55 Central points
56 Josh
57 Ahab, in the song
59 In a while
60 — vivos (among the living)
61 "Cheerio!"
62 Space drink
63 Reefers, e.g.
64 Looked over

Down

1 Fi front
2 Pilgrimage to Mecca
3 Cookie favorite
4 *The Tempest* magician
5 Beefed up
6 Be a match for
7 Arabian Sea gulf
8 Part of VHF
9 Dumbfound
10 Virgule
11 Mason's job
12 Dust Bowl refugee
13 Leaves in the bag
21 Velvet finish
22 Newsman Garrick
25 Dumas adventurer
26 Georgia product
27 Bull Moose, for one
28 A Boy of Summer
29 Pot builder
30 Get around
31 Ceiling
32 Shelled out
34 Vail sight
37 Pet shop purchase
38 Theatrical
39 Propose for an honor
45 Records
46 Kingston Trio hit
47 Hockey infraction
48 Piece of property
49 Author Jaffe
50 Object of devotion
51 Casino city
52 Disk contents
53 Sledge
54 Fill to the brim
55 Dieter's no-no
58 Unfavorable

Puzzle 1-33: Spherical Bodies

Across

1 Zip
6 Bum around
10 "Don't throw bouquets — . . ."
14 Revere
15 Workout result
16 Prepare pasta
17 Acting aggressively
20 Barrett of Pink Floyd
21 Takes one's turn
22 Hypo
23 Scorch
24 Peggy of *To Tell the Truth*
25 Opulence
28 Pass-catching wizard Art
29 Ebenezer's epithet
32 ". . . lovely as —"
33 Solo portrayer
34 Singer Guthrie
35 Circus traveler?
38 Fragrance
39 Donald Duck nephew
40 Burns flick of 1977
41 "— the ramparts . . ."
42 Caterpillar creation
43 Piglets
44 Actress Perlman
45 Part of a full house
46 All-4-One hit

49 Slight coloration
50 Hold out one's hand
53 Delectable spheroid
56 Old — (card game)
57 Over: Ger.
58 Bert's pal
59 Peppy
60 Soprano Lily
61 Tokyo trasher of film

Down

1 Does some channel-surfing
2 In an aimless fashion
3 Stow
4 React to spilled milk?
5 Intensify
6 Type of beer
7 Publisher Adolph
8 "Caught you!"
9 Abba hit of 1976
10 French clerics
11 Sticky-tongued critter
12 Gin —
13 *Vogue* competitor
18 Genesis captain
19 Clerk's spot
23 Weatherman's word
24 Like many an old joke
25 Exuberant yell
26 Chopin piece
27 Armadillo's protection
28 "Waterloo Bridge" painter
29 Actress Sonia
30 Parcel out
31 Scissors and nelson
33 Animal life
34 Loathe
36 Gets happy
37 One of Ryan's seven
42 Eastern cuisine
43 Yemeni capital
44 "Delta Dawn" singer
45 Seaside entertainment spots
46 Doctrines
47 Kind of meet
48 Australian film director Peter
49 Govt. agents
50 Word with brass or rubber
51 Director Kazan
52 Watkins —, N.Y.
54 Cable channel
55 Brother: abbr.

Puzzle 1-34: City Slickers

Across

1 Chocolate substitute
6 Carpenter's tool
9 Lasting mark
13 Bikini, e.g.
14 Exploit
16 Subdue
17 Alfa —
18 Green Gables girl
19 Bridle part
20 Sweat shop?
21 Pop vocalist/city slicker?
24 Emcee's line
26 Suitable
27 Vixen partner
29 New words
34 Journalist Guest
35 Voting locales
36 Suffix meaning "small"
37 Crowd sound
38 Sheets of glass
39 Talbot or Lovett
40 Be human?
41 1953 John Wayne flick
42 Tropical
43 Bogart-Bacall film
45 Marsh
46 MA clock setting
47 Like some seals
48 Angel/city slicker?
53 Sculpture material
56 Composer Stravinsky
57 Squirt and zip
58 Ford flop
60 Take out, as from text
61 Fencer's weapon
62 — along (drives)
63 Roebuck, e.g.
64 Japanese currency unit
65 December delivery man

Down

1 Mustang and Pinto
2 On
3 Novelist/city slicker?
4 The Grand — Opry
5 Police record book
6 Hersey bell town
7 Declare untrue
8 First Stoic
9 Levels of society
10 City of northern France
11 Surrounded by
12 Quickie-divorce mecca
15 Jumps the tracks
22 Rink great
23 Hosp. workers
25 Va. neighbor
27 Actress Bo
28 Idolize
29 Apartment type
30 Toast topper
31 Actor/city slicker?
32 Immigrants' island
33 Pomegranate interior
35 Sudden pain
38 Carrying charge
39 Come-on
41 Pilgrimage to Mecca
42 — nest (contentious situation)
44 Lascivious looker
45 — Tse-tung
47 German steel city
48 Captain — (legendary pirate)
49 The African Queen scriptwriter
50 Lacquered metalware
51 Saucer partners
52 — -jerk reaction
54 Ancient Briton
55 Hostess Maxwell
59 Edmond O'Brien cult film

Puzzle 1-35: Consonant Trigrams

 Another clue for 13 Down is "Molar."

Across

1 More remote
8 Set
11 Obeyed master, perhaps
14 Buddhist state
15 Guacamole need
17 Metrical foot
18 The former Basutoland
19 "— life!"
20 Purpose
22 Author George —
23 Seamstress
25 Texas spread
28 Donned the feedbag
29 Days off at the tourney
30 Mozart work
33 Ahead of the throw
34 Dec. day
38 Piano key
40 Swarming insect
42 Kind of drum or fiddle
43 — *Show of Shows*
45 Fresh air, informally
46 *West Side Story* gang
47 — whim
48 Cable emcees
52 Choir spots
55 Impertinence
56 Energy unit
58 Overall impression
60 Billy the Kid slayer Pat
63 *City Slickers* Oscar winner
65 "Assume the position!"
66 Me-first folks
67 Get with great effort
68 Not quite S
69 *Mommie* —

Down

1 Unforeseen obstacle
2 Dialogue parts
3 Ticked off
4 Athletic honors
5 Ginnie —
6 Make certain
7 "Doggone!"
8 "My — Sal"
9 Genesis name
10 Consolation-prize winners
11 Tuxedo trim
12 Type of committee
13 Nail partner
16 Diet-Rite, e.g.
21 Exile isle
24 List-ending abbr.
26 Very much
27 Mock
30 Govt. finance gp.
31 Zadora of *Butterfly*
32 The two Begleys
33 Coretta — King
34 1797–1798 diplomatic tangle
35 — jacket (Chinese attire)
36 Advisor Landers
37 — Felicite, Que.
39 Orbs
41 Like old LPs
44 CIS precursor
46 Deck pair
47 Golden years, to the politically incorrect
48 "Me and Bobby —"
49 Credit
50 Extreme edge
51 Wife of Zeus
53 Uptight
54 Splinter groups
57 Mimicked
59 For fear that
61 NFL scores
62 Kind of shirt
64 Mauna —

Puzzle 1-36: Say Cheese!

Across

1 Hemingway sobriquet
5 Three- — sloth
9 Otherwise
13 Actor Sharif
14 Sudden current increase
15 Pokey
16 Sausage unit
17 Elite
18 Sailor's saint
19 Pt. of speech
20 Big cheese: Ital.
22 First Lady Abigail
24 It's sometimes abstract
25 Singapore disciplinarians
27 Over
32 Extra — attraction
33 Metric weights
34 Skeleton starter
35 Grisham's *The —*
36 *60 Minutes* name
37 Switch partner
38 Cassowary kin
39 Fairly big combo
40 Serve the vichyssoise
41 Part-time ballplayers
43 Shaping tools
44 Peeples of *Fame*
45 Boxer Hector "—" Camacho
46 Big cheese
51 Arrest
54 Make eyes at
55 Put an end to
56 Play beginning
57 Indistinct sight
58 Long-eared leapers
59 Jumper or slam-dunk
60 Some kinfolk
61 North Sea feeder
62 A few

Down

1 Negri of the silents
2 In the course of
3 Big cheese
4 Place of refuge
5 Solvent, informally
6 Black-and-white treat
7 "By gosh!"
8 Bearing
9 Removes a cassette
10 — Land (Los Angeles)
11 Dolt
12 *The Time Machine* people
14 Flimflams
20 Topps offering
21 Showy flower
23 Consider
25 Latte spots
26 Stop on —
27 Little tooters
28 "— a Song Go . . ."
29 Big cheese
30 Napoleon, for one
31 Loves to death
33 Kaelin of the O.J. trial
36 Like an old record
37 Take a — (lose money)
39 Mayberry boy
40 Be in need of
42 Signatories
43 They usually are in pairs
45 Meditative one
46 Unruly bunches
47 Aptly-named fruit
48 Caveman's weapon
49 Votes of agreement
50 Stable dweller
52 Energy source
53 Sound — (brief broadcast)
56 Balaam's beast

Puzzle 1-37: Shortenin'

HINT

The title tells you to drop the G at the end of the theme entries.

57 Heat source
62 Malefactor
63 Senator Joseph's day in the spotlight?
64 Marseilles moola
65 Certain tourney
66 Flair
67 Horse —
68 Road curve
69 Fender-bender

Down

1 Escapes
2 Slangy "sure"
3 Killer whale
4 Pigeonholes
5 Masses of interstellar dust
6 Horse sound
7 Cookie king Wally
8 Question
9 A face-off starts it
10 Like some threats
11 Bust opposite
12 Mr. Rubik
13 Lascivious look
18 — tide
21 Metric — (1,000 kilos)
23 Anchored
24 Health-food store legume
25 Hilo hello
26 Pale purple
28 1995 action movie
29 Warmed up in the bullpen
30 Aesop racer
31 Mount the soapbox
32 Sample
33 Underhanded one
35 Architect Saarinen
39 Life or death
44 — Kids (Gorcey's movie gang)
47 Okra morsel
48 Tumbledown building
52 Like many fences
53 Small apts.
54 Small
55 Blood feud participant
56 Millions of years
57 Ready for picking
58 Yemeni port
59 Mah-jongg piece
60 Arabian sultanate
61 Monthly payment
63 Dylan or Dole

Across

1 City on the Rhone
5 "March Madness" org.
9 Defame in writing
14 Prefix for space
15 Deciduous hardwoods
16 Worship
17 Georgia novel?
19 Product of genetic engineering
20 Corporate reorganizations
21 San Andreas Fault event
22 Actor Mineo
23 Jane Smiley best-seller
24 Presidential nickname
27 Singer Dolly's photos?
34 What George couldn't tell
36 London district
37 Big name in wraps
38 Director's offerings
40 "It's freezing!"
41 Clear the board
42 Chicago stopover
43 Show-biz columnist Rex
45 Singer James
46 Instant-breakfast mix?
49 "A mouse!"
50 Trifle
51 Summer mo.
53 Acted the host

Puzzle 1-38: Birds of a Feather

Across

1 Huck Finn's transport
5 Dance recklessly
9 *Ghosts* writer Henrik
14 — Stanley Gardner
15 Scent
16 Grid Hall-of-Famer Greasy
17 Football birds
20 Capital gains —
21 "Beetle Bailey" pooch
22 Proletariat
23 Iowa State site
24 Sentry's cry
25 Author Rushdie
28 Fog
29 Certain mod music
32 — savant
33 L or XL
34 Tarzan's transport
35 Hockey birds
38 General Robert —
39 Christmas carol
40 Desirable trait
41 Patriotic org.
42 Peter the Great, e.g.
43 Contemptuous looks
44 Throw in the towel
45 Redcap's burden
46 Brings upon oneself
49 Be a rat fink
50 Animation frame
53 Baseball birds
56 Orange box
57 "Pogo" cartoonist Kelly
58 Taj Mahal site
59 Rusty of "Make Room for Daddy"
60 Part of HOMES
61 Word with track or swap

Down

1 Take a siesta
2 Zone
3 Linen source
4 Asian holiday
5 Like flowing lava
6 *Golden Boy* writer Clifford
7 Fair-to-middling
8 Charlemagne's letters
9 Consume quickly
10 Brutish one
11 Buzz and chain
12 Actress Sommer
13 Famed Loch
18 Warhol's soup can flavor
19 McCartney's "Maybe I'm —"
23 Martin's "That's —"
24 O'Leary of the Clinton Cabinet
25 Opposing teams
26 — Rogers St. Johns
27 Just over a quart
28 Job offerer
29 Washer cycle
30 Provoke
31 Ants, roaches, and the like
33 Summer ermine
34 Workshop clamps
36 Refuse to yield
37 Get by contrivance
42 Ted or Tina
43 Acknowledge the general
44 "Can I — you on that?"
45 Attorney Melvin
46 Backscratcher target
47 Nick Charles's wife
48 Study all night
49 Skier's tow
50 Kennel confinement
51 Brontë's Jane
52 Future atty.'s exam
54 Be in debt
55 Toast topper

Puzzle 1-39: By the By

Across

1 Bountiful state?
5 Commotions
9 Cover lightly
12 *A Doll's House* character
13 U2 front man
14 Bahrain bigwigs
17 Fan noise
18 TREADRUNG
20 Bailiwick
22 Ritz alternative
23 Dickensian epithet
24 Legendary Trojan
26 Hat
27 Phoenix's deathbed
28 ROMPPORTRAY
30 One with a handle
31 Dispatched
32 Ridge crest
33 Tai tongue
36 Ewe's milieu
37 — Jones Industrials
39 Stadium stats
40 Invalidate
42 Kind of strip
44 Casket support
45 FACEEDGE
51 Dexterous beginner

52 Inventor's monogram
53 Volleyball player, at times
54 Nichols's comedy partner
55 Spencer Davis's "I'm __"
57 Constellation near Ursa Major
58 GUSTSLAP
62 "— Three Lives"
63 Grant portrayer
64 Hungary's Nagy
65 Mudville count
66 Greek H
67 Give up
68 Pistols

Down

1 You do it on your birthday
2 Under control
3 Actress Richards
4 Hogs
5 Bodybuilder's concern
6 Shakespearean verb
7 Slugger Paul
8 Cary's *Houseboat* costar
9 Pasha's title
10 Pre-noon times
11 HARNESSIOTA
15 Keister
16 Planetarium displays
19 Beer characteristic
21 Telephone company, affectionately
25 "Auld lang —"
27 Canadian political party
29 Mom and pop org.
32 Exerted influence over
33 Los Lobos hit
34 Beasts
35 ENTIRESINGLE
37 ETO commander
38 Peepers
41 Swiss canton
43 Ecdysiast's bare essential
45 Command to Fifi
46 Poem style
47 "— in!" (card-player's request)
48 San Marino surrounder
49 Clothed
50 Chips away at
56 "L'étoile du —" (Minnesota motto)
59 Drench
60 Swimsuit part
61 Teensy

Puzzle 1-40: Starting the Day Right

Across

1 Bogart's love
7 Otolaryngology focus
10 — Na Na
13 *Clueless* star Silverstone
14 Not so wobbly
17 Started the day right?
18 Kind of irony
19 Rene's Renee, maybe
20 Longtime Mexican dictator
22 Set things square
23 Like a hedgehog
25 Started the day right?
26 Started the day right?
29 London transport until 1952
30 Daniel-Joel bridge
31 — water (catching heck)
33 LP's successors
36 Israeli guns
37 Started the day right?
38 Shipping choice
39 Shipping choice
40 Show hauteur toward
41 Guts
42 Yale Bowl squad
43 Started the day right?
45 Started the day right?
48 — Vanilli
49 Acquittal ploy
50 Water-to-wine site
51 Place for a piercing
55 Cider, et al.
57 Started the day right?
59 Conk out on the freeway
60 Peter Stuyvesant distinction
61 Corp. top dog
62 Ave. crossers
63 Calm

Down

1 Mexicali site
2 Styptic substance
3 Year in Trajan's rule
4 Gets via the Net
5 Sprawl
6 Strathclyde boy
7 Piece of Lamb?
8 All-inclusive
9 Hobby rm.
10 "— it!": Fonzie
11 Poet Heinrich
12 Followed the rainbow?

15 Biblical landing place
16 Experiment value
21 Blue dyes
24 Harper Valley gp.
25 Goad
26 As I'm showing you
27 Seep
28 Lao or Tao setting
29 — Cities (Minnesota pair)
32 — Dinh Diem
33 Olympian Lewis
34 Phony knockout
35 Husky's burden
37 Writer Bagnold
38 Did a pit-crew job
40 "— Ride" (1948 tune)
41 Cowboys' group
42 Barbecue leftover?
44 Los — (nuke site)
45 Utter devastation
46 Vibrant
47 Cinema Sal
48 Spars
50 Auto trailer?
52 Reba McIntire's home st.
53 Exemplar of redness
54 Sidle
56 HST's hopeful successor
58 Glass finish?

Puzzle 1-41: The Jacksons

 Theme entries for this puzzle include celebrities with the last name Jackson.

Across

1 "Evil Woman" band, familiarly
4 Signs to heed
9 Thumb and Jones
13 Shoe-polish name
15 Bundle of branches
16 Tartan wearer
17 Three Jacksons
20 — *You Went Away* (1944 film)
21 *Heartburn* writer Ephron
22 Grazing site
23 Eight, in combinations
26 Ultimate purpose
28 Two more Jacksons
33 —10 (blemish medicine)
34 Lane of song
35 Taxpayer's nightmare
39 Like a schnauzer's coat
41 Nonimaginary numbers
43 — Cynwyd, Pa.
44 Street ball game site
46 Madonna's "— Bonita"
47 It's nothing at all
48 Two more Jacksons
52 Backward
55 *The Time Machine* people
56 Give — whirl
57 Like chatter, perhaps
60 Bottled fuel

64 Three more Jacksons
68 The Bard's river
69 Confused
70 Point-return link
71 Ump follower?
72 Soup-kitchen patrons
73 Kindergartener

Down

1 Ticker-tape machines?
2 Leslie Caron role
3 *The Virginian* novelist Wister
4 Son — gun
5 Capt.'s superior
6 Susan of *Beauty and the Beast*
7 It's off-limits
8 Walkman, e.g.
9 "Naughty, naughty!"
10 Citrus city
11 Super 8, e.g.
12 Unbelievable bargain
14 Disguised, informally
18 Metric prefix
19 Tucker of country
24 — up (cancel)
25 Notwithstanding
27 Paint sloppily
28 Theater divisions
29 Theater sign
30 Pita sandwich
31 Embarrass
32 "— a story"
36 Comic Carvey
37 Opponent for Bjorn
38 Like most hoopsters
40 Pair of oxen
42 Leave port
45 Imminent danger
49 Jacobs Field player
50 Outlaw Younger
51 Cognizant of
52 Fix the crosshairs on
53 Cask part
54 Sierra Nevada lake
58 Up-to-the-minute
59 Move carefully
61 Kind of certificate
62 Periodic table fig.
63 Sweep's target
65 Ex-governor Richards
66 Composer Rorem
67 Thumbs-down vote

Puzzle 1-42: Precious Words

Across

1 Gospel author
5 Letterman, e.g.
9 Big name in primitive art
14 Begin bidding
15 Narcissus's admirer
16 Pueblo building material
17 Bobbysoxers' dance
19 Emulate Saint Thomas
20 Wounded-in-action award?
22 Cow catcher
23 —-twist (exert pressure)
24 Doctors' gp.
27 Nav. officer
28 Ray variety
31 Steal a glance
32 Characteristic
34 — firma
35 Jealous?
40 Saunter
41 Declare invalid
42 Icky stuff
43 April Fools' Day
45 — *Girl Friday* (Cary Grant film)
48 Truly
49 The whole shooting match
50 Animals
52 Memorable occasion?
57 Assembly instrument
59 Preserve, in a way
60 Together
61 *Born Free* lioness
62 Medicinal plant
63 Suggest
64 Newspaper department
65 Uses a Singer

Down

1 Group spirit
2 Missing link
3 Time for dodge ball, perhaps
4 Granny and Windsor
5 Austria's Lamarr
6 Folk singer Phil
7 Scattergun ammo
8 "Cheek to Cheek" musical
9 Berlin's *Call Me* —
10 Stench
11 — Methodist University
12 Wane
13 Get firm
18 P, to Plato

21 "Able was I — . . ."
25 Big name in *Wheel of Fortune*
26 Rubber-stamp
28 Mineo of the movies
29 "Muskrat Ramble" composer Ory
30 In a conflict
31 —-and-stick labels
32 Mao's Long March, e.g.
33 Robinson or Leonard of the ring
34 Calendar abbr.
35 Susan Lucci's elusive quest
36 Pout
37 French restaurant morsel
38 Social connections
39 Explosive letters
43 Ointment contaminant?
44 Undernourished
45 Gridiron gathering
46 Lined up
47 Accept a proposal
49 Red as —
50 Tall red cap
51 Fields of expertise
53 Radius neighbor
54 Perry's penner
55 *Guarding* — (1994 movie)
56 Furniture hardwood
57 Field of expertise, slangily
58 Purpose

Puzzle 1-43: Right at Home

1	2	3	4		5	6	7	8	9	10		11	12	13

58 Zion National Park home
60 *The Tempest* character
64 Nixon's 1960 running mate
67 Chang's twin
68 Eaves dropper?
69 Diamond of gangsterdom
70 West of *I'm No Angel*
71 Consider at length
72 Young woman

Down

1 Speed-of-sound word
2 Suffix with switch
3 Skater Katarina
4 Satisfies fully
5 Get droopy
6 Used-car ad word
7 Thor's dad
8 Doesn't own
9 Finishes
10 Original Beatle Sutcliffe
11 Man of parts
12 *The — of Flatbush* (1974 Stallone flick)
13 Spinning toy
18 Mont Blanc is part of it
19 Ten-gallon hat
24 "— boy!"
26 — -Bah (*The Mikado* character)
27 Crowd cheers
28 Bunches
29 Fashion mag
33 Cabinet member, for example
35 Rough husk
36 The — of Calcutta
38 Fed lines to
39 Regarding
40 Take five
42 Golfer Ballesteros
43 Act the siren
48 Wall finish
50 Milky stone
52 The Colosseum, e.g.
53 Burn superficially
54 Leaky-pen consequence
56 Under-bridge dweller of myth
57 1954 giant-ant movie
59 Opening lyrics of a children's tune
61 Concept
62 Quiche-making ingredients
63 To a smaller degree
65 Itty-bitty bark
66 Three times, in prescriptions

Across

1 Kitten cries
5 Crosses the plate
11 Prince — Khan (Hayworth hubby)
14 Operatic solo
15 Passionate
16 Dovish remark
17 Home-operated business
20 The Plaza, for one
21 Picnic pests
22 Fuss
23 It's essentially chopped pork
25 Apartment leak-fixers
27 — Dawn Chong
30 Oil-treatment letters
31 Stovetop vessel
32 ". . . and to — good night!"
34 Ernest of country
37 Lyricist Hammerstein
41 Has a good poker hand
44 "Higher Love" singer Winwood
45 Mannheim Mrs.
46 Jersey hoopsters
47 Drip-feed tubes
49 — -Magnon
51 Morse "E"
52 Balance-sheet entries
55 Held onto
57 Kovacs's Nairobi —

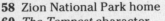

Puzzle 1-44: Diamond Skills

Across

1 Ill-gotten wealth
5 Zermatt locale
9 It may be organized
14 Lipinski feat
15 Wife of Jacob
16 Nonsense
17 Need aspirin, perhaps
20 Meathead's mother-in-law
21 Unique
22 Reading room
23 — Jima
26 Toil
27 Meas. of recording speed
30 Pipe material
32 *Casino* — (1967 film)
34 — *Shandy* (Sterne novel)
37 Its logo is an alligator
38 Win big
41 Senate worker
42 Time-wasters
43 Wizard's word
46 Stilettos of a sort
47 Mag. staffers
48 Pothook shape
50 Tippler
51 Grille protector
54 Attorney —
56 Psychologist Havelock
58 Take a break
63 Only have eyes for
64 Like khaki
65 Wood-shaping tool
66 — out (dwindle)
67 Rhythmic cheer
68 Teen's Saturday-night request, perhaps

19 Stadium sound
24 Escorting
25 Had a scull session?
27 Shaver
28 Intrigues
29 Club —
30 Calls, to an advertiser
31 Indian chief
33 Cry of dismay
34 Graham Greene's *The — Man*
35 Disneyland thrillers
36 Cocks and bulls
39 Jazz singer Laine
40 Good condition
41 Lummox
44 Tie up
45 Christiania, today
49 Like the beach
51 Shiv
52 Swank
53 Barbecue leftovers?
54 One of the lower forty
55 Used to be
57 Security problem
58 Limit
59 Sidewalk stand sale
60 Young 'un
61 Pharmacy salt
62 Crude-oil unit: abbr.

Down

1 Trimmed
2 Show aplenty
3 Ulyanov, originally
4 Highway mishap
5 Pub pint
6 Moon-vehicle acronym
7 One of the Bears
8 Wall-system part
9 Half a magician's incantation
10 Mindless memorizing
11 Gambler's marker
12 Debussy's "La —"
13 Watch closely
18 Intense desire

Puzzle 1-45: Dog Stars

Across

1 Worse, as excuses go
6 Unescorted
10 Bargain opportunity
14 Sunshine State city
15 12 to 1, e.g.
16 Attired
17 Calligraphy line
18 Verdi heroine
19 Posterior
20 Sound of disapproval
21 "Gone" singer
24 Bar food
26 Lip-smacking good
27 Ice Cube, for one
29 Does as told
31 Crocus's family
32 Take giant steps
34 Start of a one-two
37 Makes reference to
39 Enjoy the buffet
40 Alibi
42 Woodworking tool
43 In Margaritaville?
46 Geom. figure
47 Have a feeling
48 Cochise or Geronimo
50 Cupid's mate
52 You must remember this

53 One of the "Neutron Dance" group
56 GAO employee
59 Spoken
60 Ancient mariner
61 Lets the pitch go by
63 Off
64 — many words
65 Put forth
66 Hard to pin down
67 Filly filler
68 Skin, in combinations

Down

1 Disoriented
2 Old pros
3 1972 Olympics star
4 Connecticut collegian
5 Common fund-raiser
6 Brittle bit
7 Work like a slave
8 Autobahn vehicle
9 Conceded
10 Go downhill fast?
11 Prime party-goers
12 Ungracefully thin
13 Swirl in the stream
22 Corrida reward
23 Helen or Rutherford B.
25 Basilica section
27 Costa —
28 Saharan
29 Make like Cicero
30 Take the bait
33 Kinski or MacLaine role
34 Memorable Woodstock performer
35 St. Louis sight
36 8 bits, commonly
38 Win every game
41 Old London transport
44 Actor Banderas
45 Cartoon chipmunk
47 In need of air freshener
49 Split
50 1911 Chemistry Nobelist
51 — fours
52 Pal of Porthos
53 Words of Hope?
54 New York college
55 Tweed's nemesis
57 Salon treatment
58 Detective duo's dog
62 Bunyan cutter

Puzzle 1-46: New York State of Mind

Across

1 No — land
5 Low-pH solution
9 Actress Bara
14 Over again
15 Remove with a dipper
16 'Copter part
17 Jane Eyre's love
20 Turn on an axis
21 Hash house patron
22 City of southern Italy
25 Jet-setters' jet
26 Election Day day: abbr.
27 Cowboy leader
33 NYC straphangers' line
34 Huskers' units
35 Drunkard
36 Schlepper
39 Toddler
40 Bridge seats
41 — de menthe
42 Unique individual
44 Egyptian boy-king
45 Broadway composer of *Fanny*
47 Hit-leader Rose
48 Scandal's conclusion?
49 Like Capone's puss
51 "Watch This —" (billboard message)
54 Debtor
55 U.S. army scout and showman
61 Footnote abbr.
62 "Mother of Mercy, is this the end of —?"
63 Netman Nastase
64 Beau —
65 Declare positively
66 Dispatched a dragon

Down

1 Ginnie —
2 In addition
3 In-house publication
4 Valleylike tracts
5 Firm, spaghettiwise
6 Elevator unit
7 Altar vow
8 Yule mo.
9 Written discourse
10 Man, to a tapeworm
11 Cigar end?
12 Active one
13 O'Hare info
18 Capek's robot drama
19 "— Rebel"
22 Do some suturing
23 Dawn goddess
24 Patrick Henry and Daniel Webster
25 "All — go!"
28 University of Maine town
29 Valuable Hawaiian wood
30 Military roster
31 Shrewd
32 Like Matryoshka dolls
37 Funnyman Philips
38 Move to new digs
43 Put on the Rit, again
46 Affair of honor
47 Abridgment
50 Saddler's tool
51 Theater walk-on, for short
52 Cpls.' inferiors
53 Throw — (go ape)
55 Quagmire
56 ". . . man — mouse?"
57 Roy G. — (rainbow mnemonic)
58 Dry — (solid carbon dioxide)
59 Gaming cube
60 Landscaping shrub

Puzzle 1-47: Cloning Around

Another clue for 56 Down is "Word with aloe."

54 Gutter site
59 Charlie Parker's sax
60 Stooge's illegal plant?
62 Penn
63 Lotus- — (*Odyssey* figure)
64 Prima donna's tune
65 Advertising ploy
66 — bar (motorcycle part)
67 Loony

Down

1 Boom supporter
2 1969 expansion player
3 Landed
4 Astronaut Slayton
5 Start of MGM's motto
6 Dwarfs, e.g.
7 Descendant
8 Diving birds
9 Goes formal
10 Field's confederate?
11 Sylvia Plath collection
12 Smooth out
13 Rearranges a database
18 Trebek or Sajak
24 Laurel/Hardy separator
26 Pram rider
27 Dexterous
28 Opponent for Bjorn
29 "Smooth Operator" singer
30 Rock band's sound quality?
31 Dialless watch device: abbr.
33 Musical ability
34 1 on the Mohs scale
35 Gist
36 Dual-purpose mint
38 Jazzman Montgomery
41 Astonishment
42 Origins
43 Adversary
44 Olympic blades
46 Thick liqueurs
47 Kind of diet or helmet
48 Jack of *The Wizard of Oz*
49 Ready to be drawn
50 Broods
53 Laotian's neighbor
55 *Pequod* skipper
56 Miles of *Psycho*
57 Issue
58 Mineral springs
61 Snoop

Across

1 Honey of a beverage?
5 Syria's Hafez al- —
10 Fools
14 Linchpin site
15 Behave like a migraine
16 Musician Guthrie
17 Lee's catch of the day?
19 Fact-fudger
20 Tribal emblem
21 Mix, in a way
22 Time to give up?
23 City southwest of Le Havre
25 Creates a coif
27 Refusal to conform
31 Many summer babies
32 Rejoicing
33 Rejoicing
37 Rover's friend
38 Lots of money
39 Fill with cargo
40 Archie or Veronica
43 Legendary Indian Bob
45 Flock females
46 Ape
47 Picked
50 Word before love or lunch
51 Carry on
52 Raison d'—

Puzzle 1-48: Losers

Across

1 Judge Judy's garb
5 The basics
9 Magicians' props
14 — -deucy
15 Save in Tupperware
16 Naxos marketplace
17 The Beatles' "Let —"
18 It may be tall
19 "Twist and —"
20 Actress Ruby
21 Pittance
23 Freshet
25 New Mexico art center
26 Not lost, as writings
29 Susan of *L.A. Law*
33 Italian supermodel
35 "— Joe's"
37 News org. created in 1958
38 — Act (1715 law)
39 *Glengarry Glen Ross* playwright
40 Film-crew assistant
41 Wood-shop tool
42 Pitches in
43 Prepares spuds
44 Illinois River port
46 Take on, as a mortgage
48 Aware of
50 Type of piano
53 1994 Paul Newman film
58 Concert-schedule letters
59 "Brother, Can You Spare —?"
60 Dynamic start
61 Everglades denizen
62 Floor installer
63 — over (collapse)
64 On the — (collecting relief)
65 Navel orange's lack
66 Poorbox coins
67 Start of many a Shatner film

Down

1 Fridge invasions
2 Composition for eight
3 Nixon friend
4 Hand- — coordination
5 Airborne-allergen result
6 Actor Bridges
7 Composed
8 Nodded off
9 Total failure
10 Shocked

11 Twelve
12 Word with wonder or miracle
13 Glut
21 — -nine-tails
22 Lapidary's measure
24 Way out
27 Patricia of *The Fountainhead*
28 Cigar industry center
30 Ragtime dance
31 ". . . baked in —"
32 What Jack Frost does to your nose
33 Wrap tightly, to a sailor
34 Right-hand person
36 Hardy heroine
39 Like some chili
40 Vasco da —
42 Impedes
43 "Hooey!"
45 Lodged at the dorm
47 Tape reels
49 Japanese port
51 Dangerous virus
52 10K participant
53 Turner and Hentoff
54 "Garfield" pooch
55 Gall
56 "I — Good"
57 Utah city
61 Savings acct. alternatives

Puzzle 1-49: Anatomy Lesson

Across

1 Andean beast of burden
6 Healthful hangouts
10 Stars and — (Confederate flag)
14 *Great Circle* writer Conrad
15 To the — (completely)
16 Actor Baldwin
17 "I'll Never — Again"
18 Jai —
19 Nat or Natalie
20 Previously used
22 Intellectually sharp
23 "— a Song Go . . ."
24 "Go!" preceder
26 Built in advance
30 Amateur
31 Sitarist Shankar
32 *The Nazarene* author Sholem
35 Monastery head
39 Freeh man?
41 Gardener's tool
42 Round of fire, as a salute
43 Entrance-ramp sign
44 Designer Cassini
46 Stage prompts
47 Within: Prefix
49 Inquirers
51 Few and far between
54 Milne's *The House at — Corner*

56 Baseball great Hubbell
57 Barracks trunk
63 Introduction to culture?
64 Final notice?
65 Sweatband site
66 Like superior deli meat
67 American Beauty
68 Three-card — (hustler's game)
69 Medication
70 Whitetail or roebuck
71 Fencers' gear

Down

1 La Rue of the oaters
2 Peru's capital
3 Related by blood
4 Pinochle play
5 Hemoglobin shortage
6 Elm offering
7 Automatic — (navigation system)
8 "There oughta be —!"
9 Penny-pinching
10 Consecutive
11 Skin-lotion ingredients
12 U.S. Grant cosignatory
13 Bloodhound's trail
21 Napoleon's exile spot
25 Memorable times
26 Hyde Park buggy
27 Fury
28 At any time
29 Young trout
30 Fare- —-well
33 "Get lost!"
34 Honorary Ky. title
36 Like Carl Perkins's suede shoes
37 Going- — (inspection)
38 Sleep restlessly
40 Addition column
45 Liverpool lockup
48 Sportswriter Frank
50 "— State" (Missouri)
51 Burn with hot water
52 Beeper
53 Pianist Claudio
54 Composure
55 Playful aquatic mammal
58 Double-reed instrument
59 Cut short, as hair
60 Cows, in the old days
61 Villa d'—
62 Map rds.

Puzzle 1-50: Possessed

For the entry to 53 Across another clue is "Author Fleming and namesakes."

Across

1 Guinness, e.g.
6 Museum regulars
11 The — (authority figure)
14 "— You Love"
15 Loosen a four-in-hand
16 Uproar
17 Kind of bear or cap
18 Dunce's place
19 Quarterback's syllable
20 *Clermont* tag
23 Blanc, e.g.
26 Poseidon's realm
27 — noire
28 1800 symphony in C
34 Sundance's gal
35 Bellow
36 Gold-discovery site
42 Claudius I's adopted son
43 Shakespearean villain
46 "Arrangement in Gray and Black," familiarly
53 McShane and McKellen
54 Spasm
55 Johnny —
56 Rocky Raccoon's find
62 College sr.'s exam
63 Po basin city
64 Writer Joyce Carol —
68 China's — Piao
69 Doughnut topper
70 Blue jay's topper
71 Tolkien creature
72 Lugs
73 Mournful sound

24 Wimbledon call
25 Caresses
29 Upsilon preceder
30 Box-score boot
31 Turndowns
32 "I Want You" uncle
33 Calendar abbr.
37 Cable option
38 Part of AT&T: abbr.
39 Before, to Browning
40 Kindled
41 Comic Bert
44 Start to whiz?
45 Celestial body
46 Move like Jell-O
47 "Waiter! There's a — my soup!"
48 Start a paragraph
49 Compass reading
50 Con games
51 Playing marble
52 "One — Jump"
57 Skip over
58 The Velvet Underground vocalist
59 Long cut
60 Deadly poison
61 Merit
65 Gridiron gadget
66 Immigrant's course: abbr.
67 NL city

Down

1 Small taste
2 Tango need
3 Peanut product
4 B-52 gp.
5 Sweet-singing bird
6 With 11-Down, "Songs of a Wayfarer" composer
7 In the know about
8 School on the Thames
9 Ocho —, Jamaica
10 Magazine debuting in 1978
11 See 6-Down
12 Legal-age attainers
13 Maybe someday
21 Actor Gorcey
22 — -Wan Kenobi
23 Burrows of the theater

Puzzle 1-51: Metalworker's Wares

Across

1 Asparagus serving
6 Type of ranch
10 Hourglass filler
14 Where to find a gladiator
15 Oratorio solo
16 Composer Stravinsky
17 Metalworker, James Bond style?
19 Like the White Rabbit
20 — bag
21 Seagoing forces
23 Pornographic
27 Puts back in the mailbox
28 'Copter propellers
29 Supreme Court Justice Ruth — Ginsburg
30 Excursions
31 "Unforgettable" name
32 Houston ball player
36 Lend a hand
37 "My — and Only"
38 Golfer's undoing
39 Bone prefix
41 Alfred E. Neuman's publication
42 Camera manufacturer
43 Beyond the 'burbs
45 Winter driving aid
46 Created, as a cabinet
49 Far from extravagant

50 Type of tire
51 Look through the blindfold
52 "Zip — -Doo-Dah"
53 Metalworker in the dungeon?
59 Perch for Puss
60 Greeting —
61 Copse
62 Did some gardening
63 Units at Wimbledon
64 Slackened, with "up"

Down

1 Give in to gravity
2 Not con
3 Slithery swimmer
4 "— how"
5 Roof supports
6 Admirer of Beatrice
7 Yen
8 Pachisi piece
9 Deserved
10 Metalworker author Shel?
11 Encore!
12 Famous
13 Word with rehearsal or code
18 Charged particles
22 On the bounding main
23 Straight: prefix
24 Drills holes
25 Wilt the —
26 Metalworker, Dickens style?
27 X- —
29 Humdrum
31 Berber, for one
33 In a — (instantly)
34 Kentucky Derby and the Indy 500
35 Painting at MOMA, perhaps
40 — sight! (neat!)
42 Electrical problem
44 Objects from an earlier age
45 Consider
46 Wall Street event of 1929
47 Limbaugh's medium
48 Fred Astaire's sister
49 Fixes an argyle
51 Sweet wine
54 *Norma* — (Sally Field flick)
55 Older Gershwin
56 Good manners
57 Adam's madame
58 Composer Rorem

Puzzle 1-52: Here, Kitty

In crosswords, the word *kitty* refers to a pool of money more often than to Garfield's offspring.

Across

1 Necklace unit
5 Poet Walter — Mare
9 Seer's card
14 Frogner Park locale
15 Maleficent
16 Sheeplike
17 Kenton or Getz
18 Botch
19 Measured out by walking
20 Kitty in some entrees?
23 — King Cole
24 Neighbor of Ind.
25 Former grape
29 River of England
31 Fidel's friend
34 Cool
35 If not
36 Cole —
37 Kitty in a heater?
40 Actress Balin and namesakes
41 Seine feeder
42 QE 2, e.g.
43 — Moines
44 RBI, for one
45 Circe and her sort
46 Delay, with "off"
47 Heavy weight
48 Kitty in a Graham Greene novel?
56 Violin-maker Stradivari's teacher
57 Locale of Camus's *The Plague*
58 Droplet on a farewell note?
59 Canary's cousin
60 Bog
61 Killer whale
62 Wed
63 Gravy server
64 Grayish

Down

1 Bartlett's cousin
2 Bk. of the Bible
3 Kirghiz mountain range
4 Therefore: Fr.
5 Abase
6 Blessed —
7 Have ess trouble
8 Additionally
9 Overthrow
10 Profit
11 Pilaf base
12 Wad filler
13 A Kennedy
21 "Mack the —"
22 All in
25 Speedy
26 Unescorted
27 Jots
28 More than weeps
29 Desirable guests
30 "Oh, now I get it"
31 Genetic replica
32 New —, Conn.
33 Pitchers
35 Essayist Lamb's pen name
36 Recipe direction
38 Bingo's kin
39 Aid for a broken arm
44 Lying face up
45 Shakespearean form
46 — four (teacake)
47 Crown
48 Govt. agents
49 Famed spy of WW II
50 Unknown Soldier's place
51 Half a sextet
52 Greek portico
53 Share of the divorce settlement
54 Per, in pricing
55 Cart
56 Sun Devils' campus: abbr.

Puzzle 1-53: Happy Birthday, America!

58 Thurman of *Pulp Fiction*
59 Sparkler for 41 Across
64 Highway exit
66 El — (weather phenomenon)
67 *The — Is Right*
68 Home of the Mets
69 Sound of a Clydesdale
70 Before now
71 — *of Eden*
72 "Will there be anything —?"
73 Tended to the lawn

Down

1 Construction beam
2 — contendere (legal plea)
3 Dismal
4 Either of two *Paper Moon* stars
5 Patrick Rafter's sport
6 *Body Snatchers* attacks
7 Quarter, for one
8 Duck
9 Cowboys' home
10 Letterman's dental feature
11 Love, in Lyon
12 Man who left a mark
13 Crookedly
21 — and desist
22 Set of principles
26 Gave up rights to
27 *La Traviata* highlight
28 — a hand
29 Shane portrayer Alan
31 Took on cargo
34 Judges
36 Prop for *Das Boot*
38 Cartoon light bulb
39 Dunderheads
40 Bigfoot, e.g.
42 Measure of alcohol strength
43 — *On Sunday* (1960 film)
48 Musician now known as . . .?
50 Slip by
52 *The Mummy's* — (1945 thriller)
53 Brando's birthplace
54 Specifies
55 Tremolo
57 Sour
60 Hall-of-Famer Slaughter
61 Elvis's nickname
62 Behold, to Brutus
63 *The Brady Bunch* actor
65 Presidential candidate Paulsen

Across

1 Item in Fort Knox
6 — tea
10 Strip in the Mideast
14 Withstood
15 PBS science series
16 "Grand Old Man" — Alonzo Stagg
17 Sigourney Weaver thriller of 1979
18 Ampoule
19 Barrel opener?
20 Sparkler for 41 Across
23 Yorkshire river
24 *True* — (1995 film)
25 Admit a mistake
27 — *in the Family*
30 Mizzen, for one
32 H. Rider Haggard adventure tale
33 Practice palmistry
35 Controversial sitcom of the late '70s
37 Dialect
41 Theme of this puzzle
44 Cobra's cousin
45 Desert-like
46 Adroit
47 Swab
49 Take a — (lose on purpose)
51 Campfire residue
52 Monarch's wife
56 *The Fugitive* actress Ward

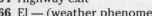

Puzzle 1-54: Wag the Jaw

The answer to 31 Down is the Spanish word for January — ENERO.

Across

1 Comic strip Viking
6 Nora Charles's pooch
10 Tucked in
14 Guam's capital
15 Post
16 "You Don't Know Me" singer Jerry
17 Luxury fur
19 Melodramatic outburst
20 Krazy —
21 Aaron of diamond fame
22 Novel by de Maupassant
24 Type opener
25 Turn informer
26 Las Vegas headliner Lola
29 Plains Indian
32 Scents
33 Life-threatening
34 The Little Red —
35 Insufficiency
36 Papal vestment
37 Type of novel
38 Adjective suffix
39 "— long, life short": Goethe
40 Chair repairer
41 Rap session
43 Regained consciousness
44 "— fast!" ("Hold it!")
45 Part of TLC
46 Luxuriant
48 Bear's home
49 Top dog letters
52 "— corny as Kansas . . ."
53 "Not by the hair on my —"
56 Beget
57 African river
58 Patterned silk
59 Actress Harper
60 Request at the barber
61 Sen. Kefauver

Down

1 Shelley of *Charlie's Angels*
2 Muslim commander
3 Trot or lope
4 Dear Abby's sister
5 Alan of *Dharma and Greg*
6 Type of acid
7 Vaccine inventor Jonas
8 "— death do us part"
9 Banjo player of song
10 "Venus" singer Frankie
11 Legendary choreographer
12 Cowboy actor Jack
13 He loved Lucy
18 Mandlikova of tennis
23 List-shortening abbr.
24 Good-natured escapade
25 Newspaper pictorial sections
26 Vitaminic acid
27 Make — for (hurry)
28 Swains, à la Sir Walter Scott
29 "Button your lip!"
30 City in southern Cal.
31 January, in Jerez
33 1980 title role for Dom Deluise
36 Flower shop sign
37 Joan Sutherland, for one
39 Matinee times: abbr.
40 "— back to ole Virginny . . ."
42 Clamors
43 Something to raise?
45 Cave — (beware of dog)
46 Shopper's aid
47 Pierre's girlfriend
48 Leslie Caron role
49 Ticket
50 Ireland
51 Wallet fillers
54 LBJ pet
55 *Fatherhood* author, familiarly

Puzzle 1-55: Notable Addresses

Across

1 Secluded valley
5 Takes five
10 Type of reader?
14 Enthusiastic, as a review
15 Seedsman Washington — Burpee
16 MBA specialty
17 They try harder
18 Fissile rock
19 Sousa instrument
20 Notable Monopoly address
23 Campaigned
24 "— is an island"
28 Open, in a way
32 Something for nothing
35 West —
36 Skin soother
37 Caviar, essentially
38 Notable Hollywood address
42 Humpty Dumpty, for one
43 "Thanks —!"
44 Orion's left foot
45 Of star quality
48 Ebb
49 Mug for Pilsner
50 *What's Up, —?* (1972 film)
51 Notable TV address
59 Eager

62 Ten-percenter
63 Home of the Bruins: abbr.
64 Fictional Jane
65 Part of LPN
66 Wilbur Post's friend of '60s TV
67 Wine label info
68 Chop off
69 Mountain cat

Down

1 Kind of bag
2 Lamp material
3 "See no — . . ."
4 Nutcracker's suite
5 Spanky was one
6 First name in patriotism
7 Eastern European
8 Vision opener
9 Detected
10 Shooting star
11 Setting for *E.R.*
12 S.F. Hill
13 Genetic letters
21 Fit to be tied
22 French article
25 Noted Vegas hotel
26 Held dear
27 Follett's *Eye of the* —
28 Unexpected victories
29 Chewy candy
30 Available, in a way
31 USNA grad
32 Genesis event
33 Disastrous defeat
34 Skinny fish
36 Up to the job
39 Make lace
40 Build up
41 Crooner Damone
46 Disney prexy
47 St. Louis-to-Chicago dir.
48 Scorecard lineup
50 Thick
52 Lacking, in Le Havre
53 Chills
54 TV's — Griffin
55 Roast cut
56 Hose shade
57 Type of school: abbr.
58 "I did it!"
59 Lock opener
60 Size up, silently
61 Period in history

Puzzle 1-56: Zoo Acts

Constructors love alliteration in clues, especially for a foreign language entry (see 46 Down).

Across

1 "—! poor Yorick"
5 Seraglio
10 Lose one's feathers
14 Occupation
15 Duck
16 Maintain
17 Lavish affection (on)
18 Papal tongue
19 Church section
20 "See See Rider" group, with "The"
22 "Happy Together" group, with "The"
24 Campus mil. group
26 Kalahari stopovers
27 Subject for Peter Maas
31 Data, for short
34 "In-A-Gadda-Da-Vida" group
39 DEA agent
40 Miss America's crowning glory
41 Rhine tributary
44 "Shambala" group
47 South African fox
48 "Bye-bye, Jose"
49 Great anxiety
53 Sailor's cry
56 "I'm a Believer" group, with "The"
59 "Ticket to Ride" group, with "The"
64 Wings, in botany
65 U.S. Grant opponent
67 Road opener
68 London art gallery
69 Tale of Achilles
70 Pound of poetry
71 Part of MIT: abbr.
72 Soothes
73 Retain

Down

1 Pierce portrayer
2 Motown athlete
3 Not pro
4 Give the impression
5 Response to a ring
6 Command from the captain
7 "I smell a —!"
8 Use a blue pencil
9 PC offering
10 Type of ray
11 Racetracks
12 "Drove my Chevy to the — . . ."
13 Lock
21 Kuwaiti, for one

23 When angry, it's raised
25 South Carolina military academy
27 Part of an hr.
28 Coach Parseghian
29 — Worth, Texas
30 2.54 centimeters
32 Emperor 54–68 A.D.
33 Shrapnel scattering, in Nam
35 Colorado natives
36 Four-in-hands
37 Sick in bed, with "up"
38 Radio antenna type
42 It precedes sigma
43 French connections
45 "At any — . . ."
46 Zip, to Zapata
49 Prized violin
50 Fireballer Ryan
51 Tiny pests
52 Trapshooting
54 Crosswise to the keel
55 Requirements
57 Guitarist Clapton
58 *The Fugitive* actress Ward
60 Journey for Mr. Spock
61 Idle
62 Joyce's homeland
63 Challenge to a duel
66 — Abner of Dogpatch

Puzzle 1-57: Between Hook and Sinker

Across

1 Sound from Rin-Tin-Tin
5 Author Mario
9 — blanche
14 Stick in the fridge?
15 Part of UCLA: abbr.
16 Then, to Pierre
17 Simba's retreat
18 Dandy's companion
19 Hindi royals
20 Meeting place for offense and defense
23 Tropical cuckoo
24 Auto of Olds
25 Savion Glover's forte
28 Board Amtrak
32 Billboard messages
35 Rodeo rope
37 Forever, nearly
38 Polish prose
39 From A to Z
42 Homeowner's proof
43 The Fab —
44 Trapshooting
45 Harris and Sullivan
46 "We should — angels do"
48 Ship initials
49 Wharton degree
50 Took by the hand
52 Zero in on

61 007, for one
62 Popular board game
63 Macadamize
64 Past or present
65 Mountain lake
66 Foreboding
67 Those: Span.
68 "Snake eyes" in crapshooting
69 Yurt

Down

1 Pod of a cotton plant
2 Jai —
3 Curb
4 Asian nation
5 Arctic bird
6 Les états —
7 Lifeguard's nose ointment
8 Finished
9 Bizet opera
10 "Remember the —!"
11 Author Jaffe
12 HS subject
13 Palindromic Latin verb
21 Actress Tatum
22 Type of setter
25 Swap
26 Felt poorly
27 Grows ashen
29 Pavarotti, for example
30 Rake
31 Cavern, to Keats
32 Parting shot, from Pierre
33 Emulates a gourmet
34 Reinstates some copy
36 Playwright Mosel
38 BPOE member
40 Gift — (chatter's talent)
41 Ruhr steel center
46 Ebbs
47 Sigourney Weaver sci-fi sequel film
49 Brainy bunch
51 Whistle stop
52 Check follower?
53 Has a birthday
54 Superman's alter ego
55 Outside: prefix
56 Vivacity
57 Entice
58 Fortune's partner
59 Pizzeria fixture
60 1996 Broadway hit

Puzzle 1-58: Pocket Change

Crosswordese, a special lingo of three- and four-letter words, consists of words you only see in the grid — like 37 Down (ENDO).

Across

1 Colgate rival
6 Johnson of *Laugh-In*
10 Lawyer Dershowitz
14 Oprah's production company
15 Quantity of paper
16 Swipe opener
17 Bird-related
18 Dish with mint jelly
19 Have no doubts
20 Cable channel
23 Unrefined metal
24 Historical time
25 Baby minder
27 Cool, to Ringo
30 Disagreement
33 Collar insert
34 Litmus changer
36 Role for Peter Fonda
38 Money at the Taj Mahal
41 Kurt Weill opus, with *The*
44 Family car
45 Word with area or penal
46 Units of work
47 China opener
49 "Arrivederci —"
51 Lush
52 Bleep out
54 Columnist LeShan
56 "So there!"
57 Woolworth's
64 Type of type: abbr.
66 Inauguration highlight
67 Bowler's beat
68 Caravel of 1492
69 Word on some diet-food labels
70 Everglades native
71 "No ifs, —, or . . ."
72 Jack of westerns
73 Farm machine make

Down

1 Martial arts star Jackie
2 Sitarist Shankar
3 Julia's brother
4 Nietzsche's *Thus — Zarathustra*
5 Copier refills
6 *Alice's Restaurant* singer Guthrie
7 Crack the books
8 Docile
9 Carve in relief
10 Inquire
11 Pre-desktop publishing machines
12 Worship
13 More fresh
21 Relish
22 Part of TNT
26 Hose shade
27 Minnesota —
28 Yearn
29 This is worth "two in the bush"
31 One of the Baldwin boys
32 General drift
35 College officials
37 Inner: prefix
39 "Cogito — sum" (Descartes)
40 Sunrise direction
42 Until the — time (eternally)
43 Red Sea republic
48 Baltimore baseball player
50 Confused
52 Limoges, for example
53 Cook your own meal?
55 Proverb
58 Colorado ski resort
59 James of jazz
60 "Excuse me"
61 Concerning, in court
62 Pitcher Johnny Vander —
63 Villa d'— (Italian estate)
65 Cruces opener

Puzzle 1-59: The Music Men

Across

1 Pianist Templeton of the '30s
5 Fulcrum for an oar
10 Noah's eldest
14 Pitcher Blue
15 Winslow the seascapist
16 Clothes for Caesar
17 Cassowary cousins
18 Place to remember
19 Tantrum
20 *South Pacific* composer
23 Longhorn
24 Broadway light
25 Watch spot
29 — *Afternoon* (Pacino flick)
33 Word ignored in alphabetizing titles
36 Year, to Yvette
38 Vision start
39 "Georgia on My Mind" composer
43 Greek vowel
44 Use a barbecue
45 Cotton fiber knot
46 Athens's foe
49 Permit
51 Polite bloke
53 Elbows on the table?
57 *Oh Kay!* composer

62 "What a shame!"
63 Related through Mom's side
64 Hercules's captive
65 Word with matinee
66 France's longest river
67 Yule tune
68 Hereditary element
69 Fed the kitty
70 *The Never Ending Story* author

Down

1 Alleges
2 Boundary
3 Draw out, as data
4 Popular nut
5 "— she blows!"
6 Keep a grip on
7 Sharif or Bradley
8 Dud
9 Wore away
10 Brawn
11 Frost
12 Breakfast order
13 Daisy — (Li'l Abner's girlfriend)
21 Spread
22 *Flubber* substance
26 Business abbr.
27 Stocking's undoing
28 — firma
30 College VIP
31 Sheltered, on the briny
32 Asta's cry
33 *All — and Heaven, Too*
34 Old-time skirt support
35 "I could — horse!"
37 Jannings or Ludwig
40 Notre Dame feature
41 Not in the pink
42 Horseshoe sounds
47 Dutch painter — Borch
48 Actress Lansbury
50 Girl in Maui
52 Companion to mortise
54 Faint
55 Like some roofs
56 Anoint, old style
57 Writer Andre
58 Harrow's rival
59 Trot is one
60 Raison d'—
61 Rex or Donna
62 Babe is one

Puzzle 1-60: Lights Out!

Across

1 Extinct bird
5 Administered medicine
10 *A — Called Wanda*
14 Citibank chairman John
15 Chou —
16 Understanding words
17 Girl of Green Gables
18 Golda and family
19 Picture of health?
20 Shady Glenn Miller theme?
23 Letter opener
24 Critical accolade
25 Señor add-on
28 *— and Old Lace*
32 Burdens
34 Eat like a cat
35 Sunless Serling series?
38 Less welcoming
41 Biblical suffix
42 Italian fashion center
43 Gloomy "Sundown" singer
46 Med. school degree
47 Jinx
48 Plentiful
51 Cable network
52 Pick up the pace, with "lively"
55 Daisy —
56 Murky Victor Young standard?
61 Highway exit
64 Minnie of Nashville
65 Gold medalist Lipinski
66 Mesopotamia, today
67 Lively: music
68 Radiate
69 Christian of fashion
70 1982 Kevin Bacon film
71 Took a canter

Down

1 Small measure
2 Wine: prefix
3 Fred Flintstone's pet
4 Danish city
5 Bad mark
6 Unique person
7 More foxy
8 "He ought to — little pay" (Robert Frost)
9 Deny
10 Idée — (obsession)
11 Neighbor of Leb.
12 Caspian, for one
13 "— there, you with the stars . . ."
21 Sermon topic
22 Overalls material
25 Tristram's beloved
26 Temporary resident
27 Get — of (understand)
28 Climb down
29 Suburban prowler: var.
30 Richard M. Nixon's veep — Agnew
31 Julia Child, for one
33 Automatic weapon
36 Ike's command
37 Norse hammer wielder
39 Teaching degree
40 Rule the —
44 Staples item
45 Earthquake
49 Shell out
50 Mandolin player Flatt
53 Nicholas Gage biography
54 — and simple
56 Letters of the Roman Empire
57 French weapon
58 — shanter
59 Parched
60 Assess
61 Devoid, with "of"
62 Jackie's second
63 — tse-tung

Puzzle 1-61: The Hourglass

Across

1 Big name in video games
6 Take a — at (try)
10 JFK sights
14 Mideast desert region
15 Diva's role
16 Winter weather hazard
17 Incense fragrance
19 Regarding
20 Poetic prizefighter
21 Cole and namesakes
22 Hit the ground
24 Senator Glenn's turf
25 Orchid tuber
26 Boxer Sonny
29 Tennis pro Testud
32 Related on mom's side
33 "— Cane"
34 Blue grass
35 Hand, to Enrico
36 Darns
37 Aspics
38 Lend a hand
39 *The Life of —*
40 — Madera, Cal.
41 Spears
43 Stopped
44 Caribbean island

45 Pick up the phone
46 Fishing nets
48 Overhang
49 Taste
52 Fail to fail, in school
53 "Teen-Age Crush" singer
56 TV funnyman Johnson
57 City and lake of Pennsylvania
58 Redwoods, e.g.
59 Box for practice
60 On a — (lucky)
61 Alamogordo event

Down

1 Looped vase handle
2 Greenish-blue
3 Hindu fire god
4 Color of a cool star
5 Sir Walter Scott classic
6 Took care of
7 Juan's uncles
8 *Much — About Nothing*
9 Sissy Spacek film: 1973
10 Black eye
11 "Guantanamera" group
12 Fatigue
13 Toboggan's kin
18 "Upon whose bosom snow has — . . ."
23 Fashion designer Gucci
24 Von Bismarck
25 Orphan Annie's dog
26 Actor Paul
27 "The bombs bursting — . . ."
28 Nicaraguan guerrilla of the '70s
29 Loudness units
30 *Prince of Tides* star Nick
31 Alleviated, with "up"
33 Softens
36 Duvall's role in *The Apostle*
37 Type of post
39 Pierre's dream
40 Piano's cousin
42 More dimwitted
43 Guinea pig
45 Dromedary
46 Health clubs
47 Wyatt of Western fame
48 Actor Jannings
49 Snick or —
50 March date
51 "Hey, you!"
54 El Dorado treasure
55 Mr. Linkletter

Puzzle 1-62: Time Keepers

Theme entries most often appear in parallel Across places within the grid and occasionally in the Down direction — for example, 5, 7, and 23 Down.

Across

1 Early spring bloom
6 Exchange
10 Coagulate
14 "It's —!"
15 "And here it is!"
16 Actor Cronyn
17 Woo-pitcher
18 Perched on
19 Pelvic bones
20 Give a hosing to
22 Military hairstyles
24 Alias letters
25 Munster mister
26 Evian, for one
29 Man on Skid Row
31 Quechuans
36 Tijuana gold
37 Ness, for one
39 Seed
40 Initial
42 One — time
43 Hike
44 Huxley's — *Hay*
45 Coverlet
47 Preschooler
48 Hidden loot
49 Lab burner
50 Retirement acct.
51 Always
54 Letter from Greece?
56 Running a temp
60 Computer screen option
64 In the thick of
65 Related
67 Prophet of the Old Testament
68 Trident prong
69 Aloha State bird
70 Mississippi has four
71 Type of collar
72 Comedian Carey
73 World's tallest tower

Down

1 Shortening
2 Composer Stravinksy
3 — rickey
4 The Cow Palace, e.g.
5 Distracted employee
6 RR stop
7 Lillian Hellman melodrama
8 Idolize
9 Type of tiger
10 Voguish
11 Humdinger
12 Skip over
13 Afternoon affairs
21 Reagan's Secretary of State
23 Rolex products
26 Divans
27 Paisley product
28 Large artery
30 Straight
32 Nonprofit radio call letters
33 Raccoon's cousin
34 Knight in shining —
35 Philly transport
38 Piquant
41 Family nickname
46 Change for five
52 Edible item
53 Glacial ridge
55 Levitated
56 Destiny
57 Exude
58 Chianti, e.g.
59 TV actress Barbara
61 Greek peak
62 Lascivious look
63 Colleen
66 Novel

Puzzle 1-63: Smorgasbord

59 Commedia del'—
60 Trattoria dessert
62 Jim Morrison was one
63 Pointed arch
64 Liability
65 Slaughter in baseball
66 One with a proxy
67 Some stable dwellers

Down

1 Gridlocks
2 Tony's cousin
3 Fenway ploy
4 Way up
5 Contemporary of Leo I
6 Jazz saxman Charlie
7 Regional flora and fauna
8 Shaker Lee
9 Hodgepodge
10 Magical phrase
11 Circuit
12 Faux pas
13 Mick's back-up
18 Dream state
22 Tends the squeaky wheel
24 Singer Celine
26 *M* director
27 Field
28 Husband of Ruth
29 Commuting conservationists
31 Word on an invoice
33 Elsie's remark
34 "You bet!"
35 Gibson film garb
36 Farm dwellers
38 Good serve
39 — and tell
42 Russian sea
43 Cordage fiber
45 Cling fast
46 Accountant's reading
47 Role for Bogart
48 Burr in Hamilton's side?
49 Tag-along's refrain
51 Boundary
53 Arm of the Black Sea
55 *The — King*
56 Hebrides island
57 Like a bug in a rug
58 Kinski role
61 "Long — and far away . . ."

Across

1 Apple computer entrepreneur
5 Coptic Church bishops
10 Mine finds
14 Lie adjacent
15 Corrupt
16 Larboard
17 Trattoria mainstay
19 Current currency
20 Tennis moment
21 Nanking dumpling
23 — the Fifth (claim immunity)
25 River through Grenoble
26 Chemist's uniform
30 Eric of *Nuns on the Run*
32 Like fans at a game
33 Taverna fare
37 Intimate
38 In unison
40 Ugandan Idi
41 Cantina order
43 American icefish
44 Popular cookie
45 Patrons
47 Margaret Mead subject
50 Charles, Prince of —
52 Cantina fare
54 Jonny Moseley, for one

Puzzle 1-64: With Apologies to Caesar

Sometimes a crossword theme containing an amusing message weaves through the grid.

Across

1 Hay measure
5 Bomb
9 Con game
13 Honeydew
14 Rickey ingredient
15 Negri of the silents
16 — *There* (Peter Sellers film)
17 Arab commander: var.
18 Actor Thicke
19 Beginning of a quip
22 "A Shropshire —" (A.E. Housman poem)
23 Houston team
24 Second part of the quip
30 French soldier's place
31 Prizefight setting
32 Coast of Del.
35 Teen follower
36 British weapons
37 La — Tar Pits
38 Bagel accompaniment
39 Evel strong suit
40 Strange
41 Third part of the quip
43 Film festival locale
46 Note in Guido's scale
47 End of the quip
54 Anklebones
55 Fe
56 Hodgepodges
57 "L' —, c'est moi"
58 Uncool one
59 Sierra —
60 Studies
61 Turns right
62 Author Ferber

Down

1 Complain
2 Touched down
3 More homesick
4 Emulate Dürer
5 Tire
6 Bridal carriage, for short
7 Skip
8 Relates
9 Lacedaemon
10 Feature of most TVs
11 Avis competitor
12 "Reins" for early Indians

13 Wharton degree
20 Despot Amin
21 Greek peak
24 River in South Africa
25 Cogito-sum connection
26 O'Keeffe country: abbr.
27 Input
28 "Goodnight" girl
29 Twenty, in Turino
32 Sutherland solo
33 Seabird
34 Cheryl or Alan
36 Packrat's pastime
37 Lamented
39 Keel part: var.
40 British author Hugh
41 Eskimos
42 Black or Yellow, for example
43 Quoted
44 Lessen
45 He was "The Man Without a Country"
48 Arboretum display
49 Oliver's request
50 Split or loose
51 Hill in Jerusalem
52 Playwright Gale
53 Peer Gynt's mother

Puzzle 1-65: So Long!

Across

1 Form-fitting
5 Sampras, for one
9 Fakir's faith
14 Exhortation to Nanette
15 — *Man* (1984 Estevez film)
16 Laminated rock
17 Barbershop quartet member
18 Fortitude
19 Greek isle
20 Philip Roth best-seller
23 Actress Ward
24 Wingtip width, for some
25 Down in the mouth
28 Early communications satellite
31 "You —!"
34 Golf shoe feature
36 DDE's opponent
37 Gymnastics coach Karolyi
38 Ernest Hemingway novel
42 Runner's measure
43 Baton Rouge-to-New Orleans dir.
44 Where some socks end
45 Favorite
46 Tapioca source
49 A crowd, in Capri?
50 Loo, in London
51 Vatican resident
53 Mario Lanza song

61 Down East
62 Indochina locale
63 Shortly
64 Proposal
65 DC strip, with "The"
66 Keyhole
67 Howard of shock radio
68 "— in Boots"
69 Role for Joan Fontaine

Down

1 Hidden obstacle
2 — contendere
3 Golden Rule preposition
4 Merchandise
5 Sort of sock
6 Battle Creek export
7 The *Iliad,* for one
8 Tiller opener
9 Credit card provider
10 Ignominy
11 Mary had a little one
12 Matty, Felipe, or Jesus
13 Jumble
21 The Divine Miss M
22 Last but not —
25 Mischief-maker
26 Role for Michael Caine
27 Attended to, with "with"
29 In January they're white
30 — Aviv
31 Tête topper
32 Fudd of cartoons
33 Demi follower
35 Real estate measure overseas
37 Forbid
39 Use a loom
40 Curlicue
41 Giraffe's cousin
46 Carlsbad attraction
47 "Oh, to be in England now that — there . . . "
48 Singing parts
50 *Titanic,* notably
52 Rub out
53 Cookie man
54 Place for Huck Finn
55 Abounding
56 Dungeon description
57 Biblical name
58 "— the Lonely"
59 8th-century conqueror of Spain
60 Poker prepayment

Part II
Sunday Puzzle Fun

The 5th Wave   By Rich Tennant

Puzzle 2-1: The Sundance Kid Grows Up

Across

1 *Show Boat* author Ferber
5 "Get lost!"
9 Ferrari covers
13 Blues singer James
17 Bring back, as a ruling
19 Part of an economic cycle
21 One of 62 Across
23 The — of two evils
24 Immersed, as with a hobby
25 U.S.-Canada canal
26 Brooklyn follower
27 One — million
29 It may be paper or plastic
31 Spirits from Jamaica
33 One of 62 Across
38 One of 62 Across
43 Isle off Eire
44 Paper purchase
46 "Xanadu" rockers
47 Gawk

48 Pressure-measuring device
50 Involves in litigation
52 Mom and Pop org.
54 Singer Adams
55 Vegas opener
57 Oaf
59 *A Nightmare on — Street*
61 Neighbor of Syr.
62 Theme of this puzzle
68 Start for cure or center
69 Gift from a wahine
70 Palm starch
71 Evian or Vichy
72 Gulf of Greece
74 Some sets
76 Exasperated sound
78 Drastically reduce, as costs
82 *To — a Thief* (Hitchcock thriller)
84 U.S. Open champ Ernie
86 Rip
88 *On the Waterfront* director Kazan

89 One of 62 Across
92 One of 62 Across
94 Partner to Adam
95 Hoosegow on Old Ironsides
97 Matterhorn, for one
98 Doctrine suffix
101 Finis
103 The Bard's stream
105 Small cavity, in botany
110 One of 62 Across
114 Heavenly
115 Like Cassandra
116 "I — to see you go!"
117 Ultraspeedy planes
118 — ball (arcade game)
119 Diner sign

Down

1 Regarding a particular historical time
2 Editorial manuscript notation
3 Rocker Lofgren
4 Picnic pests
5 More rigorous
6 — d'Antibes (Riviera resort)
7 Longfellow's bell town
8 High-schoolers
9 French breakfast bun
10 Comedic Skelton
11 Passes the exam easily
12 Mexican matron
13 Slalom curve
14 Henry Luce's weekly
15 Ticklish things
16 — of the Thousand Days
18 Valentino role
20 Sizes for corpulent men
22 RBI, for example
28 God of war
30 Seaweed
32 Remote control option
33 Droop
34 Pro-arms group: abbr.
35 — de Cologne
36 Slant
37 Worcestershire or soy
39 Famous
40 Circle spokes
41 Get up
42 Groucho-type looks
45 Pinochle scores
49 Warren of the Supreme Court
51 Where couch potatoes thrive
53 "— for the poor!"

56 Opposite of 2 Down
58 Drag one's heels
60 Swabs
62 Change chemically
63 First name in talk shows
64 Please, in Berlin
65 The Bridge on the — Kwai
66 Man of many words?
67 Car parker
73 Yearn
75 Oscar Madison, for one
77 Laugh track sound
79 "Thrilla in Manila" winner
80 Transgress
81 Crone
83 Moves like a helicopter
85 Many John Hancocks
87 Health problem
90 Credos
91 Pueblo meeting place
93 Shopper's indulgence
96 Plays at Augusta
98 The Seven Year —
99 Mets' home
100 Tuna-cheese sandwich
102 Platform
104 Bismarck's state: abbr.
106 Blunted foil
107 Sight-related suffix
108 Time before Easter
109 Work units
111 Word with whiz
112 Do needlework
113 Bauxite, for example

Puzzle 2-2: Put Up Your Dukes

Sometimes a theme's entries all answer to a common clue. You'll see what I mean as you solve this puzzle. By the way, the theme clues are easy to spot in this puzzle because they are all capitalized.

Across

1 Damon of *Good Will Hunting*
5 Stocking's undoing
9 *Misery* star James
13 Tater
17 Happily-after connection
18 Mister in Munich
19 Aware of
20 Turner or Sinatra
21 DUKE
25 Family vehicles
26 "— Together" (1969 Beatles hit)
27 Preminger and Kruger
28 Fashion designer Perry
31 Lucy's husband
32 West African nation
34 DUKE
41 Loser, with "ran"
42 Mars's counterpart
43 River into the Tatar Strait
44 Pie — mode
45 West of screen fame
46 Engages in litigation
47 "Get lost!"
49 Italian wine center
50 Rock group of yore Hot —
51 *Duck* — (Marx Brothers movie)
52 Choir members
53 DUKE
59 Cultural values
60 Long division word
61 Hankerings
62 *Underboss* author Peter
63 Like the Pillsbury doughboy
65 Quilting and spelling
66 Writer Bradbury
69 Actress MacGraw
70 Upkeep
71 *Thunderball* agent
72 Ticklish spot
73 DUKE
78 Angler's equipment
79 Fad
80 Diminish, as rain
81 Perplexed

84 Carry on
85 Bedouin
87 DUKE
94 *The — Warrior* (*Mad Max 2*)
95 Mercury or Saturn
96 Beer ingredient
97 Zilch
98 Farm dwellers
99 Datum on a wine bottle
100 Freudian topics
101 Fortitude

Down

1 Tom Seaver, once
2 City map abbr.
3 — Aviv
4 Lee of the links
5 It's below the knee
6 Home of a Loch monster
7 Hero of *Exodus*
8 Food suppliers
9 Stupendous
10 Chip in the kitty
11 — loss for words
12 Neither's partner
13 Kind of cling
14 Early British P.M. Sir William
15 Do — others . . .
16 Calendar boxes
22 Item from the Ming Dynasty
23 Like a yenta
24 Kind of bear
28 Dutch cheese
29 Kinks hit, 1970
30 Take it on the chin
31 Membership fees
32 Michelle Phillips or Cass Elliot
33 Boxing promoter Bob
35 Place to sweat it out
36 Porgy cousin
37 Cast member in 51 Across
38 Toothsome
39 "Candle in the Wind" singer John
40 Poker move

46 Phoenix five
47 Pushover
48 Stephen King thriller
49 Cry of despair
50 Holyfield stats
51 Top-40 number
52 Barley beards
53 River in Belarus
54 Author Calvino
55 College department head
56 Down from a duck
57 Laughing scavenger
58 Requirements
63 Keep up the —
64 Russian range
65 Reward for Lassie
66 Carrot, basically
67 Baseball family name
68 Excited bark
70 Use crib notes
71 Major-league
72 The whole —
74 Where rubber meets the road
75 Cicero was one

76 Actress Turner
77 Statesman Henry
81 Pearl Mosque site
82 Disney 1982 sci-fi film
83 Theater ticket designation
84 Beatles' meter maid
85 He sings about Alice's restaurant
86 Decays
88 Botany or Hudson
89 Actress McClanahan
90 Browbeat
91 Strongman Ferrigno
92 TBS alternative
93 "Owner of a Lonely Heart" group

Puzzle 2-3: Ancient History

 A palindrome is a word (or phrase) that reads the same way from right to left as it does from left to right (see 37 Down).

Across

1 Brewer's ingredient
5 Soft focus
9 Sonoma County neighbor
13 Captain of the Pequod
17 Traveling with 13 Across
18 Drill sergeant's command, with "at"
19 In the thick of
20 Joyous celebration
21 Pillow —
22 Sicilian spouter
23 Dorothy's dog
24 Potpourri attribute
25 Ancient laws of Babylon
29 Johnny —
30 Pitchblende, e.g.
31 Frost, as a cake
32 Hearing aid?
33 Notions case
35 Mother —
37 Pays for
40 Delete
43 Black or orange tea
45 Mucho
47 Ancient Andean
48 First name in sitcoms
51 Bert's *Sesame Street* pal
54 Remote button
56 Make a lap
57 Christmas Island, for one
59 Short and to the point
61 Large parrot
63 Lummox
65 Render useless, as a Jeep

67 Kilt folds
70 Gave the once-over to
72 "No way, Jose!"
74 Shoelace end
75 "Shiny Happy People" group
77 Sector
79 Cut off
81 A Fitzgerald
82 "Ding-dong, — calling!"
84 Pathfinder's destination
86 Tomato blight
88 Actress-director Marshall
90 Hit the sack
93 Geiger counter, e.g.
97 Tournament rank
99 Nabokov heroine
100 Valuable item
101 Godzilla was one
102 Highway sign
104 Legendary symbol of imminent threat
109 Spread on the table?
111 The third man
112 The Taj Mahal, really
113 Take on
114 "My word!"
115 Poolside attire
116 Biographer Leon
117 Inside-trader Boesky
118 December 26th event
119 "The only thing we have to — . . ."
120 Ted's mother
121 History

Down

1 Mule, to the Army
2 On the beach
3 Pacesetter
4 Obedient, as a pet
5 Photo from Muscle Beach
6 Potter's wheel
7 Annapolis letters
8 Juice-making device
9 First throw of 7, in craps
10 Eros's Latin counterpart
11 Falafel holder
12 Town near Phoenix
13 "Four score and seven years — . . ."
14 Ancient fortification in England
15 Skin soother
16 Fishhook feature
26 Seine feeder
27 W.C.'s costar in *My Little Chickadee*
28 Native: suffix
34 Psychic Geller
36 Closing section of a drama
37 Palindromic principle

38 Twain hero
39 Florist's unit
41 — -fi
42 Raid the fridge
44 Table scrap
46 Grab, with "up"
48 Hammarskjold
49 Letters at O'Hare
50 Symbol from the Bible
52 Press
53 — Park, Colorado
55 Alma mater for Aikman
58 Temptress in *Damn Yankees*
60 Roof overhang
62 Arm of the Mediterranean
64 Four years, for the President
66 Flood foiler
68 — Aviv
69 Stop on the B&O
71 Expensive
73 Checkers choice
75 Grammy category
76 First lady?
78 "Who — you kidding?"
80 Take after
83 St. Louis-to-Chicago dir.
85 1982 Masters champ
87 Interoffice directive
89 Thumbs up
91 Bachelor's last words
92 River sportsman of a sort
94 Doggie dribble
95 La Scala productions
96 Carry a grudge
98 Tower over
100 1998 Winter — (Nagano event)
102 Says, in teen talk
103 Sea lettuce
105 Mitch Miller's instrument
106 First name in C&W
107 Extinct bird
108 *My Three Sons* brother
110 Typical Keats piece

Puzzle 2-4: Legendary Ladies

Across

1 Asset
5 Hemingway, to friends
9 James of jazz
13 Famed coach — Alonzo Stagg
17 Fall shade
18 Type of exam
19 Like Felix Unger
20 Price for a cab ride
21 Downwind
22 Tooth's companion
23 Unload, as merchandise
24 Off the hook
25 Legendary lady of TV
28 Type of luggage
30 Wimbledon word
31 Exhaust, with "out"
33 Snail-like
34 Giant great
37 AFC division
40 Use clippers
42 *The — of Kilimanjaro*
45 Rap's Dr. —
46 Beverage bottle
48 "Good grief!"
50 Arbor Day honoree
51 Dethrone
53 Highway features
55 Length times width
57 Three, in Turin
58 Phys. therapy
60 Tommy of the Falcons
62 Robin Hood, for one
64 Legendary lady of film
68 Money, in Mexico
71 Live and —!
72 Get-go
76 Timetable abbr.
77 Type of pickle
80 Box score figures
82 Shred, with "up"
83 Camera's eye
85 *Guiding Light,* for one
87 Pilfer
89 Elizabethan, e.g.
90 Moderator
92 Dennis the Menace, often
94 First name in courtroom mystery
95 Word on a tissue box
96 Lee Dorsey hit, 1961

98 Had the answer
100 New Deal agcy.
102 Like a circle
105 Legendary lady of fiction
111 Twelve Oaks neighbor
112 Noel pageant prop
114 He loved Lucy
115 Ore deposit
116 Unwrap
117 For — and a day
118 Harbinger
119 Hot spot
120 First name in D.C.
121 — precedent
122 Telegram
123 Outdoor wedding protection

Down

1 Baby buggy
2 "Little" girl of the funnies
3 PC person
4 Measures
5 Hairstyle
6 Riyadh resident
7 Poker holding
8 Give the green light to
9 Trap
10 Type of shirt
11 Après bain powder
12 Where to find Europe?
13 Insult
14 Legendary lady of comics
15 Nabisco nibble
16 Caught in the act
26 Command to Fido
27 Rainy
29 *Treasure Island* author's monogram
32 Baltic seaport
34 Scent
35 — *Lies*
36 Connie Selleca's spouse John
38 Show respect
39 Placido Domingo, e.g.
41 Deface
43 "— in the money . . ."
44 Cassandra, for one
47 Ole Miss student
49 Letter opener
52 G-rated, for films

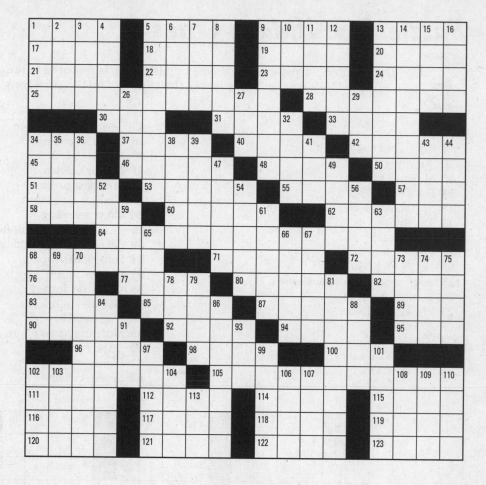

54 Squares have four
56 Sacramento arena
59 *The — Cage* (Robin Williams film)
61 Domestic tiffs
63 "Red" coin
65 Superman's lady
66 Furious
67 Computer key
68 Editor's direction
69 Agenda unit
70 Legendary young lady of mystery
73 Trickle
74 Rank below marquis
75 Butler's burden
78 Tennis ploy
79 Escapade
81 Symbol of drudgery

84 Waterproof coating
86 Box owner of myth
88 Jeans-maker Strauss
91 Spud sprout
93 Oolong, for one
97 *Angela's —* (Frank McCourt best-seller)
99 Black or Merry one
101 Give one's share
102 Prince William's school
103 Scruff
104 Bullpen statistic
106 Big rig
107 North Sea feeder
108 Songdom's most popular topic
109 Perfect place
110 Flat fee?
113 Permit

Puzzle 2-5: Hidden Cities

The "hidden" element of the theme in this puzzle is reflected in the way the clues are presented. (Rearrange the letters of the clues to find the answers.)

Across

1 Bottom of the barrel
6 Surveyor's nail
10 Munster mister
14 Esth's neighbor
18 — *Adams* (Booth Tarkington)
19 Toothless
20 Not aweather
21 Habituate
23 LEONA'S LEGS
25 Source of zest, in the kitchen
26 Be in the cast of
27 Waste allowance
28 *Home* —
29 ABOUT GOREN
31 *A — of Two Cities*
33 Greek letters

35 German connection
36 Llama's cousins
39 Alma —
41 Author LeShan
43 Breakfast order
47 Roaring, in a way
48 More revealing
49 — *in Black* (1997 hit film)
50 Barrymore's granddaughter
51 Some inheritors
52 IN CON'S FRACAS
56 Deauville donkey
57 Like a — of bricks
58 Laura and Bruce
59 More unctuous
60 Tuck's companion
61 Clams
63 Seven, in Siena

65 Midshipman
67 Come up
68 Mindful
69 Where to find King Solomon's mines
71 Out of order
73 Winged, in botany
74 Lawsuit starter
77 Yore
78 *A — in the Sun*
81 Monster
82 Unadulterated, in Nimes
83 Bank acct. amount
84 I'D NAP IN A SILO
87 Astronaut Sally
88 Leave out
90 Cape —, Mass.
91 Egghead
92 Chunk, as of Brie
93 Diamond bag
94 Seine sight
95 Dough that's not for baking
96 Colleens
97 Title opener
99 "Te —" (hymn)
100 Entertainer d'Orsay
101 SWAN O' NIGHT
106 — fixes (obsessions)
109 Dashboard element
113 Fix, as a hem
114 Crucifix
115 SENATOR MAC
117 City in Pennsylvania
118 Actress Meara
119 Poet Pound
120 Bury
121 Head "Untouchable"
122 Homeowner's document
123 Pas — (ballet solo)
124 Phillips of *Dateline NBC*

Down

1 Disney
2 Swan genus
3 Shine's companion
4 Disperses
5 One below jack
6 Inscribed pillar
7 — Alto
8 Final word
9 Turncoat
10 Where sailboats gather
11 Author Canetti
12 Current Broadway hit musical
13 Decorate again
14 Live and —
15 Like a cryptogram
16 Nobelist Bishop Desmond
17 HS math course

22 Vane direction
24 Guys' counterpart
30 Shade of difference
32 Brew
34 Olympian queen
36 Tosses
37 Happening right now
38 IMPS ON A LINE
39 Herbie and Horace
40 Canine comments
41 *South Pacific* role
42 Mr. Arnaz
44 DRAGS PINDAR
45 Sidekick for Aladdin
46 Won every game in a series
48 Wilkes —, Pa.
52 Goes out with
53 University of — Dame
54 Quote
55 Exotic flower
58 Composer Shostakovitch
62 Island group of Indonesia
63 Proust character
64 Relish, with "up"
66 Purpose
68 Inter — (among other things)
69 Liquid part of fat
70 Certain camera shots
71 Shish —
72 Color-changing lizard
73 Digression
74 Caterpillar hairs
75 Elbow gently, for a hint
76 Shoe inserts
79 — régime (pre-Revolutionary France)
80 Golden calf, for one
81 Stable newborn
85 Aladdin's pet
86 Vows
87 Unspecific addressee
89 Ties up
92 Female flyers, for short
95 Patched up
96 Elvis's daughter — Marie
98 Employs
99 *Lorna —*
100 Like a tiger
101 Used to be
102 Greenspan of the Fed
103 Eye affliction
104 Reunion attendee, for short
105 Word with dial or muscle
107 Stupefied feeling
108 Unbleached linen color
110 Sondheim's — *the Woods*
111 ". . . dollar, — o'clock scholar"
112 Traditional knowledge
116 Badly: prefix

Puzzle 2-6: Corporal Punishment

An alternate clue for 47 Down is "Author Melville."

Across

1 Jamie of *M*A*S*H*
5 Imply
10 Uses a sunfish
15 Window part
19 A Great Lake
20 Nonsensical
21 Disentangle, as a knot
22 Ratio words
23 Clown's noisemakers
25 Buttery desserts
27 Landlord's sign
28 Perry's aide
30 Chewing gum flavor
31 Pop fly's path
33 Pick on
35 *One Day — Time*
36 Integers: abbr.
37 Garb
40 Like the pampas
44 Cousteau's domain
45 Don't fold, spindle, or mutilate these
49 Flower part
53 Brewer's ingredient
55 Girder material
56 Did a doggie trick
59 Garden pest
60 Tops in seniority
62 Smeltery input
64 Greek H
65 Related
66 Actress Keaton
67 — tai (cocktail)
68 Direct route
70 Rudolph's boss
71 Police units
74 Put on, as a play
77 Convinced
79 Kind
80 Sticks in the mud
81 After deuce, in tennis
83 Mont Blanc, for one
84 Coward in the theater
86 Gathers info, in the army
87 "— Dimittis" (song of Simeon)
88 Measures
91 Madrid museum
93 Chapter of the Koran
94 Beats by a nose
96 Informal discussion
99 Napoleon's marshal

100 The USS Enterprise
103 Hair nets
105 She played Maude and Dorothy
108 Pub potable
109 Mythical giant
113 Ostrich's cousin
114 Edmonton natives
118 "Ora pro —"
120 Nuclear experiment
124 Moola
126 Where to find argyles
128 Clockmaker Thomas
129 Rene of *Tin Cup*
130 "The bombs bursting — . . ."
131 Jewell of *The Facts of Life*
132 Cream-filled cookie
133 Watch surreptitiously
134 "I Am Woman" singer
135 Historical intervals

Down

1 Ending for song or slug
2 Guthrie of folk
3 Irani coin
4 Summer TV fare
5 Command to Nellie
6 Author Bagnold
7 Be silent: music
8 Easily sprained spot
9 Electronics pioneer Nikola
10 Enjoy a midnight meal
11 Years, in the Yucatan
12 Chalk — to experience
13 Of direct descent
14 Far from excitable
15 *The King and I* locale
16 Invite for coffee
17 Gregg system expert
18 Party givers
24 Sunset, for one
26 Boorish
29 *The Thin Man* canine
32 Pizza perimeter
34 Drops the ball
37 Region in Turkey
38 Soft shoe, for example
39 *The Lord of the Rings* creature
41 Author LeShan
42 Regard highly
43 English major's subject
44 Backyard structures

46 Corporate VIP
47 Novelist Wouk
48 Golf shoe stud
50 Rummage
51 "Rope-a-dope" boxing great
52 Novelist Deighton
54 Suspended things, sometimes
57 Western Indians
58 Chum
61 Scorch
63 Peaceful protest
68 Cookie makers
69 "Woe —!"
71 Season
72 Windshield —
73 Run off, romantically
75 Categories
76 Effort
78 Classroom helpers: abbr.
81 Donkey, in Deauville
82 Lemon
85 — Cruces, NM
86 TV VIP Arledge
89 Oom — band

90 Rotisserie part
92 Insult, '90s style
95 — raving mad
97 DC doctor
98 Baseball's Garciaparra
101 Does tailoring
102 React like Nellie
104 Defeated in a pie contest, perhaps
105 Deep voice
106 Mr. Fudd
107 Let up
110 — *With Love*
111 Have — to pick
112 Battery type
115 Canyon comeback
116 Like a busybody
117 Mediocre
119 Lose traction
121 Wide spouter
122 IV fluids
123 Hall of Fame Speaker
125 Prodigal —
127 Without butter

Puzzle 2-7: Top of the Deck

Some clues imply that the entry is in a language other than English by referencing a location where English is not spoken, as in 58 Across.

Across

1 Bar to pry with
6 Hebrew prophet
12 Mrs. Nixon
15 — Paolo
18 Ammonia compound
19 Iterate
20 Actress Arden
21 "Rule, Britannia" composer
23 Frank Sinatra/Natalie Wood film
25 Burgess Meredith/Molly Ringwald film
27 Before, to Byron
28 Shoe-size measure
29 Poetry of a people
31 Visited casually
32 Artist Magritte
33 Film noir, for one
35 Trooper's monitors
36 Bumpkins
39 Elect
41 Lights-out bugle call
42 Shakespearean sprite
43 Bolivian's broad bean
44 U.S. diplomat Silas
46 Arabic letter
49 The Swedish Nightingale
50 Yul Brynner/Deborah Kerr film
53 Playwright Howe
54 Outfit
55 Bichon — (dog breed)
56 Singer Redding
57 Kind of boom
58 Year, in Juarez
59 They rest on tholes
60 Ruler in *Salomé*
62 Treat a sore throat

63 *Noises Off,* for one
65 Dead duck
66 Lose it
67 Say no to
69 Babbles on
70 Wilbur's equine co-star
71 Estes of *Melrose Place*
74 Without — in the world
75 Henry's was Golden
76 With merriment
77 Norse goddess
78 '60s supermodel Parker
79 Cecil B. De Mille epic
82 Silent screen star Negri
83 La —, Bolivia
84 Related to bristles
85 Corned beef order, perhaps
86 After-Christmas events
87 Hold back
88 Before Taureans
90 Oceangoing vessels
91 Abase
94 Uses scissors
95 Herb for turkey
96 One of the archangels
97 Flits
98 French actor Delon
100 Yorkie remark
103 Jessica Lang/Jeff Bridges film
105 Robert DeNiro/Jerry Lewis film
109 Grafted, in heraldry
110 Black sheep's lament
111 *Seinfeld* regular
112 Fierce badger
113 Neighbor of Leb.
114 "— getting better all the time . . ."
115 Franz of *NYPD Blue*
116 Rebel

Down

1 Louise or Ladoga
2 Eastern potentate
3 Tarzan's transport
4 Chang's Siamese twin
5 Expand again, as a wave
6 Wear away
7 *My — Foot*
8 Major city of Malaysia
9 Sun. talk
10 Pillbox or Easter
11 Acropolis site
12 Tea type
13 Rara —
14 Half a score
15 Waldorf and Caesar
16 Boston Garden, for one
17 Sign in a broadcast studio
22 Shore birds
24 Cotton-processing machines

26 Fruit sacred to Bacchus
30 Hunter
32 Film critic Rex
33 Mongolian desert
34 Relating to the dawn: poet.
35 Rangoon royal
36 Conference site, 1945
37 Hunter constellation
38 Bing Crosby film with the Rhythm Boys
39 Bobby Fischer's game
40 Codlike fish
41 Small fry
45 Tennyson girl
46 Elvis Presley film of 1958
47 Source of indigo
48 — */Off* (1997 Travolta/Cage film)
50 Expanse of land
51 Put on the payroll
52 Second Family of D.C.
53 Singer Amos
55 Compel
57 Alomar of baseball
60 John Wayne picture of 1953
61 Medical specialty: abbr.
62 Scottish Celts
64 High flyer's nest: var.
65 The underworld
66 Prude
67 Emery board
68 Its capital is Quito: abbr.
69 *Five Women* author Jaffe
70 Manfred and Herbie
72 Slippery basketball player?
73 Orchestra section
75 "What a —!" ("Too bad!")
76 Composer — Carlo Menotti
79 Actor Edmund of old English theatre
80 Somersault
81 New Zealand parrots
82 Glazier's insert
84 Unit of celery
86 Mrs. in Milan
87 Folk singer Pete
89 Stuck one's neck out
90 Secular
91 Wayne's nickname
92 Moran and Gray
93 Like a julep
94 Tales of dynasties
95 Strongboxes
97 No-see-um
98 In opposition, Dogpatch style
99 Burt's ex
100 The Abominable Snowman
101 Midmonth date
102 Gomer of TV
104 Kimono accessory
106 — du Diable
107 Socialite Kempner
108 Deface

Puzzle 2-8: Museum Tour

Across

1 Soft drink choice
5 — Rica
10 Great graduation gift
13 An Alaskan native
18 Word removed from a wedding oath
19 Synthetic fabric
20 Game at Caesar's Palace
21 Flora and —
22 *Mona Lisa* portrayor
25 Winter Olympics sleds
26 Actor McKellan
27 One-pot entree
28 "Ditto!"
29 Stroke gently
30 Unfair player
32 Lady Bird or Phil Gramm, e.g.
33 Name, in ancient Rome
34 — Abner
35 Precious veins
36 Sirens of folklore
39 Amtrak unit
42 Prelude to divorce, perhaps
44 JFK's predecessor
45 Cameo, for one
46 Chinese: prefix
47 Items in a boathouse
48 Lugosi of fright films
49 Holiday night
50 Potter or carpenter
54 Oregon's capital
55 Qualities, as of fabric
58 — *of Two Cities*
59 Old type of telephone
60 Colorado ski site
61 Not — (no way)
62 Tangier's country, to a Frenchman
63 Relative on Dad's side
65 Leaflet
66 Directed from one doc to another
69 San —, Cal.
70 Man on the flying trapeze
72 Raw minerals
73 Donkeys: Fr.
74 Muck
76 "Woe is me!"
77 Latvia's capital
78 Abbr. on a sale item
79 Alpine phenomena
83 City on the Nile
84 *The Spy Who Came in from the Cold* author and family
87 Personal logbook

88 Prefix with function or pepsia
89 Territories
90 Annie of *Designing Women*
91 "— very confidentially, ain't she sweet?"
95 Finally!
97 TWA competitor
98 Gunpowder and BB's
99 Elevation: abbr.
100 Inner group of personnel
101 *Coronation of the Virgin* painter
104 Pick up the tab
105 Sweet syrup brand
106 Primp
107 Compact car from Germany
108 Categorizes
109 *60 Minutes* network
110 Condor's nest
111 Wall St. letters

Down

1 Pediatrician's diagnosis
2 Witchcraft in the West Indies
3 Sierra — (African land)
4 Author Rand
5 Group like OPEC
6 Law and —
7 Singer Phoebe
8 Sen. Kennedy
9 Walkway in the Southwest
10 Church law
11 Exxon rival
12 "Vive le —!"
13 Burning
14 Hardy's pal
15 *Massacre at Chios* painter
16 French "ones"
17 Soviet news agency
20 Healthy phrase, with "fiddle"
23 Actor Sean
24 Irritating person
29 Treats meat
31 What young George couldn't tell
32 "On — Old Smokey"
33 Queen of Jordan
35 Miss Horne et al.
36 Jungle vine
37 Slacker
38 Sordid
39 Weight allowance
40 Wander
41 *Lobster Trap and Fish Tail* sculptor
42 Alarm sound

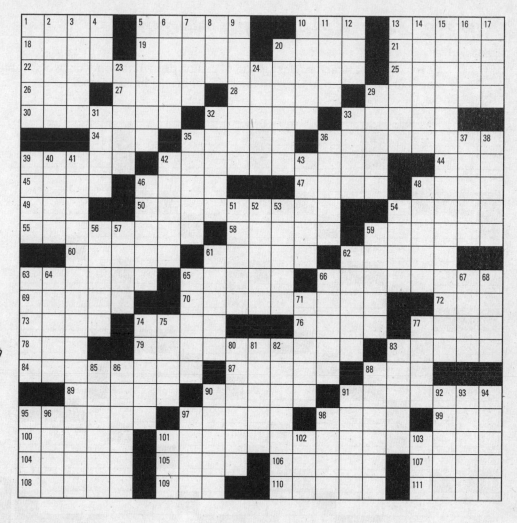

43 "And — a good night"
46 Mountainside rubble
48 Ulan —, Mongolia
51 Turkic language
52 Keanan in *Going Places*
53 Island in the Mediterranean
54 Bent out of shape
56 Ivan and Peter
57 As far as
59 Navigates whitewater
61 Dizzy
62 Tablelands
63 "To fetch — of water . . ."
64 Category of art or literature, e.g.
65 Gogol hero, — Bulba
66 Jeannie C. of country music
67 Thus, to Cicero
68 Precious
71 Comic Bert and family
74 Corday's victim
75 Folk singer Burl

77 Statesman Dean —
80 Italian fashion designer
81 Al Capone's "Enforcer"
82 Tree with heart-shaped leaves
83 Brand of disinfectant
85 Noah's landfall
86 Fixes the VCR
88 Singer Vic
90 Bosc and Anjou
91 Noted Chinese-American architect
92 Like a Yorkie
93 Greek flasks
94 Serving a purpose
95 Performs on stage
96 Type of root
97 Colorless
98 Copycat
101 Federal agcy.
102 Anger
103 Charged particle

Puzzle 2-9: Relocating Nearby

Crosswords attract a select group of celebrities whose one- or two-syllable names may appear more often in the grid than in real life, as in 75 Across.

Across

1 *Sing — With Mitch* (popular show of the '60s)
6 Hautboy
10 Alliance of 1955–1976
15 Saves, with "aside"
19 Fishing net
20 Shape
21 Agra's country
22 Joie de vivre
23 Legendary Greek beauty at musicfest?
26 Other, to Jose
27 Marlene's *The Blue Angel* co-star
28 Galley propellers
29 Straight as an —
30 Selected
33 Furiously
35 Ropes at the rodeo

37 1995 Nicolas Cage film changes location?
39 One of Columbus's three
40 Runs in neutral
41 Outs counterpart
42 Cenozoic and Mesozoic
43 — *Gun: Will Travel*
47 Look at closely
48 Felt in one's bones
51 Chianti, for one
52 Sara Lee equipment
53 1968 Glen Campbell hit moves away?
56 Hide
57 Onetime abbr. for Lith. or Ukr.
60 *Star —*
61 Aching
62 Uncle Miltie
63 Commit perjury

64 Rock producer Brian
65 Borgnine role, 1955
67 "We — the World"
69 Big —, Cal.
70 Skips over
72 Casino game
73 Elvis — Presley
74 German river
75 Ms. Lollobrigida
76 Wild West showman relocates?
81 Baldwin or Guinness
82 Mild reproof
83 Stuck-on-oneselfness
84 — buco (Italian dish)
88 Pianist Peter
89 Biblical preposition
90 *The — Man and the Sea*
91 Reach the dock
92 He hit 61 in '61
94 Old Don Johnson show finds a new town?
97 Reaches
100 Bridge support
102 Westerns
103 Believer
104 Like two — in a pod
105 Indigo dye source
106 Fervor
107 Lindbergh's other plane?
115 Raison d'—
116 Scoops, to a gossip
117 Type of bag
118 Raccoon's cousin
119 *Rich Man, Poor Man* author
120 Analyze a sentence
121 Hardy girl
122 Mohammed's sacred book

Down

1 Wood for a Louisville Slugger
2 Director Spike
3 Persian Basin product
4 Wind dir.
5 "Invisible Touch" group
6 In the — (coming soon)
7 Orange or Gator
8 Guadalajara gold
9 Funnyman Philips
10 Strong fiber
11 Page in a diary
12 Fusses
13 Start of an X-O game
14 Once an acorn
15 Hospital drama opens new facility?
16 Violet opener
17 Fortune-teller's deck
18 Makes a white Christmas
24 Portent
25 Blockhead

29 Garfunkel
30 Give up
31 Skipper in *Gilligan's Island*
32 Out in the open
33 Egghead association
34 Photographer Adams
35 Climbing plant
36 Potsie of *Happy Days*
37 Back talk
38 Where to see Kings with Rangers
39 Highest grade meat
42 "— man for himself!"
44 Opposed (to)
45 Parchment
46 Comes on stage
48 Thumb-to-pinkie measure
49 Architect Saarinen
50 Take it all off
54 Has markers out
55 *Wayne's World* catchword
57 Adman's phrase
58 Metaphor's kin
59 Carl or Rob
62 Flex
65 Testosterone-rich
66 Parseghian of Notre Dame
67 Rainbows
68 Den, for one
71 1977 Triple Crown also-ran?
72 Clenched hands
73 Actress Valli
76 Driving maneuver
77 Mediterranean port
78 Stravinsky and namesakes
79 Lounges about
80 "— got to be kidding!"
85 Recipe instruction
86 Sets the Doberman on
87 Single
91 Church supper
93 River isle
94 Kick out
95 Breaches of etiquette: var.
96 Legislature in Eire
97 Carving tools
98 Bicuspids
99 Crown for Miss America
100 — *of Endearment*
101 Poker action
104 Marina
105 Pretends
107 Little taste
108 School org.
109 Giant great Mel
110 Enemy
111 Comment from Bossy
112 Legal profession
113 "Give — rest!"
114 Rhone tributary

Puzzle 2-10: Wanderlust

Detective Perry Mason and his creator are popular puzzle fodder, as you see in 91 Down.

Across

1 Where Rainier rules
7 Foreign correspondent?
13 Admired, in a way
18 Dodger
19 John of *A Fish Called Wanda*
20 Belief
21 Disgust
22 Travel, in a way
24 Wheelhouse dir.
25 Oahu gift
27 City in Manche department
28 Hale's partner
29 Current producers
31 Tiger's disappointments
32 Travel on Sunday
35 Term of endearment
36 Common catch-all abbr.
40 Cuckoopint plant
41 Start of a paper-and-pencil game
42 Cleaned the yard
44 Spock's org.
45 Distant
46 Kim's husband
48 Minotaur's challenge
49 Dying fire
51 Venus' —
53 Make tracks
55 Halloween mo.
56 Miter joint
57 — and tuck
58 Travel by foot
62 Sweet Portuguese wine
66 Irregular, as a leaf
67 Mount near Reno
68 Cracker spread
69 Did a marathon
70 Egg —
71 English naval hero
73 Computer of film fame
74 Bumpkin
75 Cinch
77 Good serve
78 Travel the briny
81 Tax
83 City on the Garonne

84 PC user's salvation
87 Bottom of the barrel
88 Actor Robbins
89 *Babe* role
92 Follow the map
95 Soup server
97 Used a VCR
98 Liturgical vestments
99 *The Hairy Ape* playwright
100 Nest, to a robin
101 Beliefs
102 Sales incentive

Down

1 Pierre's mom
2 Hot spot
3 Wheel hub
4 *Much — About Nothing*
5 Wine storage place
6 Former Nicaraguan leader
7 Lender's abbr.
8 Flexible
9 Small sea swimmers
10 Rinds
11 Regarding
12 Composer Delibes
13 Yellow-brown pigment
14 Travolta musical
15 Regan's dad
16 Cut and splice
17 Hunky- —
23 Macbeth, for one
26 Top of the foot
29 Hillary, to Chelsea
30 *Titanic,* for one
31 Fireplace tool
32 Nautical hook
33 Rev. Roberts
34 Rage
35 Eye color
37 Off-limits: var.
38 "You said it!"
39 Crust ingredient
42 *Bolero* composer
43 Make fun of

46 Like an angry cat's back
47 Too — in the day
48 Cineplex offering
50 Brood
52 Preschoolers
53 Companion to desist
54 Sign of summer
56 On one's uppers
58 Barnyard dwellers
59 Press agent?
60 Caesar's garb
61 Funny lady Ullman
62 Croquet player's need
63 Rainbow goddess
64 10-K, for one
65 Singer Paul
68 Stamp on a receipt
72 Poe subject

73 Stubborn
74 Put a spell on
76 Gave a performance
78 Point of origin
79 Alterations expert
80 Compassionate
82 Lyric poem
83 Boston athlete
84 "¿Como — usted?"
85 Attempt
86 *Underboss* character
87 Bump into, with "across"
89 Essayist Lamb's nom de plume
90 Cobbler's strip
91 Perry's creator
93 Dr. Seuss animal
94 Curved letter
96 Jr. miss

Puzzle 2-11: Puzzle People

You won't get stuck on 60 Down if you remember this hint: Some letters of the alphabet look exactly like numbers, and constructors take advantage of this resemblance. All's fair in love and crosswords!

Across

1 Film projector's input
6 Peacock Throne ruler
10 Nest egg funds: abbr.
14 Revenuer
18 First name in swashbuckling
19 Cabbage
20 Place for a pager
21 Film for which Geoffrey Rush won Best Actor
22 Movie hero from Down Under
25 Pierre's aunt
26 As yet
27 MBA subject
28 Spontaneous
30 Baseball's Hershiser
31 Playpen item
33 Natasha, to Lynne
35 NYC subway line

36 LBJ pet
37 "That explains it!"
38 Real estate measure
39 Dutch uncle
42 Dapper western lawman of 1958–1961 TV
48 Barbie's friend
49 Spanish dessert
50 Wandering
51 — Yankees
52 In good shape
53 Sham
54 Shell out
55 Bog
56 — of this world
57 Grill sound
58 H.H. Munro's pen name
59 Darker than ecru
60 Believers: suffix

62 *Lorenzo's —*
63 Scottish county
64 Architect of St. Paul's Cathedral
69 Cleopatra's nemesis
72 Lose vigor
73 Fluctuate
74 Rubber tree
75 Mosque prayer leader
79 Win over with charm
81 Anti anti
82 A sib
83 Singer Baker
84 Make into law
85 Chart representation
86 April forecast
88 Low in hemoglobin
89 *— Rider* (Clint Eastwood flick)
90 Shipping weight
91 House leader
93 Actor Roth
94 Worthies are dubbed this
95 Flat-top, out West
96 Keats's preferred format
97 Pet for Ursula, the sea witch
98 What -vore means
99 Monogram for the *Cats* poet
100 Tar
104 Giving in
108 June 6, 1944
110 More gray
112 Civil rights leader Medgar
113 Classic character of kiddie TV
116 Count of music
117 One of HOMES
118 Russian veto
119 Council of —, 1545–1563
120 Old dagger
121 Spotted
122 Sound of surprise
123 Squares have four

Down

1 Right-hand page
2 Boo-boo
3 Wear away
4 It makes all the stops
5 Vegas machine
6 What to do in Vail
7 Author of *Hotel*
8 Brother of Adam, Daniel, and Billy
9 Carefree philosophy
10 — Saud
11 Diet
12 Coeur d' —, Idaho
13 Interfere, with "in"
14 Former UN leader
15 Neighbor of S. Dak.
16 Pay to play poker
17 Require
21 React to a popped balloon
23 Abhor
24 In — (all together)

29 Simba
32 Scrap for Fido
34 Poetic time of day
36 Applause
38 Allow
39 *My Fair Lady* girl
40 Virile
41 Response to a knock
42 Mrs. Truman
43 Angelic instrument, to Dante
44 *Star —*
45 In a frenzy
46 Lord and Lady Anthony
47 Kurosawa epic
48 A Carson
49 Shriner's cap
52 Something to blow
53 Rank's partner
55 *— Safe* (Fonda flick)
56 Roman emperor in A.D. 69
57 Royal address
59 In good shape
60 A grand
61 Double agent
62 Wise tree dwellers
65 Hockey's MVP trophy
66 Ancient Phoenician port
67 Regretful
68 Forty— (football player)
69 Deft
70 Biblical mount
71 King David's form
76 *La Boheme* soprano
77 Kind of: suffix
78 Jet speed measure
80 Role for Jim Carrey
81 Wrestling fall
82 Command to Fido
83 Heavenly being, in Brest
85 — favor (please, in Tijuana)
86 Flowering shrub
87 Giving, as an Oscar
88 Related to a South American range
90 Pinball peril
91 After taxes
92 Moon of Jupiter
94 Detect
95 Blackbird
97 Ghostly
98 Finnish lake
99 Little ones
100 Lamb Chop's Lewis
101 Broadcast
102 Sierra —
103 Horse gaits
104 CSA members
105 Author Hunter
106 — majesté
107 Sorbets
109 Author Seton
111 Cpl.'s bosses
114 Bo Derek score
115 Cell's energy chemical, for short

Puzzle 2-12: Musical Letter Drop

Dropping a letter from a well-known title often leads to surprising results!

Across

1 Deep sleep
6 Wine server
12 Killer fly from Africa
18 Evergreen
19 Titania's husband
20 Or's partner
21 Prokofiev's noble-with-lobo piece?
24 Preliminary draft
25 Guido's notes
26 — *Africa* (Streep-Redford film)
27 Tease
29 Drive the getaway car
30 First-born of two
32 Revealing
33 Stretch, for short
34 Spanish queen and namesakes
35 Edna Ferber book
37 Indian P.M. Narasimha
39 Inflate, as T & E
41 Map abbr.
43 Thurman of *Pulp Fiction*
46 Czech statesman Eduard
48 Schubert's racetrack five?
52 Brunch setting
54 Radio wave emitter
56 Drives
57 Not fooled by
58 Music for sitar
61 Cockney idol
62 Cash endings
63 Author James
64 Pull — (err)
66 "Tapestry" songwriter King
69 Rocky peak
70 Wagner's perjuring sailor?
73 — Moines
76 Passed, as a rumor
78 Whalebone
79 Dear — (columnist)
80 Cookout veggie
81 Globe
84 Mortgages
85 Pressing need?
86 Duplicated
88 Like some fruitcake
90 Excursion
92 Saint-Saens's morbid Hamlet?
94 Hobo
97 Word to complete 104 Across
98 Funnyman Philips
99 Brouhaha

100 Osaka sash
102 Journalist Stewart
104 "In the twinkling — . . ."
106 Detail
109 Surrender
111 Perfume base
115 Armenian border river
116 Related on Mom's side
117 Wonderland girl
119 Marathon, e.g.
120 Baker's tool
122 Tchaikovsky's nest in a tree?
125 Trapped
126 Appoint an agent
127 Less strict
128 Snub
129 Wipes out
130 Ruling body of France

Down

1 Participate in a bee
2 Mountain nymph
3 Racetrack prize moneys
4 Wood sorrel
5 Cabinet member Janet
6 Type of cheese
7 Dislike intensely
8 Double-breasted coat
9 London blitz civilian aide: abbr.
10 Partner of fancy-free
11 Chou —
12 Lab work
13 "— transit gloria"
14 Allen or Hawke
15 Smetana's traded cheese?
16 School calendar units
17 Part of QED
18 German battleship, the *Graf* —
22 Add to the sound track
23 Word in a fairy tale giant's exclamation
28 Lineup after M
31 Judge Judy's outfit
34 First — (original printing)
36 Two-time
38 Wd. in NATO
40 Vienna's land: abbr.
42 Space visitors, for short
43 WW II menace
44 Low-grade wool
45 Debussy's matinee for an enthusiast?

47 Directly, Dogpatch-style
49 Onetime Mideast initials
50 Poetic foot
51 1970 Physics Nobelist Louis —
53 Opponent
55 Secondhand
59 Anne Nichols hero
60 Venice transport
65 — the wrong way (antagonize)
67 Prayer ender
68 Kidnappers' demands
70 Bell Atlantic employee
71 One of Scheherazade's 1,001
72 Gene's *Absolute Power* costar
74 Piano key material
75 *The Playboy of the Western World* playwright
77 River past Caen
79 Island in the stream
80 Public outcry
82 Johnny —
83 Weatherman's gauge
86 Between B and F

87 June honoree
89 Coming-out girl
91 Second word of "The Raven"
93 It's often flipped
95 Roots, in botany
96 Smart guy?
101 Unwise flyer of myth
103 Individual
105 Texas athlete
107 Author of *The Joy Luck Club*
108 Chopin piece
110 Put on cloud nine
112 Mrs. Gorbachev
113 Musical group
114 Wolfish look
115 Species of holly
116 *Das Lied von der* — (Mahler)
118 Slippery ones
121 Eternal, to Eliot
123 Apr. overtimer
124 Caviar

Puzzle 2-13: Nothing Heavy

Across

1 — Hari
5 Driveway entrance
10 Average
13 Some surreal paintings
18 Tell it like —
19 Actress Glenn
20 Part of a bridle
21 "Für —" (Beethoven piece)
22 Mariner's guide
25 Where to find Niamey
26 Bullfight cheer
27 Amusement park attraction
28 Classroom fixtures
29 Cozy corners
30 Overexerts
32 Singer Isaak
33 French forest
34 Comic turn
35 Flies like an eagle
36 Russian ravioli
39 Removed, as from a text
42 101 animated characters
44 "Do I dare to — a peach . . ."
45 Like the Sahara
46 Flying-related
47 Composer of "Rule, Britannia"
48 Stutz Bearcats
49 Tom Hanks hit film of 1988
50 Matriarchs in the stable
54 Toggle-buttoned coat
55 *ALF* actress Anne
58 Former Giant
59 Award-winning Rita
60 Britisher's "boot"
61 Metric weights

62 Got on
63 Regis, to Kathie Lee
65 Glimmered
66 Unseasonable chill
69 Win by —
70 Three-cornered headgear
72 Comedian Philips
73 Steak order
74 Seine sights
76 Eyeball movements during sleep: abbr.
77 Ivan the Terrible, e.g.
78 Ice: Ger.
79 Lunar plain
83 Billiards stroke
84 Dissertation
87 As red as —
88 Bill, to Chelsea
89 Takes on
90 Former Secretary of the Treasury
91 Place for an overnight guest
95 Trapper
97 *Dead Souls* author
98 Points, in math
99 Actress Gardner
100 Spelling of Hollywood
101 Easy to tote
104 Walk like a rooster
105 Dill herb
106 "— is an island"
107 River in England
108 Axton and family
109 Law graduate's hurdle
110 Like some gases
111 Nutty

Down

1 Director Forman
2 Tipped
3 William Blake's "burning bright" beast
4 Hardwood tree
5 Yearning
6 Trudges
7 Rake
8 WW II spy group
9 Stuntman Hal
10 Reaches a maximum
11 Goals
12 ICU employees
13 *Wag the Dog* star Robert
14 — *Restaurant*
15 Flu symptom
16 "Oh, that's it!"
17 Sun. talks
20 Fend off
23 Group of three

24 Well-known Yogi
29 From Oslo
31 Like fine wine
32 Panama seaport
33 *Huckleberry* —
35 Popular wrap
36 Analyze a sentence
37 Valentine or Carpenter
38 "— trouble at all"
39 Applies, as makeup
40 Julia's older brother
41 Henry Lee, familiarly
42 Bo of *Ten*
43 Metrical feet
46 Author's rep
48 Prepares Granny Smiths
51 Type of hog
52 Imbibed
53 — Semple McPherson
54 Owner of the manor
56 Worn away
57 Legendary actress Eleanora
59 Fountain orders
61 Swayze-Moore blockbuster of 1990
62 Like a mug of beer
63 Printer's mark
64 Sign in Howard Stern's studio
65 Public tantrum
66 Deal from the bottom, e.g.
67 Latin I word
68 Study, with "over"
71 Casey of '60s TV
74 More remote
75 Subtraction word
77 Magician's syllables
80 Type of iron: Scot.
81 Monastery leader
82 "Sweet —, heavenly flower . . ."
83 Subject of *Underboss*
85 Open the windows, for example
86 Sen. Lott and namesakes
88 Museum tour guide
90 Mudd on TV
91 Up to now
92 Brazilian seaport
93 Chris Mills, née —
94 Challenges
95 Obi
96 Western alliance
97 Burt's costar in *Trapeze*
98 Unconvincing
101 HS science room
102 Charles, to Elizabeth
103 Something to pick up

Puzzle 2-14: Big Brags

Across

1 Reasoning
6 Between Roosevelt and Wilson
10 Dental tool
15 Shade trees
19 Put on a pedestal
20 Happily — after
21 Calm down
22 Milk, to Pierre
23 Big brag, to a peacemaker
25 River past Grenoble
26 Actress Meara
27 Before, to Frost
28 Do a bank job?
29 Identical
31 Where to find Ottawa
33 "Drink to me only with — eyes . . ."
35 Big brag, to a rock-and-roller
38 Most base
40 Stair guard
41 Quotes
42 Like a watchdog
43 Mill intake
45 Wife of Menelaus
46 — *Max* (Mel Gibson role)
49 Cause for overtime
50 Leads for Sherlock
51 Seethed
52 Package sealer
53 Big brag, to a freshman
56 Buddhist monk
57 *Three Musketeers* author
58 Honkers
59 Big brag, to an employee
62 Siouans of Nebraska
64 More timid
65 Alter, as text
66 Big brag, to a movie star
68 Athenian lawmaker
69 Setting of *The House of the Seven Gables*
70 GI dining
71 Big brag, to an athlete
75 Scheme
76 *Seascape* playwright
78 Predecessor of e-mail
79 Hydrogen's atomic number
80 Pronounce
81 Political power
82 Tampico tips
83 Silverheels role
85 Fountain orders
86 Type
87 Anglican cleric

88 Big brag, to a soldier
92 Proofreader's symbol
93 Brunch order
94 It's east of Java
95 Potato —
96 Well-known ring leader
99 Feral
100 Gunther Gebel Williams, notably
103 Big brag, to an equestrian
106 Fashion magazine
107 Clear the tape
108 Behindhand
109 Claw
110 Someone always brings it up
111 Threw down the gauntlet
112 Jug
113 *The 39 —* (Hitchcock classic)

Down

1 *Daily Planet* reporter
2 Reputation
3 Messenger
4 Aer Lingus dest.
5 Yo-Yo Ma, for one
6 Roofer's material
7 Zealous
8 City in Morocco
9 Walk on forbidden ground
10 Type of therapy, with "scream"
11 Change the alarm
12 Cheer for a toreador
13 Salad or candy
14 Implemented
15 African antelopes
16 Luau setting
17 Cares
18 Barbecue order
24 Confined, with "up"
30 Dismounted
32 Last word
34 "Get — out of my heart" ("Rhonda" lyric)
36 Word in an O'Neill title
37 River through Cairo
38 Chair back part
39 Melange
40 Cambodian currency
43 Like an 8 x 10 photo
44 Make a judgment
45 Sense of —
46 Cass and Bear
47 Speedily
48 Student's place

50 Scone topping
51 Destined
52 Whitewater sport
54 Region of Somalia
55 Fix a skirt
56 Safe havens
57 English county known for 50 Down
59 Aspect
60 Where to find treasures
61 DNA strand
62 Florida city
63 Indonesian peninsula
64 — as sugar
66 Vipers
67 Catch offguard
68 Unaccompanied
71 For fear that
72 Landscape painter
73 "Do — others as . . ."
74 Drudge
76 Parceled out
77 Idle

78 Like some two-year-olds
81 Singer Natalie
82 Lottery
83 La Brea —
84 Neighbor of Cal.
85 Mobile sculptor Alexander
86 Caught
87 Poker holding
88 Lawn —
89 Writer Zola
90 Mason's Street
91 Heavyset
92 Hip, hip!
95 — as a button
97 Skating maneuver, with "toe"
98 B & B's
101 Southern constellation
102 Damage
104 F. Lee Bailey's domain
105 Fenway club?

Puzzle 2-15: Fruity Flavors

A surname may read as a common noun at first, as in 23 Across.

Across

1 Aries and Taurus
6 Mashed potato serving
10 — the hand that feeds you
14 Facade of sorts
19 Characteristic
20 German industrial center
21 Concert halls, to Caesar
22 Broadway sponsor
23 Post of etiquette
24 Kazan of film
25 Source of wax
26 Les girls
27 Fruity flavor
29 Fruity flavor
31 Goes to a restaurant, with "out"
32 Telephones
34 Pen name?
35 Type of knife
39 Medical school course: abbr.
40 Bowling item
44 Chicago hub
45 Onetime city of witches
47 Mongrels
49 Teed off
50 Pumice stone
51 Fruity flavors
54 Kettle and Rainey
55 Raw material
56 Clear, as a plane's wing
57 "Able to — tall buildings . . ."
58 Blessed or main
60 Crackers
62 Part of USNA

64 Sponsorship
65 Ejects from office
66 Indonesian textile
67 Papal headdress
69 Throat problem, for short
71 IOU's
72 Word with health
75 — and desist
76 Space lead-in
77 Headquartered
78 Hill of San Francisco
79 Abby's sister
80 Fruity flavors
84 Stable mom
85 Records
87 Lalique or Coty
88 Former labor leader George
89 With "noster," The Lord's Prayer
90 — *to a Kiss*
92 Snaps
93 Least inhibited
94 I, to Caesar
95 Inspire with happiness
97 Designer Gucci
99 Citrus flavors
103 Tropical fruity flavors
109 The alpha and —
110 B&O stops
111 Take-out phrase
112 — of no return
113 Yields, with "in"
114 See 14 Down
115 Novelist Wister
116 Ford, for one
117 Rundown
118 Film critic Rex
119 Unusual
120 Legal papers

Down

1 Irish —
2 Cookbook writer Rombauer
3 Gallop or lope
4 Ibis's habitat
5 Rubber ingredient
6 Wave to
7 Down times
8 Buckeye State
9 Unopened
10 Snow vehicle
11 Paragon
12 The wonder years?
13 — *of Eden*
14 Old language of Scotland
15 Uses a combination
16 Dome home: var.
17 Ooze

18 Ultimatum word
28 *Mad* or *Time,* for short
30 Go to extremes
33 Metrical foot
35 Western neckwear
36 Maureen of film
37 Citrus flavor
38 Retiree's letters
39 Wings, for Pegasus
40 Party pooper
41 Fruity flavor
42 Man from Qum
43 Cozy spots
45 Pens
46 Parts of circles
47 Haunted house sound
48 Russian river
51 Posted
52 "The King"
53 Acted as usher
56 Assuage, as fears
59 Go off-course
61 Elect. day
62 Bigwig
63 Letters on a business letter
66 Swiss city
67 Amble
68 Folksinger Burl
69 Resell, as a theater ticket
70 Carreras, e.g.
71 College VIP
72 Adam's eldest
73 Al and Tipper
74 Siskel's partner
76 Author James
77 Bikini parts
81 Give this to the waiter
82 Radiate
83 Antenna, basically
84 West of Hollywood
86 Hiked a muddy trail
89 Supported, with "up"
91 In a dither
92 Didn't bid, in bridge
93 Govt. agency
95 — nous
96 Landlord's offering
97 Tick off
98 Sierra —
99 Clothing
100 Pierre's girlfriend
101 Area above a glacier
102 Czech river
104 Hawkeye State
105 Skin opening
106 Toe the —
107 Geraint's love
108 Holy women: abbr.

Puzzle 2-16: Animal Atlas

 Celebrity names expand the vocabulary of crosswordese and add color to the solving process. Some folks become immortal through crosswords. (See 52 Across.)

Across

1 Porcine film star
5 Facilitated
10 Bar, at the bar
15 Festive party
19 As strong as —
20 Kukla and Fran's friend
21 Desist
22 Unique person
23 Antelope's hometown?
25 Pet rodent's hometown?
27 Filter off
28 Jekyll's servant
30 Kayak's cousins
31 Quote
32 Mr. Karloff
33 Zilch
34 Jaunty
37 Related to a lake tribe
38 Parade attraction
43 Have — for news
44 Steer's homeland?
46 Mil. offense
47 Well-groomed
48 High time?
50 Stupid
52 A Gabor
53 Mailing tube: abbr.
54 Swoons
56 Leader
57 Gent's gent
59 The way arguments are conducted
61 Like — from the blue
63 Loose-fitting jackets of yore
64 Veins in stone
65 Marry in haste
66 Companion to mortise
67 Trance
69 Clear the board
70 Insult
73 Lancelot's mail?
74 Gung-ho
75 Peaceful
77 Go gray
78 Once around the track
79 Jellied meat dish
81 Tardy
82 God in *Aida*
83 EEC currency
85 Wildcat's hometown?
89 Scribbled

90 Ivory's filmmaking partner
92 Harridan
93 Actress-dancer North
94 Victor Hugo drama — *Blas*
95 Assumed name: abbr.
96 Pub selections
97 Stellar
100 "Ars gratia —" (MGM motto)
101 Violinist Erica
104 Simian's home region?
106 Sheep's hometown?
110 Staunch
111 Chews the fat
112 Ancient Roman magistrate
113 Bit for the gossip column
114 Teen dances
115 Foyle or Hawk
116 Was overly fond (of)
117 On the briny

Down

1 Carry-on piece
2 Sothern and others
3 Ring event
4 Jason Miller role
5 Early stone tool
6 Coeur d'—, Idaho
7 Patty Hearst's abductors: abbr.
8 German article
9 Plunder
10 Like a yodel
11 Pod group
12 Emulate Petruchio
13 CIA precursor
14 Funnel-shaped blooms
15 Thug
16 *3 Men — Baby*
17 Security problem
18 Venus de Milo's loss
24 Poker move
26 Kuwait bigwig
29 Type of exam
32 Main force
34 Western spread
35 Keep — on (look after)
36 Marsupial's hometown?
37 Ivory's piano partner
38 Oct. 31 option
39 Prime a yo-yo
40 Another sheep's hometown?

41 Range —
42 Blind features
45 Designer Simpson
48 Consumer advocate Ralph
49 Medium for Monet
51 Reveal
54 Soft hat
55 Tossed dish
56 Aspirations
58 Run — (go bananas)
60 "— the morning to you!"
62 Derek and Diddley
63 Where to float your bateau
65 Conductor Leinsdorf
66 Waste allowance
67 Hawthorne's birthplace
68 Hint
69 Oust, as a tenant
70 Danish astronomer Tycho
71 Type of type
72 Giggle
74 Neat as —

76 Resident of 23 Across?
80 Overworked horse's problem
82 Soviet Politburos
84 Reacts to a horror flick
86 Agony's counterpart
87 "Able was I — saw Elba"
88 Undressed, as hair
89 Journalist's question
91 Cast, as an epithet
93 On a slant
95 Snapshot
96 Walk in the park
97 Window frame
98 Capable of
99 Kind of show
100 Make — (succeed)
102 Violin knobs
103 Fortune-teller's phrase
105 Phi follower
107 Fuss
108 Cambridge campus, for short
109 *I — Camera*

Puzzle 2-17: Home Stretch

Across

1 Roseanne's former name
5 Raised pulpit
9 Writer Mumford
13 White poplar
18 Sunburn soother
19 "Still waters run —"
20 Rhone tributary
21 Turned on the pilot again
22 Home stretch on stage
24 Home stretch in the darkroom
26 Gets ready to shower
27 Makes a reservation
28 Between shake and roll
29 Peeves
30 Identifies, in police lingo
31 Way opener
32 Slippery one
33 *Angela's* —
36 Delete the message
38 Accepts a contract

40 Relinquished
42 Home stretch at the patisserie
48 Nimbus
49 Ring-shaped reef
51 Celestial calendar equalizer
52 Russian river
53 Home stretch at a chess match
55 Psychoanalyst Fromm
56 Not trustworthy
57 Haw's partner
58 Tears
59 Torso
60 Sappy tree
61 Native Canadian
62 Pasta order
63 Football Starr
64 Dingbat
66 French —
67 Julie Christie role
68 Newt
71 Less cooked

72 Figure of speech
73 Home stretch for a gladiator
75 Yipes, to Yorick
76 Twilled cotton
77 Tether for Toto
78 Italian bread
79 Home stretch at the hairdresser's
82 Emulate Earhart
84 Lilliputian
85 Uses a prie-dieu
87 Map feature
88 Faux —
91 Bad grade
92 Angler's basket
94 Like yesterday's roll
96 Puts down
98 Trademark
99 Hot pepper
103 Home stretch in a duel
105 Home stretch for a student
106 Carrie's dad
107 Horse opera
108 BPOE members
109 Small, medium, or large
110 Controls, with "in"
111 Washed away the gray
112 Pry
113 Tommy's gun

Down

1 Like Kojak
2 Jai —
3 Supremes leader
4 Fido's trick
5 Hacienda material
6 Collar of a goblet
7 Hospital units
8 Photo — (media events)
9 Western lake
10 Cup hangers
11 Termites
12 "— Gratias" (hymn)
13 She helped Theseus
14 Crooked
15 Crème de la crème
16 Cotton thread
17 Legendary Merman
20 Oral
23 Not so good
25 Ugly thing
27 Pesto herb
30 Twinned crystal

31 Conductor Miller
33 Flooded
34 Prepare mushrooms, in a way
35 King of Tyre
37 Melees
38 Midnight —
39 Emulate Rodin
41 Belgian missionary
43 Noun ending in -ing
44 Offer a view
45 Seed cover
46 Glacial sand deposit
47 Bridge expert Culbertson
50 Use a VCR
54 Goof
55 Bert's pal
56 "The Divine" Bernhardt
59 "I'm a little —, short and stout . . ."
60 Choreographer Graham
61 Kind of card
62 Part of a fork
63 Sounds from the meadow
64 Wise men
65 Algerian port
66 Like the sea
67 American admiral
68 Inventor Howe
69 One's strong suit
70 Canary call
71 Court figure, for short
72 "Drink to me only with — . . ."
73 Sticker
74 Deliberate ignorance
76 Say this to the camera
77 Used a spinner
80 Pulls out
81 Jacks or better
83 Type of infection
86 Cuts of beef
88 Indy 500 feature
89 Dwelling
90 Riyadh resident
92 Jalopy
93 Competed with Unser
95 Humiliate
97 Emulate Rumpelstiltskin
98 Donkey's remark
99 Hawaiian bay
100 *No* — (Sartre)
101 Knock down
102 Writing on the wall
104 Olympian
105 Bog

Puzzle 2-18: Heave, Ho!

Across

1 Office fill-ins
6 Chase of stage and screen
10 "— luck!"
15 Rough file
19 Related to the hip bone
20 Lizard: suffix
21 TV oldie *Green* —
22 "This can't be!"
23 Heave ho tableware?
25 Heave ho barbecue fare?
27 *Peter Rabbit* author Beatrix
28 Quick-witted
30 Draftsman's tool
31 "— my party and I'll cry . . ."
32 Marsh gas
34 *The Name of the Rose* author
36 Down — (Australia)
37 Octoberfest quaff
38 Nest egg acct.
40 "— you loud and clear"
42 Place for cappuccino
45 Cribbage scorekeepers
49 Slackens
53 Saber handle
54 "Your turn," in CB speak
55 Ravi Shankar's instrument
57 Oxford, for one
58 Fix a story
59 Ceremonial act
62 Free-for-all
64 Genetic code letters
65 Send an e-mail again
67 Author Murdoch
69 Dole organization
71 "No more seats" abbr.
72 Albatrosses have big ones
75 Playing marble
76 Cork native
79 Oil cartel
80 Souped-up auto
83 Gallivant
84 Surpass in performance
86 Do a slow burn
89 Sousaphone cousin
90 Galena and bauxite
92 Canyon of comics
94 Bangkok native
95 Opposed, in Dogpatch
96 Bowling alley buttons
98 Bank account records
101 "First star — tonight"

102 Romantic rendezvous
104 Beltway VIP
105 And others: abbr.
107 Take a sip
110 Half a dance step?
112 Do a bank transaction
115 Word to a doctor?
118 Not explicit
120 Diminish
122 Big name in cocoa
124 Heave ho exercises?
126 Heave ho jiggers?
128 Pre-Soviet ruler
129 Fencing needs
130 Workplace watchdog: abbr.
131 Ditties
132 Rel. schools
133 Shorthand taker
134 City near Tahoe
135 Cubic meter

Down

1 Actress Hedren
2 *The Waste Land* poet
3 Gloves for Yogi
4 Formal agreement
5 Lay plans
6 Prefix with metric
7 Coniferous tree
8 Fran and Ollie's friend on old kid-vid
9 Former late-night host Hall
10 "Chantilly —"
11 Earthy hue
12 Capote one-man show
13 Piece of a pie chart
14 Poses, as a question
15 Domed rooms
16 Upcoming
17 Part of Buddy Rich's set
18 Word with face
24 Bahamian city
26 Pigeon on a menu
29 Miles in Hollywood
33 Famous Roman fountain
35 Rainwater catcher
37 Exacta players
39 "— gratia artis" (MGM motto)
41 Dog-— (folded down)
42 *Moonstruck* star
43 Gal or guy Friday
44 The "B" portions of 45s

46 " — a life!"
47 Beantown skater
48 Headlights setting
50 Floor coverings
51 Millennia
52 Salty seven
56 English festivals
60 Jason's vessel
61 Thpeakth like Daffy
63 Plasm opener
66 London neighborhood
68 *Graf* — (German battleship)
70 Kind of comb
72 Light bulb measure
73 Thorough
74 Vinegar: prefix
76 Maestro Stravinsky
77 Seldom seen
78 Tussy — garden
80 Felon's activity
81 Broadway stage award
82 Victor Borge, for one
85 Caesar's breakfast order?

87 However, for short
88 Cod relatives
91 Colonists
93 Psychic ability
97 Trapped, like a cat
99 Repairs the lawn
100 Sneeze observer, perhaps
103 Screenplay
106 Bomb try-outs
107 Clumps, as of hair
108 Licorice flavoring
109 "Get lost!"
111 Woody of film
113 1902 Martinique erupter
114 Bermuda, for one
115 Make amends
116 Take in or let out
117 *Steppenwolf* author
119 Mars, in Athens
121 Gas station sign of the '50s
123 Boarded up
125 Pinky or Spike
127 Sgt., e.g.

Puzzle 2-19: Tee Off

A question mark at the end of a clue indicates wordplay in the entry. If a question mark appears after every theme clue, check the puzzle's title for further insight on the theme.

Across

1 Where grass roots
4 Vicar
10 *The Paper* —
15 Detest
19 Fly-by-night type?
20 Type of cracker
21 Surgeon's high-tech tool
22 Not "fer"
23 Arikara Indian
24 2, 4, 6, 8?
26 1996 Broadway hit musical
27 Leader in foot comforts
29 Chemical used in plastics
30 *Sesame Street* regular
31 Threatening words
32 Stick-to-it-iveness
33 Loose-leaf insert
35 It's worth two points
37 Insincere hearing organs?
39 They're a pain
40 Pipe type
42 Open and aboveboard
43 Run — (go wild)
44 Prepare Parmesan
45 Least in number
47 Crash site
50 NBA official
51 Sewing machines?
53 Early Roman general
55 Springs
57 Gets a good workout
59 Take a cruise
60 Parmesan alternative

62 Dr. McCoy
64 Number that starts a Jules Verne title
66 Patron saint of Norway
67 St. Francis's birthplace
70 "— humanum est"
72 The brainy bunch
74 Coventry clairvoyant?
77 Elect, with "for"
80 Cosmic time period
81 Fancy suit
83 Root beer brand
84 '60s hairstyle
85 Toward sunset, in Sevilla
86 Like some seals
87 Made a pass at
88 Animated synagogue leader?
93 Where Marco Polo ventured
94 Suggests
95 Natives of Tirana: abbr.
96 Medium's state
98 Confuse
99 Orderly
100 Kidnaps a crew
103 Obsession, with 45 Down
104 Lost a scarf?
107 Poker stand
108 Scorch
109 Palette pigment
110 Not so hard
111 Nero, to Nero
112 Linemen
113 1936 Cooper role
114 Corrects
115 Conciliatory offering

Down

1 Conrad's Jim
2 Pitcher
3 Brews by Offenbach?
4 Document seals
5 Profane
6 Tehran tender
7 Off by — (not even close)
8 Cures leather
9 Rock group, for short
10 4 Across, for example
11 Must
12 Floating
13 D.C. VIP
14 Ambulance destinations: abbr.
15 Ricky's mom
16 To-do list
17 More minuscule
18 Goes on stage
25 Hoo-ha

28 Battle —, Michigan
30 Turns inside out
32 Go light
33 Strip (of)
34 St. Lawrence sights
35 German coal region
36 Peak
37 Refer to
38 Widow's inheritance
40 Imp
41 Trans World team
44 Sausage variety
45 See 103 Across
46 Vane directions
47 Gorillas' transport?
48 Landed
49 She played Lacey
51 Back burner, at times
52 Smart guys, to Caesar
54 CompuServe customer
56 Bumblers
58 Scatter about
60 *Tosca* locale
61 Dairy case item
62 *The Most Happy Fella* tune
63 Olympics host: 1952
65 Hawk's hope, perhaps
68 Trio times two
69 Show contempt
70 Feudal fieldhand
71 Funny Foxx
73 Commander's command
75 Volvo rivals
76 Mata —
78 Malay outrigger
79 Actor's award
82 Stamp on a side of beef
84 It's between gee and eye
85 Stable work force
86 Fell off
87 Buildings for Boeings
88 — longue (poolside chair)
89 Jockeyed (by)
90 Roger Corman film subject
91 Put up
92 Birch relatives
93 Paddled the Potomac
96 "— are a few of my . . ."
97 1994 Peace Nobelist
99 New tennis stadium in Queens
100 Counterfeit
101 Venetian villain of drama
102 Road sign
104 Not a rocker, in the '60s
105 Cleaver's *Soul on* —
106 Drink from a bag

Puzzle 2-20: First Names

Roman numerals can supply a variety of consonant-vowel entries in puzzles sometimes. (See 96 Down.)

Across

1 Ointment
5 Enumerates
10 Studio sites, often
15 Dune material
19 Celebes ox
20 Sign up
21 Negatively charged atom
22 Mine, to Marie
23 Playwright Bagnold
24 An Allman
25 — the Greek
26 Put on a long face
27 Clooney
29 Yalie
31 Thatcher
33 Love trailer
34 Sales pitch
36 High-schooler
37 Opens the gate
40 Exonerated
42 Irish —
46 Red Badge of Courage author
47 Fan's sound
48 Wayne's World buzzword
50 Flagstone, for one
51 Inflection
52 The Niña or the Pinta
53 Submarine-detection system
55 Partner of crafts
56 French article
57 Dance of the Jazz Age
58 Fixes a pump
60 U.S./Canada canal
61 Nag
63 Popular pie filler
65 Russell
67 Literary collections
69 Contaminated ground element
71 — contendere
72 Longet
76 Helen of Troy's suitor
78 Pack it in?
82 "I've — it!"
83 Sly laugh
85 TV actress Annie
87 After Blynken
88 Batman West
90 Practices in the ring
91 Top dog in D.C.
92 Burlap fiber
93 Pertaining to the kidneys

95 Tokyo, once
96 Use crib notes
98 Evita
99 Sawed wood by night
101 Keyboard buttons
103 Restaurant patrons
104 Jolts
106 Inventor Howe
107 Neighbor of S. Dak.
108 Hamel
112 "Put a — on it!"
113 Woolf
117 Outlawed orchard preservative
118 Answer in some quizzes
120 Ghostbusters weapon
122 Ward (off)
123 Bus or skirt start
124 Bride's follower
125 Desert stops
126 Sea eagle
127 — de foie gras
128 Sunflower and pumpkin
129 Celebrity function
130 Supreme Supreme

Down

1 Boxer Max
2 Part of A.D.
3 Clark's gal
4 Kahn
5 — of Lebanon
6 Bury
7 Waiter's burden
8 Times out of mind
9 Woody Allen film of 1973
10 More indolent
11 Lennon's lady
12 Grisham subject
13 Go — for (defend)
14 Some drums
15 Eggar
16 Love, Lisbon style
17 Slangy refusal
18 Scarsdale, for one
28 Speck
30 Role for Jim Carrey
32 The Bee —
34 Important prop in Cinderella
35 Jay and others
37 Misbehave
38 Male bee

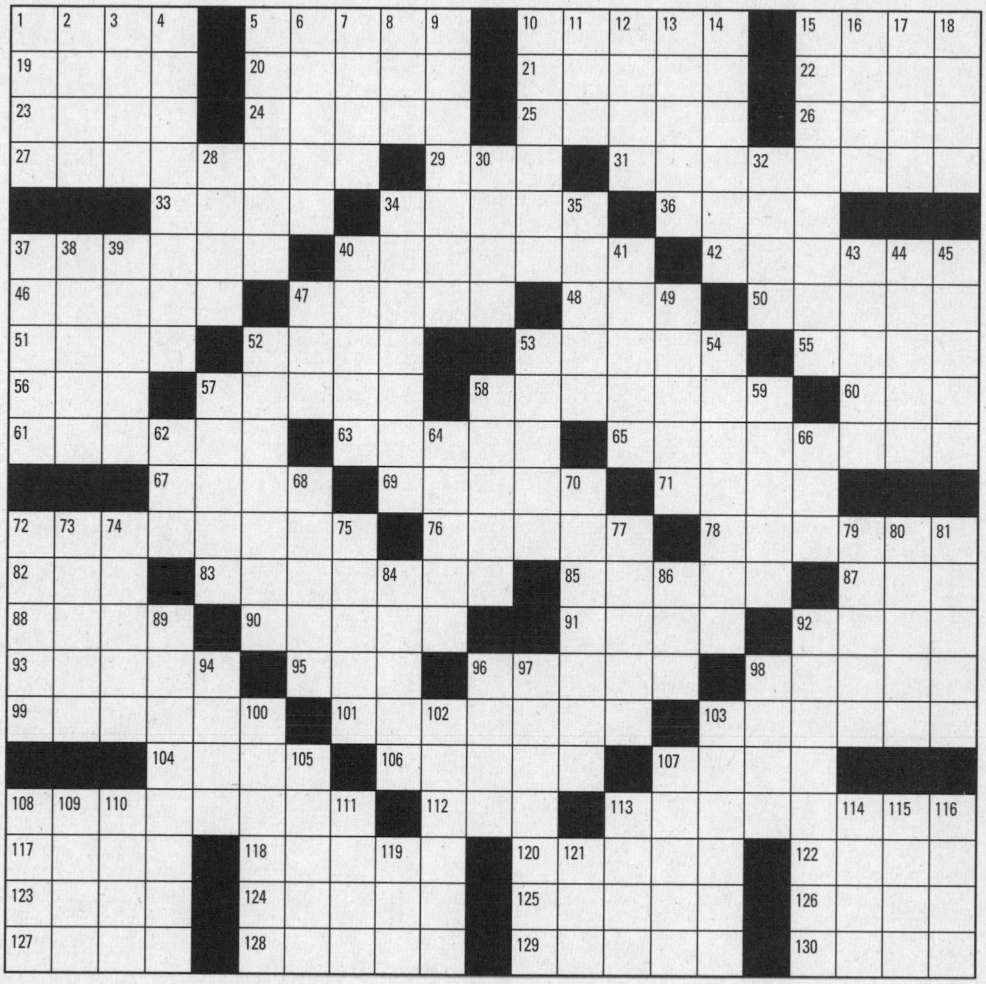

The crossword grid with numbered cells appears here.

39 Bareback riders' handholds
40 Cutup at the zoo
41 Generous one
43 Ankles
44 John of rock
45 Fix the lawn
47 Legendary rockers, with "The"
49 Eagle's claw
52 Uses a sieve
53 Madrid mister
54 Vacation venues
57 Uses e-mail
58 *M*A*S*H* role
59 Post-holiday highlights
62 Greek letter
64 Cod and Hatteras
66 "Thanks a —!"
68 Sandpiper's cousin
70 Tots
72 Cleans the chimney
73 Burdened
74 Hersey's *A Bell for —*
75 Mild oaths
77 Marsh birds
79 Habituate

80 Copter blade
81 Perfect places
84 Feel one's way
86 Asian holiday
89 Merriweather post
92 Jason leigh
94 Director David
96 202, to Cicero
97 "— tails?"
98 Suspicious engine sound
100 Piles of snow
102 Funt and Ludden
103 Most desperate
105 Say "boo!" to
107 Street performers
108 Part of a shoe
109 Essayist Lamb
110 Rave's partner
111 Wings: Lat.
113 MasterCard rival
114 Fictional sleuth Wolfe
115 B & B's
116 Fruit drinks
119 TV's Caesar
121 Buddhist Thai

Part III
Stepping Away from the Crossword

The 5th Wave   By Rich Tennant

Turn... Likes... Mental... Pleased...

No need to unjumble the words Mr. Coff, just recite the letters.

UTNR
SLEKI
EALMEN
SEDALEP

Puzzle 3-1

HINT

Fill in the letter E whenever you see V in the puzzle.

DPXYRIVQZ LQV MVCWGWIVOT ZXLQIVQ INLG

_____ ___ _____ _____ ____

YVPYOV. JNVG NLAV TPR VAVQ NVLQM PC ZWS

_____. ____ ____ ___ ____ _____ __ ___

DPXYRIVQZ EVIIWGE IPEVINVQ IP CPQX L

_____ _____ _____ __ ____ _

DPXXWIIVV?

_____?

Puzzle 3-2

HINT

Fill in the letter A whenever you see L in the puzzle.

RLXXL IVNHM NT ONWM FS GPTHFLX. TVM HLWMT

_____ _____ __ ____ __ _____. ___ _____

ONKM PXM OMHHMQ LH L HNFM.

____ ___ _____ __ _ ____.

Puzzle 3-3

HINT

Fill in the letter O whenever you see Z in the puzzle.

OZA SVF OXAJS-SXHF NZEY-TEYPFA, SVF TVZYF

___ ___ _____ ____ ____ _____, ___ _____

AXSBEY TEJ E OFFS ZO NZBAEMF.

_____ ___ _ ____ __ _____.

Puzzle 3-4

 Fill in the letter E whenever you see P in the puzzle.

SWP SRNL MPGPLZP JRXXPJSRM UREPSDEPU IRZLB

___ ____ _____ _____ _____ _____

WDU KRC RGPMXA SVTDLO.

___ ___ _____ _____.

Puzzle 3-5

 Fill in the letter T whenever you see O in the puzzle.

ORT IDCWWSMO VEEM-PSDLTF UGXO BEGDAM'O XTMXT

___ _____ ____-_____ ____ _____'_ _____

ORT KFSYCOZ EI ORT XCOGSOCEM.

___ _____ __ ___ _____.

Puzzle 3-6

 Fill in the letter N whenever you see B in the puzzle.

BRTVZGKX AW NUFB XRS TSB RSC RJ VRBFX;

_____ __ ____ ___ ___ ___ __ _____;

ABWRGYFBKX AW NUFB XRS TSB RSC RJ FIKSWFW;

_____ __ ____ ___ ___ ___ __ _____;

PZBLTSMCKX AW NUFB XRS TSB RSC RJ CRNB.

_____ __ ____ ___ ___ ___ __ ____.

Puzzle 3-7: 15 x 15 Squares

1 Across begins in the 10th square from the left in the top row.

Across

1 Agree
7 Major or Minor in the heavens
11 *Crocodile* —
12 Thai cash
13 Farthest point in an orbit
14 Baby — (those born in the '50s)
17 She sheep
18 "Sweet as apple cider" girl
19 Feel poorly
20 Mongrel
22 Wager
23 Street in Paris
24 Regions
27 Pie topping
29 Iron source
32 Step in dance
33 Frequently, poetically
34 Foolishness
37 Go in
38 Like 1, 3, or 5
40 Spigot

43 Existed
44 Not old
45 Eggs
46 Runner in Aspen
48 Refinery
50 Street urchins
53 Soother in lotions
54 Good luck charm
55 Close loudly
56 Oriental temple

Down

1 City in Oklahoma
2 Part of the psyche
3 Winter fall
4 Rim
5 Maiden-named
6 Golfer's prop
7 WW II submarine
8 Aries is one
9 Reap wool
10 Courtyard
14 Apron part
15 Lyric poem
16 Children's pajamas
20 Two-wheeled ammunition wagons
21 Vase
25 — Wiedersehen (Fritz's farewell)
26 Jet or Scrabble —
28 Hurried
29 First number
30 Howard or Reagan
31 Interwoven
35 — biscuit (hardtack)
36 Tomato blights
39 Reside
40 Tribal emblem
41 NYC's Mad. or Lex.
42 Golfer's goal
46 Self-satisfied
47 1,000 gms.
49 Mauna —
50 Delaware Water —
51 Doctors' org.
52 Local post office: abbr.

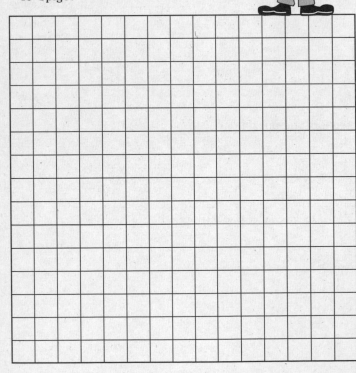

Puzzle 3-8: 19 x 19 Squares

1 Across starts in the 6th square from the right in the top row.

Across

1 Young men
5 Diva's rendition
6 Lost color
11 Wartime action
13 Hurok, the impresario
16 Kate Nelligan title role, 1985
17 Bob and Elizabeth
18 Mine find
19 Makes port
20 Author's collected writings
23 Morsel in a valentine gift
25 Learned one
27 As a whole
28 Leather workers' tools
29 Wall cover
34 Panelists' comment on *Family Feud*
38 Foldable baby cart
40 Like Chicago's weather
42 Not illicitly
43 *Wheel* request
49 Promotional giveaway
50 Cornell's astronomer
51 Catalysts
53 Miami's slogan
60 Ain't right?
61 Eleventh President
63 Crying words
64 Russia's Boris
67 In the direction of
68 Sizes up wrongly
72 Touching king?
74 I-95 is one: abbr.
75 Nebraska city
76 Rodeo sharpshooter Oakley
77 Expressions of delight
78 More docile
79 Intends
80 Objective
81 Facile

Down

1 Runged climber
2 Pointed projectile
3 Need assistance?
4 Morley — of *60 Minutes*
6 Jai alai ball
7 A.A. affiliate
8 Dawson or Dykstra

9 Closes down
10 CD or LP
12 "Shame on you!"
13 Edna Ferber book
14 Maine college town
15 Slowly, to Solti
20 Out, as the tide
21 Woes
22 Passing corridor
24 Physique, to an admirer
26 Bound books
29 Walt Kelly's possum
30 "There oughta be — !"
31 — -et-Vilaine (Rennes' department)
32 Jodie Foster role in 1994
33 Attempt
35 Fragrant climber
36 Gagster
37 Son of Seth
39 Gun the motor
41 Car from Eastern Europe
43 Annoys

44 *Superman* Cain
45 Kids' snap-together blocks
46 "Oh yeah!"
47 Relatives
48 Holiday potato
49 Pt. of TGIF
52 Realtor's dream word
54 Get
55 Hangman's ropes
56 — Jones average
57 Mrs. Butler's maiden name
58 Value
59 Protuberances
62 They rank under Capt.
64 Every twelve months
65 Muslim title
66 Baseball team number
68 Witty remark
69 View in the mirror
70 Margaret Mead's isle of study
71 Ostrich relatives
73 Genetic marker

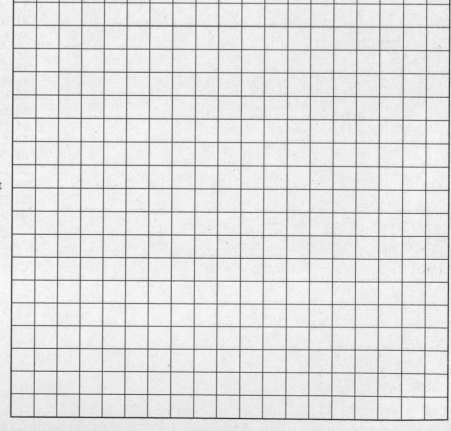

Puzzle 3-9: 17 x 17 Squares

1 Across starts in the 3rd square from the left in the top row.

Across

1 Fed. pollution control gp.
4 Funny person
5 Roast hosts, briefly
8 First name in old horror films
9 *Vogue* competitor
13 —— *22*
16 Not too well
17 Bosc or Anjou
18 Toddler
19 Tickled pink
21 O'Toole's role in *The Lion in Winter*
23 Toolshed item
24 Anatomical network
26 Branch of biol.
27 Fourth notes
28 Racer Bobby's brother
32 Military mix-up
34 "— Clear Day . . ."

35 Oafs
36 — Miller of orchestral note
38 Everything
39 Revered figures
40 St. Louis's — Arch
45 Pen point
46 Computer data unit
47 " — a Kick Out of You"
49 Private's goal
52 Matter-of-fact
54 This kind of puzzle: abbr.
57 Amorous eyes
59 This, in Mexico
60 Put a match to
61 Say yes
62 Molecule component
63 Ye — Tea Shoppe
64 Money dispenser, for short
65 Honey maker
66 Apr. 15 collectors

Down

1 *The Seven Year Itch* costar
2 Supporting column
3 *One Day — Time*
5 1102, in dates
6 Rogue
7 Criteria: abbr.
8 Word before Apple or Ben
9 Destination of an epistle by Saint Paul
10 Grant's opposite
11 Mario who played Caruso
12 Swashbuckling Flynn
14 Cloak-and-dagger org.
15 Fell
18 Oven for ceramics
20 Neglect a payment
22 Last word of the golden rule
25 27th U.S. President
29 Pepys diary phrase
30 Send-along in a letter: abbr.
31 Cheerleader cheers
32 Smeltery dross
33 Vincent Lopez's theme song
36 On-location video recorder
37 "Got it!"
41 River of Spain
42 Cheyenne is its cap.
43 Cruising
44 Baker's need
48 It gives a ship direction
49 Golf org.
50 Low clouds
51 Bil and — Baird
52 Lyrical composition
53 "How was — know?"
55 Helpers
56 Telecom giant
58 Obtain
63 Sash for Madame Butterfly

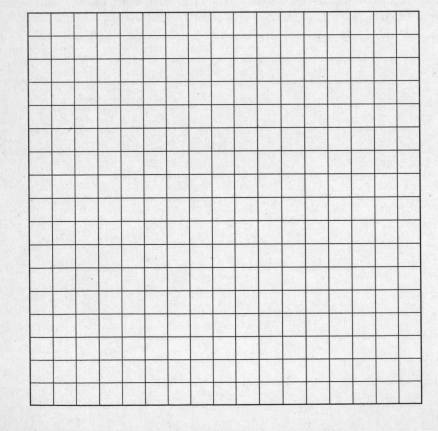

Puzzle 3-10: 15 x 15 Squares

HINT

1 Across starts in the 4th square from the left in the top row. Instead of the usual top-to-bottom symmetry, this puzzle's symmetry is left-to-right. If you divide the puzzle vertically down the middle, the right side is a mirror image of the left side.

Across

1 Big — theory
5 Nuisance
9 Baal, for one
10 Early stringed instrument
11 Rating on an egg carton
13 Spiny shrub
16 Not feel so well
17 Wallop
19 DDE followed him
20 Tickle Me Elmo is one
21 Unlock, to poets
22 — du Diable
23 SAT org.
24 Forrest's friend
26 Very wide, shoewise
27 Sweden's cont.
28 Paddle
30 German port
33 Multitude
37 Ballpark nibble
38 Steak selection
40 Verdi's Ethiopian slave princess
41 Cake decorator
42 Trundle or bunk
43 — -la-la
44 Somewhat, informally
49 Pandas' main food
53 Chess champ
55 Dubbing anew
56 Florida city

Down

1 Bagels' cousins
2 Say further
3 Refusals
4 Fashion magazine
5 Inactive dose in controlled tests
6 Jan van —, Flemish painter
7 Mrs., below the border
8 Computer guru
11 Where racehorses line up
12 Melee
14 Man, for one
15 Suit to —

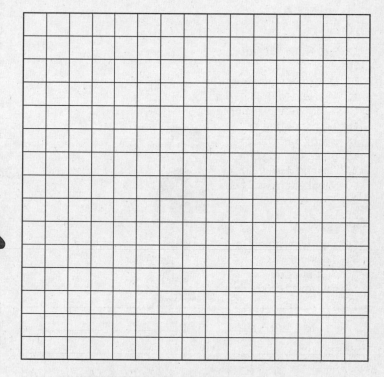

18 Announcement to patrol cars, briefly
24 ". . . on a sesame seed —"
25 Sound from a Jacuzzi user
27 Comic-strip squeal
29 Decay
30 Ohio Indians
31 Nickname for baseball's Bill Madlock
32 Paternity test material
34 Slugger's stat
35 Fix up
36 January, in Juarez
37 The — Four
39 Chapter in history
45 Elementary requirements, initially
46 Light bulb inventor's monogram
47 Aware of
48 Savings insurer: abbr.
49 Ump's silent call
50 China setting?
51 Mauna Kea or McKinley: abbr.
52 Seek alms
54 Transit abbr. in many cities

Puzzle 3-11: 15 x 15 Squares

HINT

1 Across starts in the 4th square from the right in the top row.

Across

1 Cops' org.
4 *Live From Lincoln Center* network
7 Thus
9 Surrealist Salvador
10 Hen
11 Don't get stuck in this!
12 "— Help Myself" (Four Tops hit)
13 — down (make a note of)
16 Trapshooting
18 Horne and Olin
19 Black cat, to some
21 Coach Parseghian
23 Silents actress Theda
24 Tractor-trailer
26 Use scissors
27 Gives off
29 *Casablanca* heroine
33 Toss out
35 Soft mineral
36 Pilgrimage to Mecca

37 Clothing maker Picone
38 Journalist — Rogers St. Johns
42 Not connected
47 Printemps follower
48 Vaccine developer
49 Per
50 With regard to
51 Horse carriage
52 Corporate benefit
53 CIA predecessor
54 Ave. crossers

Down

1 Slogan from the '60s
2 William Jennings —
3 Satellite launcher
4 Central or Balboa
5 Feeling down
6 Location
8 Table crumbs
9 Marx's — *Kapital*
10 Spring bloom
13 Classified ads section
14 Neighbor of Yemen
15 Actress Garr
17 Lemony
20 Most of baby's day
22 Yeltsin's home: abbr.
24 One-ninth of an iceberg
25 Flying toy
27 Time of importance
28 Goya's *The Naked* —
30 Wash
31 Narrow wood strip
32 Teen trouble
34 Intone
38 Now!
39 Odense residents
40 Siskel's colleague
41 Golf course
43 Small change in Chile
44 Sighs of pleasure
45 Some VCRs
46 Quaker pronoun

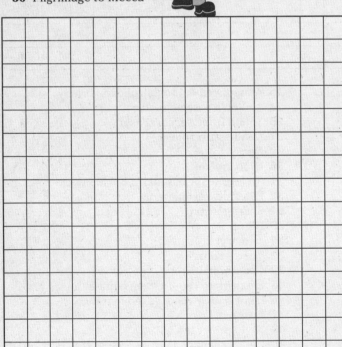

Puzzle 3-12: Poetry

Just to get you started, word J is LIVIDITY.

1B	2E	3H	4F	5A	6C	7K	■	8L	9E	10C	11F	■	12H	13F	■	14O	15D	16G	17B
18P	19J	■	20H	21M	22B	23F	24D	■	25L	26O	27H	■	28B	29Q	30M	■	31B	32F	33R
34G	■	35A	36F	37G	38L	39D	40K	41B	42I	■	43F	44G	45A	46P	■	47Q	48R	49D	50A
51P	52C	■	53A	54C	55E	56G	57N	■	58B	59K	60D	61M	■	62N	63P	■	64G	65C	66Q
67F	■	68H	69A	70I	71B	72D	■	73R	74H	75E	■	76C	77J	78A	79F	80M	■	81J	82H
■	83I	84N	85G	■	86E	87Q	88M	■	89E	90O	91Q	92I	■	93P	94D	95B	■	96D	97F
98J	99I	100G	■	101K	102I	103A	104M	■	105I	106Q	107M	108C	■	109I	110D	111M	■	112I	113P
■	114C	115L	116D	117F	■	118I	119M	120O	121R	■	122E	123C	124I	■	125J	126A	127F	128L	129I
■	130K	131N	132E	■	133Q	134A	135G	136M	■	137J	138M	■	139I	140J	141H	142M	143R	■	144H
■	145H	146R	147A	148N	■	149F	150N	151R	■	152D	153E	154I	155A	156J	157B	158L	159C	160K	■

A Roger Williams perennial favorite (6, 6)

$\overline{134}\ \overline{50}\ \overline{53}\ \overline{103}\ \overline{69}\ \overline{5}\ \overline{155}\ \overline{78}\ \overline{147}\ \overline{35}$
$\overline{126}\ \overline{45}$

B Pandas' dinner

$\overline{28}\ \overline{22}\ \overline{58}\ \overline{157}\ \overline{41}\ \overline{31}\ \overline{17}\ \overline{1}\ \overline{95}\ \overline{71}$

C Favored practice of English worship (4, 6)

$\overline{52}\ \overline{10}\ \overline{114}\ \overline{54}\ \overline{76}\ \overline{123}\ \overline{65}\ \overline{108}\ \overline{6}\ \overline{159}$

D Off limits (3, 2, 6)

$\overline{94}\ \overline{110}\ \overline{15}\ \overline{116}\ \overline{24}\ \overline{152}\ \overline{49}\ \overline{39}\ \overline{60}\ \overline{96}\ \overline{72}$

E Name for a theater employee, once

$\overline{132}\ \overline{75}\ \overline{9}\ \overline{2}\ \overline{89}\ \overline{153}\ \overline{122}\ \overline{86}\ \overline{55}$

F Terrier bred from crossing a bulldog and an English terrier

$\overline{11}\ \overline{149}\ \overline{79}\ \overline{23}\ \overline{43}\ \overline{32}\ \overline{97}\ \overline{117}\ \overline{13}\ \overline{67}$
$\overline{36}\ \overline{127}\ \overline{4}$

G Exposer of scandal, like Ida Tarbell

$\overline{64}\ \overline{16}\ \overline{37}\ \overline{100}\ \overline{56}\ \overline{44}\ \overline{135}\ \overline{85}\ \overline{34}$

H Greedy for riches

$\overline{44}\ \overline{141}\ \overline{68}\ \overline{3}\ \overline{74}\ \overline{145}\ \overline{12}\ \overline{82}\ \overline{27}\ \overline{20}$

I Kind behavior of a lord to his liege (8, 6)

$\overline{99}\ \overline{102}\ \overline{105}\ \overline{154}\ \overline{124}\ \overline{42}\ \overline{83}\ \overline{92}\ \overline{112}\ \overline{109}$
$\overline{118}\ \overline{70}\ \overline{139}\ \overline{129}$

J Grayish-blue, to a medical examiner

$\overline{77}\ \overline{140}\ \overline{125}\ \overline{137}\ \overline{19}\ \overline{98}\ \overline{81}\ \overline{156}$

K Salt's assent (3, 3)

$\overline{40}\ \overline{130}\ \overline{7}\ \overline{59}\ \overline{101}\ \overline{160}$

L "Beam me up, —"

$\overline{128}\ \overline{158}\ \overline{115}\ \overline{38}\ \overline{8}\ \overline{25}$

M Playground fixture (6, 6)

$\overline{61}\ \overline{136}\ \overline{107}\ \overline{111}\ \overline{88}\ \overline{104}\ \overline{21}\ \overline{119}\ \overline{30}\ \overline{138}$
$\overline{142}\ \overline{80}$

N "Poetry Man" singer Snow

$\overline{48}\ \overline{150}\ \overline{131}\ \overline{84}\ \overline{62}\ \overline{57}$

O Sculler's needs

$\overline{26}\ \overline{90}\ \overline{120}\ \overline{14}$

P Fourscore

$\overline{63}\ \overline{18}\ \overline{51}\ \overline{113}\ \overline{46}\ \overline{93}$

Q Heavy jungle knife

$\overline{133}\ \overline{29}\ \overline{66}\ \overline{87}\ \overline{106}\ \overline{91}\ \overline{47}$

R Turned to another track

$\overline{143}\ \overline{146}\ \overline{33}\ \overline{48}\ \overline{73}\ \overline{151}\ \overline{121}$

Puzzle 3-13: New World

HINT If you want help, you can pencil in MINGY for word G.

1L	2A	3B	4N	5J		6M	7C	8B	9P		10A	11H
	12B	13J	14H	15C		16O	17H		18B	19J	20F	21M
	22J	23A	24O	25D		26C	27D	28K	29E	30O	31B	32G
	33G	34K	35I	36C		37C	38F	39P	40L	41G	42I	43J
44P		45E	46G	47M	48L	49O	50F	51N	52P	53D	54B	55L
56J		57C	58N		59H	60F	61I	62M		63K	64A	65O
66P		67K		68L	69H	70A	71E	72K		73I	74N	75M
	76F	77C	78I	79D	80L		81A	82G	83N	84C	85L	86E
87K	88F	89D		90F	91P	92D	93O	94E	95B	96L	97A	98N

A A quaff of ale

$\overline{81}$ $\overline{97}$ $\overline{23}$ $\overline{2}$ $\overline{10}$ $\overline{64}$ $\overline{70}$

B Standard of unimportance

$\overline{95}$ $\overline{54}$ $\overline{18}$ $\overline{12}$ $\overline{3}$ $\overline{31}$ $\overline{8}$

C Bicycle tricks

$\overline{84}$ $\overline{77}$ $\overline{37}$ $\overline{7}$ $\overline{26}$ $\overline{57}$ $\overline{15}$ $\overline{36}$

D Followed as a result

$\overline{53}$ $\overline{92}$ $\overline{79}$ $\overline{27}$ $\overline{25}$ $\overline{89}$

E Piece of chewing gum

$\overline{94}$ $\overline{86}$ $\overline{45}$ $\overline{71}$ $\overline{29}$

F From former days (3, 4)

$\overline{60}$ $\overline{50}$ $\overline{90}$ $\overline{76}$ $\overline{20}$ $\overline{38}$ $\overline{88}$

G Meager and sparse in quantity

$\overline{33}$ $\overline{82}$ $\overline{46}$ $\overline{41}$ $\overline{32}$

H Wanderer

$\overline{17}$ $\overline{11}$ $\overline{59}$ $\overline{69}$ $\overline{14}$

I Put two and two together

$\overline{42}$ $\overline{35}$ $\overline{73}$ $\overline{78}$ $\overline{61}$

J Cowardly one

$\overline{55}$ $\overline{19}$ $\overline{13}$ $\overline{22}$ $\overline{5}$ $\overline{56}$ $\overline{43}$

K Tack on

$\overline{34}$ $\overline{63}$ $\overline{87}$ $\overline{67}$ $\overline{28}$ $\overline{72}$

L Dirgelike musical piece

$\overline{40}$ $\overline{48}$ $\overline{1}$ $\overline{96}$ $\overline{85}$ $\overline{80}$ $\overline{68}$

M Close-fitting tartan trousers

$\overline{47}$ $\overline{75}$ $\overline{83}$ $\overline{6}$ $\overline{98}$

N Science that deals with smells

$\overline{74}$ $\overline{58}$ $\overline{83}$ $\overline{51}$ $\overline{4}$ $\overline{98}$

O John's *Grease* costar

$\overline{93}$ $\overline{49}$ $\overline{16}$ $\overline{24}$ $\overline{30}$ $\overline{65}$

P Raise unnecessary and trivial objections

$\overline{66}$ $\overline{91}$ $\overline{44}$ $\overline{52}$ $\overline{9}$ $\overline{39}$

Puzzle 3-14: A Letter

To give you a little help, here's one hint: Word S is LAPIDATE.

1M	2H	3B	4C	■	5K	6S	7D	■	8C	9M	10R	■	11A	12E	13J	14F	■	15D	16M	17T	18G	19H
■	20T	■	21A	22H	23F	24M	■	25O	26P	27F	■	28R	29N	■	30I	31C	32G	33T	■	34G	35I	36N
■	37C	38H	39I	40Q	41J	42G	43E	■	44A	45R	■	46I	47D	48G	49C	■	50P	51K	52L	■	53L	54O
55R	■	56O	57S	58B	59K	■	60S	61J	■	62A	63I	64Q	■	65Q	66M	67H	68T	■	69E	70G	71S	72P
73R	■	74I	■	75R	76P	77J	78H	■	79O	80D	81I	■	82B	83P	■	84C	85B	86T	87L	■	88I	89G
90J	■	91S	■	92F	93E	94D	95S	96B	97J	98H	■	99G	100K	■	101J	102Q	■	103R	104H	105B	106A	■
107A	108O	109R	110J	■	111R	■	112I	113A	114Q	115E	■	116K	117N	118A	■	119F	120K	■	121C	122R	123D	124O
■	125A	126N	127K	128B	■	129I	130O	131L	132J	133B	■	134A	135O	136P	137N	138B	139P	140C	141D	142M	■	143L
144F	145Q	146O	■	147D	148O	149H	■	150D	151K	152P	153S	154N	■	155R	156I	■	157S	158J	159A	160G	161E	■

A Feelings of ill will

$\overline{113}\ \overline{118}\ \overline{159}\ \overline{107}\ \overline{11}\ \overline{62}\ \overline{125}\ \overline{21}\ \overline{44}\ \overline{106}\ \overline{134}$

B Make a love slave of

$\overline{105}\ \overline{3}\ \overline{96}\ \overline{128}\ \overline{82}\ \overline{58}\ \overline{85}\ \overline{138}\ \overline{133}$

C Suffering from poverty, pain, etc.

$\overline{84}\ \overline{31}\ \overline{4}\ \overline{37}\ \overline{49}\ \overline{121}\ \overline{140}\ \overline{8}$

D Pesky thing

$\overline{47}\ \overline{7}\ \overline{141}\ \overline{94}\ \overline{147}\ \overline{15}\ \overline{123}\ \overline{150}\ \overline{80}$

E Wandered in search of food

$\overline{93}\ \overline{69}\ \overline{12}\ \overline{161}\ \overline{115}\ \overline{43}$

F Like the pearls in a necklace

$\overline{144}\ \overline{119}\ \overline{27}\ \overline{23}\ \overline{14}\ \overline{92}$

G Resourceful and creative thinking

$\overline{18}\ \overline{160}\ \overline{70}\ \overline{42}\ \overline{32}\ \overline{89}\ \overline{99}\ \overline{48}\ \overline{34}$

H Asset for a marathon runner

$\overline{78}\ \overline{19}\ \overline{98}\ \overline{149}\ \overline{38}\ \overline{22}\ \overline{104}\ \overline{67}\ \overline{2}$

I Burr under the saddle

$\overline{88}\ \overline{35}\ \overline{129}\ \overline{30}\ \overline{156}\ \overline{46}\ \overline{63}\ \overline{112}\ \overline{74}\ \overline{39}\ \overline{81}$

J Fitting that passes through the end of a twisted wire (4, 6)

$\overline{132}\ \overline{61}\ \overline{41}\ \overline{110}\ \overline{101}\ \overline{158}\ \overline{13}\ \overline{77}\ \overline{97}\ \overline{90}$

K Foe

$\overline{51}\ \overline{5}\ \overline{116}\ \overline{151}\ \overline{127}\ \overline{59}\ \overline{120}\ \overline{100}$

L Like an unkempt yard

$\overline{52}\ \overline{143}\ \overline{131}\ \overline{87}\ \overline{53}$

M Pestered with the same old stuff

$\overline{66}\ \overline{9}\ \overline{16}\ \overline{142}\ \overline{24}\ \overline{1}$

N Provides, as with talents

$\overline{137}\ \overline{29}\ \overline{154}\ \overline{36}\ \overline{117}\ \overline{126}$

O Made light of (4-6)

$\overline{25}\ \overline{108}\ \overline{148}\ \overline{56}\ \overline{79}\ \overline{54}\ \overline{135}\ \overline{130}\ \overline{146}\ \overline{124}$

P Cruel to animals

$\overline{72}\ \overline{50}\ \overline{139}\ \overline{152}\ \overline{136}\ \overline{76}\ \overline{83}\ \overline{26}$

Q Eerie

$\overline{145}\ \overline{40}\ \overline{102}\ \overline{65}\ \overline{114}\ \overline{64}$

R Adversity

$\overline{75}\ \overline{109}\ \overline{28}\ \overline{155}\ \overline{55}\ \overline{10}\ \overline{122}\ \overline{45}\ \overline{111}\ \overline{103}\ \overline{73}$

S Pelt with stones

$\overline{153}\ \overline{57}\ \overline{95}\ \overline{91}\ \overline{157}\ \overline{71}\ \overline{60}\ \overline{6}$

T Minneapolis suburb

$\overline{68}\ \overline{33}\ \overline{20}\ \overline{86}\ \overline{17}$

Puzzle 3-15: Question for Willard Scott

HINT If you want some help getting started, word B is ATTACHE.

1N	2J	3D	4O	■	5C	6R	■	7A	8D	9H	10O	■	11R	12G	13H	14W	■	15Q	16O	■	17W
18B	19D	■	20J	21S	■	22K	23A	24N	25J	26P	27M	28D	■	29G	30P	31V	32L	33J	34S	35K	36E
■	37I	38R	39A	40C	■	41M	42Q	43F	44E	■	45A	46B	47P	■	48Q	49V	■	50Q	51L	52O	■
53H	54K	55J	56U	57C	■	58S	59T	■	60K	61I	62F	63A	■	64N	65A	66V	67I	68U	69E	70C	71P
72F	73W	74L	75J	76M	■	77W	78A	79J	80C	81G	82T	83P	84E	■	85B	86W	87R	88J	■	89O	90L
91J	92C	■	93Q	94G	■	95B	96S	97R	■	98A	99T	100X	■	101W	102J	103S	104M	105I	■	106Q	107G
■	108N	109O	110H	111U	■	112C	113H	■	114J	115N	116V	117L	118C	119G	■	120M	121T	122P	123J	124L	125X
126K	127T	128A	129W	130R	131E	132U	■	133X	134T	135L	■	136A	137H	■	138A	139J	140C	■	141J	142V	143U
144L	145A	146B	147G	148E	149P	150V	151W	152K	153Q	■	154E	155F	156B	157K	158I	159S	160P	161J	■	162J	163D
164I	165B	166C	■	167R	168P	169M	170J	171O	■	172R	173A	174T	175F	■	176D	177J	178C	179A	180P	181V	182E
■	183G	184J	■	185L	186C	187W	■	188J	189A	190K	191R	192Q	193L	194W	195P	196E	■	197U	198Q	199K	■

A Out of the spotlight (6, 3, 6)

$\overline{138}\ \overline{173}\ \overline{65}\ \overline{179}\ \overline{98}\ \overline{145}\ \overline{7}$
$\overline{128}\ \overline{39}\ \overline{136}\ \overline{78}\ \overline{23}\ \overline{189}$
$\overline{63}\ \overline{45}$

B Embassy worker

$\overline{46}\ \overline{156}\ \overline{85}\ \overline{95}\ \overline{165}\ \overline{18}\ \overline{146}$

C Indispensable aide (5-4, 3)

$\overline{70}\ \overline{80}\ \overline{57}\ \overline{166}\ \overline{140}\ \overline{186}\ \overline{118}$
$\overline{40}\ \overline{5}\ \overline{178}\ \overline{112}\ \overline{92}$

D Debate again

$\overline{28}\ \overline{19}\ \overline{163}\ \overline{3}\ \overline{176}\ \overline{8}$

E Beatles' megahit ballad

$\overline{44}\ \overline{69}\ \overline{148}\ \overline{36}\ \overline{131}\ \overline{182}\ \overline{196}$
$\overline{154}\ \overline{84}$

F Comedian Chase

$\overline{155}\ \overline{72}\ \overline{43}\ \overline{62}\ \overline{175}$

G Remainder

$\overline{119}\ \overline{12}\ \overline{29}\ \overline{183}\ \overline{107}\ \overline{81}$
$\overline{94}\ \overline{147}$

H Get even for

$\overline{13}\ \overline{110}\ \overline{9}\ \overline{113}\ \overline{53}\ \overline{137}$

I Flag-holder's activity

$\overline{37}\ \overline{61}\ \overline{158}\ \overline{164}\ \overline{67}\ \overline{105}$

J Capra Best Picture Oscar winner (3 ,4, 4, 2, 4, 3)

$\overline{161}\ \overline{102}\ \overline{188}\ \overline{33}\ \overline{91}\ \overline{123}\ \overline{141}$
$\overline{25}\ \overline{114}\ \overline{170}\ \overline{75}\ \overline{55}\ \overline{79}$
$\overline{162}\ \overline{177}\ \overline{20}\ \overline{2}\ \overline{88}$
$\overline{184}\ \overline{139}$

K Alternatively

$\overline{54}\ \overline{190}\ \overline{60}\ \overline{152}\ \overline{126}\ \overline{22}\ \overline{157}$
$\overline{35}\ \overline{199}$

L Guarantee financial support

$\overline{117}\ \overline{144}\ \overline{124}\ \overline{32}\ \overline{135}\ \overline{74}\ \overline{51}$
$\overline{193}\ \overline{185}\ \overline{90}$

M Spoiled

$\overline{76}\ \overline{169}\ \overline{120}\ \overline{41}\ \overline{27}\ \overline{104}$

N Rolex, e.g.

$\overline{1}\ \overline{24}\ \overline{64}\ \overline{115}\ \overline{108}$

O Pardon for political offenses

$\overline{109}\ \overline{89}\ \overline{16}\ \overline{52}\ \overline{171}\ \overline{4}\ \overline{10}$

P Student lodging abroad (5, 6)

$\overline{47}\ \overline{168}\ \overline{122}\ \overline{83}\ \overline{26}\ \overline{149}\ \overline{30}$
$\overline{71}\ \overline{160}\ \overline{195}\ \overline{180}$

Q Consign to the circular file (5, 4)

$\overline{106}\ \overline{42}\ \overline{153}\ \overline{15}\ \overline{93}\ \overline{50}\ \overline{48}$
$\overline{192}\ \overline{198}$

R Dazzle

$\overline{6}\ \overline{172}\ \overline{97}\ \overline{191}\ \overline{130}\ \overline{38}\ \overline{87}$
$\overline{167}\ \overline{11}$

S Oddments of information

$\overline{58}\ \overline{96}\ \overline{103}\ \overline{21}\ \overline{159}\ \overline{34}$

T Indiana hoopster

$\overline{121}\ \overline{59}\ \overline{99}\ \overline{127}\ \overline{82}\ \overline{134}\ \overline{174}$

U Put up with

$\overline{111}\ \overline{56}\ \overline{68}\ \overline{143}\ \overline{132}\ \overline{197}$

V *Walden Pond* author

$\overline{116}\ \overline{142}\ \overline{150}\ \overline{31}\ \overline{49}\ \overline{181}\ \overline{66}$

W Dry, in a way (2, 3, 5)

$\overline{73}\ \overline{194}\ \overline{17}\ \overline{86}\ \overline{187}\ \overline{151}\ \overline{77}$
$\overline{101}\ \overline{129}\ \overline{14}$

X Buddy or Socks

$\overline{133}\ \overline{125}\ \overline{100}$

Puzzle 3-16: Policing the Barn

HINT

Word G is DUGONGS.

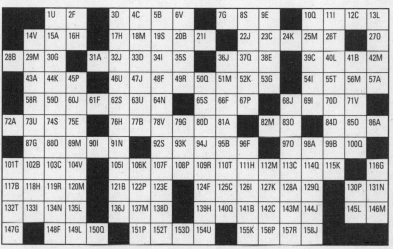

	1U	2F		3D	4C	5B	6V		7G	8S	9E		10Q	11I	12C	13L	
14V	15A	16H		17H	18M	19S	20B	21I		22J	23C	24K	25M	26T		27O	
28B	29M	30G		31A	32J	33D	34I	35S		36J	37Q	38E		39C	40L	41B	42M
	43A	44K	45P		46U	47J	48F	49R	50Q	51M	52K	53G		54I	55T	56M	57A
58R	59D	60J	61F	62S	63U	64N		65S	66F	67P				68J	69I	70D	71V
72A	73U	74S	75E		76H	77B	78V	79G	80D	81A		82M	83O		84D	85O	86A
	87G	88O	89M	90I	91N		92S	93K	94J	95B	96F		97O	98A	99B	100Q	
101T	102B	103C	104V		105I	106K	107F	108P	109R	110T	111H	112M	113C	114Q	115K		116G
117B	118H	119R	120M		121B	122P	123E		124F	125C	126I	127K	128A	129Q		130P	131N
132T	133I	134N	135L		136J	137M	138D		139H	140Q	141B	142C	143M	144J		145L	146M
147G		148F	149L	150Q		151P	152T	153D	154U		155K	156P	157R	158J			

A Wisconsin Bay

$\overline{31}\ \overline{128}\ \overline{98}\ \overline{72}\ \overline{86}\ \overline{43}\ \overline{15}$
$\overline{57}\ \overline{81}$

B Yearly celebration

$\overline{121}\ \overline{5}\ \overline{41}\ \overline{95}\ \overline{99}\ \overline{20}\ \overline{117}$
$\overline{141}\ \overline{28}\ \overline{77}\ \overline{102}$

C Left-wingers

$\overline{23}\ \overline{113}\ \overline{39}\ \overline{103}\ \overline{125}\ \overline{4}$
$\overline{12}\ \overline{142}$

D Like country roofs

$\overline{84}\ \overline{3}\ \overline{70}\ \overline{33}\ \overline{80}\ \overline{59}$
$\overline{153}\ \overline{138}$

E Founder of Christian Science

$\overline{38}\ \overline{123}\ \overline{9}\ \overline{75}$

F Bancroft, in *The Graduate*

$\overline{96}\ \overline{148}\ \overline{124}\ \overline{48}\ \overline{2}\ \overline{61}$
$\overline{107}\ \overline{66}$

G Manatee's cousins in the Indian Ocean

$\overline{147}\ \overline{79}\ \overline{53}\ \overline{7}\ \overline{87}\ \overline{116}\ \overline{30}$

H Does a bouncer's job

$\overline{118}\ \overline{139}\ \overline{111}\ \overline{76}\ \overline{17}\ \overline{16}$

I Greedy to taste, old-style

$\overline{69}\ \overline{11}\ \overline{34}\ \overline{133}\ \overline{21}\ \overline{54}\ \overline{126}$
$\overline{105}\ \overline{90}$

J Letter order

$\overline{136}\ \overline{158}\ \overline{144}\ \overline{47}\ \overline{32}\ \overline{22}\ \overline{94}$
$\overline{36}\ \overline{60}\ \overline{68}$

K 144 tile game (3-5)

$\overline{106}\ \overline{24}\ \overline{93}\ \overline{155}\ \overline{44}\ \overline{52}$
$\overline{115}\ \overline{127}$

L Completely tired out (3, 2)

$\overline{145}\ \overline{135}\ \overline{13}\ \overline{40}\ \overline{149}$

M Sewer's use this for basting (7, 6)

$\overline{112}\ \overline{143}\ \overline{120}\ \overline{146}\ \overline{82}\ \overline{137}\ \overline{89}$
$\overline{42}\ \overline{56}\ \overline{51}\ \overline{29}\ \overline{25}\ \overline{18}$

N Art Deco illustrator

$\overline{134}\ \overline{64}\ \overline{91}\ \overline{131}$

O Oscar winner for *Network*

$\overline{97}\ \overline{88}\ \overline{83}\ \overline{27}\ \overline{85}$

P Hurt

$\overline{156}\ \overline{122}\ \overline{130}\ \overline{108}\ \overline{45}\ \overline{151}\ \overline{67}$

Q Impassioned, as a speech

$\overline{50}\ \overline{140}\ \overline{37}\ \overline{150}\ \overline{10}\ \overline{100}$
$\overline{114}\ \overline{129}$

R Monroe's *Seven Year Itch* co-star

$\overline{49}\ \overline{58}\ \overline{119}\ \overline{109}\ \overline{157}$

S City east of South Bend

$\overline{74}\ \overline{8}\ \overline{62}\ \overline{35}\ \overline{65}\ \overline{19}\ \overline{92}$

T Chattered

$\overline{152}\ \overline{55}\ \overline{26}\ \overline{132}\ \overline{101}\ \overline{110}$

U Archie's dingbat

$\overline{63}\ \overline{154}\ \overline{1}\ \overline{46}\ \overline{73}$

V Broadway events

$\overline{104}\ \overline{14}\ \overline{78}\ \overline{71}\ \overline{6}$

Part IV
The Part of Tens

The 5th Wave   By Rich Tennant

"Exiting, one of the limousines is a person whose name is synonymous with stage, screen, and crossword puzzle clues."

In this part . . .

1 take you beyond the puzzle grid into the wider world of puzzledom. Specifically, I give you some solving tips from the experts (okay, I give you tips on how to cheat), and I answer a few of the questions I most often hear about creating puzzles.

Chapter 1

Ten Solving Tips

Don't be fooled into thinking that either you've got it or you don't (at least when it comes to puzzles). In my 20 years of professional crossword experience, I've met natural-born acrossionados, and I've seen dedicated newcomers turn into good, competent solvers.

Just like with any sport, you need practice to become a great solver. In this chapter, I give you some tips and hints, culled from my years of experience with puzzles, that should give you a leg up when it comes to tackling the puzzle.

Consulting Reference Books for the Answer

When you encounter a clue that stumps you, turn to the following reference books:

✔ **A standard desk dictionary and the world atlas:** These books set you on the path to most answers. However, because these general-reference books aren't written with the crossword puzzler in mind, searching for answers in them requires the most effort on the solver's part.

✔ **Crossword puzzle dictionaries:** Unlike standard dictionaries, crossword puzzle dictionaries don't show you how to use the word or define the word. Instead, crossword puzzle dictionaries lead you to the selection of typical crossword entries by matching clues to entries. You find the clues listed alphabetically, and after each clue is a number of corresponding entries, organized from shortest entry to longest.

✔ **Word finders:** These books take you directly to the answer by listing all possible letter combinations that you run across in crosswords. For example, if you have a series of four squares that look like T (blank) A (blank), the word finder shows you all the letter combinations that could make a word with the letters you know. You can then test out each possible entry by cross-checking it with the other entries that cross it. (You won't find the meaning of the word here, just the entries.)

Because crosswords use proper names and letter combinations not included in the standard dictionary, solvers definitely benefit from using references geared towards solvers.

For information and recommendations on specific references for puzzlers, pick up a copy of *Crossword Puzzles For Dummies,* by yours truly, published by IDG Books Worldwide, Inc.

Looking words up along the way brings you up to speed with key repeaters. Puzzle VIP Stan Newman, who wears two large hats in puzzledom (as the managing director of puzzles for Times Books and Puzzle Editor for Creators Syndicate), says that he built his success on a simple principle: He looked up words he didn't know before. You won't be surprised to find that he has an amazing vocabulary.

Keeping in Good Form

Playing any sport requires putting in a little time every day. With puzzles, the time investment can be as small as you wish. It can become part of your morning routine after brushing your teeth. Or, you can squeeze in good practice time during a commute or during lunch.

By the measure of magazines missing their puzzle pages in waiting rooms, I know that lots of people are getting in practice. But librarians take note: Nothing is more exasperating for an acrossionado than making the trip to the local library to check the solutions for last week's puzzle only to find the answer page missing from the reference room copy! (I should know — it's happened to me on several occasions.)

Observing the Great Solvers at Work

Crocuses aren't the only sign of spring! Once a year, after the vernal equinox, the American Crossword Tournament draws solvers from around the nation for some solving fun. (Of course, entrants are welcome from any country if they're game!)

Over the course of three days, nearly 200 puzzle lovers have the chance to shoot the breeze about clues and themes they've seen over the past year, and to solve a series of six specially designed crosswords (the puzzles are put together by world class constructors). Will Shortz, puzzle editor for *The New York Times,* acts as emcee of the event, which is sponsored by Official Publications. More than a dozen puzzle pros serve as judges. The final round of the Tournament involves the three top contestants who solve in a "lightning" round working against the clock at upright boards in front of the entire assembly. Whoever solves the puzzle correctly first wins both a cash prize, 15 minutes of fame on the local news, and the eternal admiration of those who know. Additionally, winners tend to get involved with puzzles on the professional level as constructors, editors, or proofreaders.

Even if you don't enroll in the competition, watching how the nation's top acrossionados attack the grid can be a fascinating study. The first entry they insert and the special handwriting tricks they develop in order to improve their solving time offers insights on how to conquer the grid. That doesn't mean that you'll follow their lead, but watching a speed solver's technique is a sport in itself.

You can access the puzzles used in the Tournament on the Tournament's Web site if you want to participate long-distance. For more information visit the Web site at http://www.crosswordtournament.com. Or you may use pencil and paper and write to Will Shortz at *The New York Times,* 229 West 43rd Street, New York, NY, 10036, Attention: Puzzle Editor.

Playing Scrabble®

Scrabble, the popular board game by Milton Bradley, offers the following two insights to crossword solvers:

- ✔ **Frequency of letter usage:** The tiles help you understand which letters appear most often in the grid, with E in the top slot.
- ✔ **Letter combinations:** Looking at a rack of randomly selected letters gives your eye some training on useful letter combinations. When you look at a rack of four E's and three I's and wonder who will pick that lone Q, you come to appreciate the dilemma that constructors sometimes face when they combine letters in the grid.

Crosswords cut a wider swath than Scrabble, which excludes proper names, foreign terms, and geographical locations.

Cheating!

I call it "reading solutions." Novice solvers always worry about so-called "cheating" in crossword solving. Cheating doesn't exist! Forget about grades.

Yes, puzzles measure your instant recall on a variety of subjects, but you're allowed a lapse. If geography isn't your bag, the occasional river or mountain range may throw you — at first. But if you look up the answer in the solution grid and find out that river's name when it first stumps you, you have a much better chance of remembering it the next time you see the same clue.

Of course, books of puzzles (like this one) supply the answers, so you can look up an entry any old time you want to. But if you're deliberating over daily, weekly, or monthly puzzles, you have to depend on delayed gratification.

Writing Down Key Words

Writing something down in your own handwriting often proves a great memory device. If you discover a word, and you want to keep it in your special lexicon of crosswordese, just jot it down.

Some champs find that a file card system works best. You write the entry at the top of the card, with the clues below. Then you can store the cards in a shoe box for easy reference.

Writing Clearly

An H can easily look like an N in the small square allotted to each letter. This sounds mighty obvious, but if you can't read your handwriting, neither practice nor word lists nor outside reference books can come to the rescue. I recommend writing in all capital letters for best results.

Some speed solvers develop faster writing techniques to help cut their solving times. For example, a cursive capital E (which looks like a reversed 3) is quicker to insert than an E that takes four strokes to write.

Strolling through the Dictionary

Contrary to popular belief, crossword solving doesn't enhance your everyday vocabulary. Instead, you become familiar with a strange assortment of short words and abbreviations. Crossword words only come in handy when you're watching *Jeopardy!* on TV. (One panel of three players was stumped by the often used crossword clue "Spanish queen," which any acrossionado knows is ENA.)

Still, the dictionary makes great bedtime reading for solvers. I'm not recommending that you read it from cover to cover — just scan the pages on a regular basis. You may find that you boost your solving skills as you notice prefixes, suffixes, and words that weave through the grid.

In *Crosswords For Dummies,* I recommend a parlor game called Fictionary for three or more players (the more, the merrier). All you need is a dictionary (the larger, the better), paper, and pencils. The first player selects a word from the dictionary and spells it aloud. Then each player writes down a definition, with the first player writing the actual dictionary definition. The first player reads each definition aloud, and the other players must select the correct definition. I guarantee a good laugh after each round. Of course, along the way, you also pick up some words for the crossword.

Taking Your Mind off the Puzzle

Reading the newspaper or watching TV may bring to your attention some repeaters that you weren't aware of before. Also, you find out about what's "in" with clues these days (brand names like ALPO), and what's "out" like "Celebes ox" (ANOA).

Retired champ David Rosen suggests that puzzles measure your general knowledge. Simply reading the newspaper and staying on top of popular culture (film titles, celebrities, and government officials, for example) may be all the effort necessary to fill in the average 15 x 15 daily crossword.

Knowing When to Let Go

If a crossword just doesn't tickle your fancy, try another puzzle. Above all, puzzles should be fun — you won't get anywhere, and quickly, if you feel like you're drudging through a puzzle.

Puzzle legend Margaret Farrar (long-time editor of *The New York Times* crossword) was a great advocate of the unfinished puzzle. She believed that if it's not falling into place, move on to another puzzle before frustration sets in. Use the same principle you do when reading a novel: If it doesn't move you, find one that does. Pleasure is the key here. You become a better solver when you recognize that a puzzle is (or isn't) for you.

Chapter 2
Ten Fun Facts about Crossword Creation

*W*henever someone finds out I'm involved with puzzles on a professional level, I get barraged with the same questions about the way things work in puzzledom. (I bet you have a few of those same questions swimming around in your head right now.) In this chapter, I address some of the main queries I've heard over the years.

What Do You Call a Puzzle Maker?

People who write conventional crosswords are called *constructors*.

By "conventional crossword" I refer to the sort that you find in this book. Typically, the conventional crossword operates as a sort of synonym-matching game with clues listed by number Across and Down and entries inserted in the grid.

Who Writes Crosswords?

Unbelievably, most people who ask me this think that jail prisoners write crosswords. The implication, I suppose, is that you need a lot of time and solitude to construct the average crossword puzzle. Although I can understand that prisoners may try their hand at construction, I don't know of any who are published. But one of my close colleagues knows of two!

Curiously, a small pool of folks are responsible for the amusement of millions of solvers. Of course, the same is true of just about every art form.

The kind of folks who write crosswords are those who love words more than financial remuneration. In fact, former puzzle pro Mike Miller has compared the wages of a crossword constructor unfavorably to that of a babysitter.

Certain professions do seem more likely to produce the types of people who find themselves fashioning grids and poring over clues. Among conventional crossword constructors, I've noticed large contingents of computer whizzes and teachers who moonlight with the grid.

In fact, the man who inspired me, Ira Marienhoff, was my high school social studies teacher. When he passed away several years ago, he left a huge endowment to his college, much to everyone's surprise. I like to think that he accumulated his fortune by investing his crossword earnings wisely.

Who Wrote the First Crossword?

The very first crossword was created by newspaperman Arthur Wynn in 1913. As editor of the Fun supplement of *The New York World,* Wynn was charged with amusing the readership with a variety of word games.

An Englishman by birth, Wynn was practiced in the clever word puzzles of his Victorian boyhood. So, at holiday time, he took the liberty of designing a diamond shaped grid with clues that he dubbed the "Word Cross."

Within weeks of its debut, the syllables of this newspaper feature switched position and the game became known as Cross Word. It remained known only to its immediate readership for the next decade until a collection of crosswords hit the bookstores in 1923 and created an international sensation.

Can Computers Construct Crosswords?

Some constructors use computer programs to create crossword puzzles. In fact, some professional constructors have never put pencil to paper.

It's no question that the computer has had a major impact on the puzzle industry. The issue has split the industry into two distinct camps.

Acrossionados like Eric Labert, a former computer scientist for Bell Laboratories, designed some seminal puzzle software. He believes that computers create puzzles faster and better than people.

On the anti side are puzzle experts who believe that computers can't match the quality of purely-human work. Some holdouts on this issue, including master constructor Henry Hook, won't even own a computer!

Both camps agree that computers only serve as a tool for the constructor. When it comes to ingenuity and creativity with puzzles, you still need the human element.

Which Comes First — the Clues or Grid?

It's a trick question. Generally, the constructor begins by figuring out a theme for the puzzle. The theme may be straightforward (titles, categories of items, idioms) or tricky (involving wordplay like anagrams or double meanings).

After deciding on the theme, the constructor determines which size grid fits his theme clues the best. Of course, the more complex the theme, the larger the grid must be to accommodate it. The average daily size is 15 x 15 squares, while Sunday expands to 21 x 21 squares.

After the constructor selects the grid, she inserts the words that comprise the theme into the grid. Then she fills in entries that interlock correctly with those theme entries. After she fills the grid, the constructor composes clues that match the entries.

I walk you step by step through the process of creating a puzzle in *Crossword Puzzles For Dummies,* published by IDG Books Worldwide, Inc. Pick up a copy of that book if you're really into the idea of creating your own puzzles.

Who Writes British Crosswords?

British crosswords (also known as *cryptic* crosswords) take the conventional, American-style crossword and turn it into a game of complex wordplay. Not long after the crossword landed in Great Britain in 1923, constructors replaced the synonym type clues with the anagrams, puns, and charades that have become a staple of the British crossword. (See *Crossword Puzzles For Dummies* for a detailed look at the British crossword.)

A strain of musical folks write cryptic crosswords, among them leaders of the American musical stage such as Richard Maltby, Jr. and Stephen Sondheim (Maltby's variety cryptic puzzles are a regular feature in *Harper's* magazine). Clever use of words in a creative format makes it a natural playground for lyricists.

Can You Write Crosswords in Languages Other Than English?

Yes, indeed! Acrossionados may be found around the world, from China to Israel to Scandinavia. The standards vary according to the language — for example, if you write a puzzle in Hebrew, a language that reads from right to left, then you put the first Across entry in the upper-right-hand corner (rather than the upper-left corner, where it resides in English).

If you're interested in writing a puzzle in a language other than English, you should locate a puzzle in that language and use the grid as a model.

Where Can I Get More Tips on Constructing?

I recommend *A Puzzlemaker's Handbook* (Times Books) by experts Mel Rosen and Stan Kurzban. This serves as the industry handbook as well. You'll make your money back if you sell one puzzle after buying this book.

Developing a library of reference books requires a greater investment. For a complete list of recommended dictionaries and other resources, consult *Crossword Puzzles For Dummies.*

Part V
Appendixes

The 5th Wave   By Rich Tennant

"Lookout? You're right, here it is — a 7-letter word for 'An observant'."

In this part . . .

After you complete a puzzle (or yield to the urge to see the solution), turn to Appendix A for confirmation. In Appendix B, I tell you everything you need to know about working the puzzles you find in Part III of this book, including cryptograms, diagramlesses, and acrostics.

Appendix A
Answers

Puzzle 1-1: Giant Steps
Page 4

Puzzle 1-2: Have You Read . . .
Page 5

Puzzle 1-3: Seeing Double
Page 6

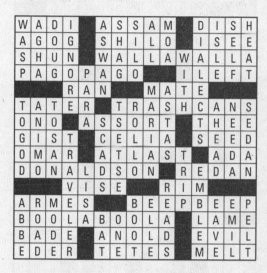

Puzzle 1-4: Seaside Sights
Page 7

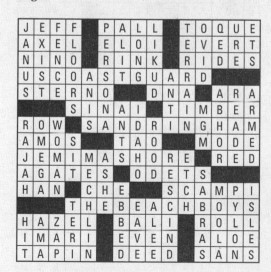

Puzzle 1-5: Masterful Mix
Page 8

```
R I M S ■ ■ T E E N ■ S A L T
I R A Q ■ O R A T E ■ A R I A
N A N U F I R S T C L A S S
D E S I ■ F A N ■ T R A M P S
■ ■ U R K E L ■ E L I ■ ■ ■
T R E M O R ■ P R E S A G E
R O T ■ L E V I N ■ P L A N S
A P U S ■ D I N E R ■ E L A L
M E D I C ■ B A S E R ■ S T E
■ S E R A P E S ■ S T O W E D
■ ■ L A S ■ S E E T O ■ ■ ■
E A S T E R ■ P A N ■ I R I S
F L A M B O Y A N T ■ O T T O
T I G E ■ D E L E S ■ S H E M
S T A N ■ Y S E R ■ ■ E Y R E
```

Puzzle 1-8: Dessert Menu
Page 11

```
R A P ■ A S T A ■ F E E S
I T E ■ S L A M ■ L A S T
T O E ■ S E R B ■ A C T I
A P P L E P O L I S H E R
■ ■ ■ A R T ■ I R K ■ ■ ■
S P E N T ■ O N E ■ R Y E
P O N D ■ F I G ■ L A O S
A I D ■ A L L ■ R E N D S
■ D N A ■ A A A ■ ■ ■
L E M O N M E R I N G U E
O D I N ■ I N E S ■ A N D
S I L O ■ N O N E ■ I D E
S T E R ■ G L A D ■ T O N
```

Puzzle 1-6: Use Your Noodle
Page 9

```
H A D T O ■ R S V P ■ B A S S
A R E O N ■ E L I A ■ I L K A
C O P P E R H E A D ■ G L U M
K A T S ■ E O E ■ P H I L O
■ H E A D O V E R H E E L S
T W E E D ■ K E S H I A ■ ■
I R A D E S ■ D E O ■ D R A G
K I D ■ S O S ■ R D A ■ O N O
I T S A ■ L E E ■ A B O U N D
■ ■ H E D A Y A ■ E R N E S
L O S E S O N E S H E A D ■
E R I A S ■ C I O ■ T H E A
P O N D ■ H E A D P R I E S T
E N T O ■ O G R E ■ T O A S T
W O O F ■ W O E S ■ E N D O N
```

Puzzle 1-9: Rhyme Scheme
Page 12

```
R E A D S ■ P A C T ■ B A R S
A C T U P ■ L I R E ■ U L A N
F R O M E ■ O D I N ■ M E T E
T U M B L E W E E D ■ B R I E
■ ■ O L D S ■ R E A L T O R
A B A ■ S O H O ■ D D E ■ ■
C A S H ■ M A P S ■ E B B E D
T I T U S ■ R E Y ■ N E E D Y
S L I M E ■ E R L E ■ E R I E
■ B A A ■ A L A S ■ N E D
S T A L L E D ■ A R I A ■ ■
N I N E ■ R U M B L E F I S H
A T O P ■ O R A L ■ S T O N E
C A L I ■ B A K E ■ T E N O N
K N E E ■ E N O S ■ A R A B S
```

Puzzle 1-7: Family Affair
Page 10

```
T A R A ■ F I R M ■ A G A N A
A G O G ■ O L I O ■ E A G E R
F A T H E R K N O W S B E S T
T R E A T ■ G N A T ■ E S S
■ ■ S C O T ■ S H E ■ ■ ■
■ M O T H E R O F P E A R L
R I D ■ R A M A ■ T R A I N
E N D U P ■ D E M ■ E L I T E
B E L L I ■ E G O S ■ S E W
■ R Y A N S D A U G H T E R
■ ■ N A E ■ S T O W ■ ■ ■
R O D ■ F L O W ■ P E A C E
A S O N O F T H E C I R C U S
F L O O R ■ T I T O ■ P E L T
T O R T E ■ O M A N ■ S R T A
```

Puzzle 1-10: Comedy Teams
Page 13

```
U S E S ■ E G G E D ■ A V O N
R E N T ■ L A R V A ■ M O P E
A P S O ■ A L I A S ■ A I R E
L A U R E L A N D H A R D Y
S L E E K ■ D E E R E ■ ■ ■
■ ■ S E E P ■ R E T T O N
S A M ■ R E S T ■ S T A R E
T H E T H R E E S T O O G E S
A M O R E ■ K W A I ■ S O T
R E W I N D ■ R E E K ■ ■ ■
■ ■ F I A T S ■ N A D I A
C H E E C H A N D C H O N G
E R I C ■ A R T I E ■ U L A N
L E S T ■ P E A C E ■ N O N E
M E S A ■ O W N E R ■ A R E S
```

Puzzle 1-11: Plain Geometry
Page 14

```
P I N O N | B L A H | R A P S
A D E L A | L O L A | E L A L
N A W A B | U T E S | A F R O
T H E F I R S T C I R C L E
S O L | S O H O | D O T A G E
| R C A | P I C | N O T
D I A M O N D B A C K | D R U
E M U S | O R A | V O I D
N B C | S Q U A R E D A N C E
I R T | A U G | R E N
S O I G N E | A G E R | A P B
| G O L D E N T R I A N G L E
U L N A | N E R O | N O N E T
M I E S | I L I A | G R E B E
P O D S | E L A N | E A S E L
```

Puzzle 1-12: Weekend To-Do List
Page 15

```
A L T A | M E L T | R A J A S
D I A N | O B O E | E M I L E
I C K Y | D O L E | W O M A N
T I E | R U N A N E R R A N D
S T A T E L Y | T O E
| D E L E | S C O T S M A N
P A R T Y | S T O N E | O L A
E R I E | S L I M S | G W E N
E N V | L A U R A | L U T E S
P E E L I N G S | C A S H
| A C T | A R C H E R Y
W A T C H A M O V I E | L I E
A W O K E | E L E M | F A V A
D O N E E | W I R E | A W E T
S L E D S | S O T S | A N T S
```

Puzzle 1-13: Take the Day Off
Page 16

```
I N S T | T E D S | A P A R T
D O E R | U R A L | P O L A R
E L L A | R I T A | E L A T E
S O F W I N E A N D R O S E S
| L A D | T A I
H I M | N O E L | S T O L I D
A M I D | W R I T | I N A N E
S A T U R N I G H T F E V E R
I R E N E | C H E R | S E R B
D I R E C T | T E A L | S T Y
| O N O | I O U
S O F F U T U R E P A S S E D
A L I E N | T A T S | H A L E
S P L A T | E Y R E | E L I A
S E E R S | R E E D | R E E F
```

Puzzle 1-14: Duffer's Course
Page 17

```
F O R E | S L I P S | B O A R
A B E D | T O N I C | A N T E
N I N E T E E N T H | S T E N
| T E N S E S | S O O T H E D
| A D S | O G E E
A N G E R S | D O L L | G A L
L O O P S | R A N E E | R B I
L I L I | C I T E D | G E E S
A R F | T O L E R | C H E L A
Y E S | O M E R | A L I N E S
| C O O P | P G A
P E O P L E S | A E R A T E
R A R E | T O U R N A M E N T
O N E R | E A T I T | E T O N
M E S A | D R E S S | N E S T
```

Puzzle 1-15: Biography
Page 18

```
S E A S | S A I L S | T B A R
E X I T | A G L O W | R E D O
C E D A R V I L L E | I N D O
| C A N Y O N | L E A N E S T
| A R G | T G I F
C A N O N S | C R E E | A B E
I D O L S | P A U S E | C O X
T O B E | C A R E T | A T O P
E R E | T A P E S | A D O B E
D E L | A N A S | C H E R Y L
| P O N D | A R E
P R E P A Y S | B E A D L E
S E A T | J A N E A D D A M S
A N C E | A D U L T | A M M O
T O E D | R A N E E | Y E A S
```

Puzzle 1-16: Sightseeing
Page 19

```
W R I T E | K U N G | F E E L
A A R O N | O R A L | L I M A
G R A N D C A N Y O N A R I Z
S E N | I L L S | W I N E R Y
| N C A A | O W L S
A B L O O M | A M O S | L E W
C L O U T | L I A R | G I N A
M O U N T R U S H M O R E S D
E A T S | O L L A | V A G U E
S T S | K A L E | R E S E E D
| W E D S | A I R S
S K I E R S | E L L A | R A E
L I B E R T Y B E L L P E N N
A L I D | E E O C | L I N E D
M O S S | R A N K | S T O W S
```

Puzzle 1-17: Plays on Words
Page 20

```
L A G O S | O L I O | Z I P S
A D R O P | R E N D | U R A L
P L A Z A | A W E D | N O S Y
P A P E R C L I P J O I N T
S I E S T A | S T O P
      A I M | B A H A M A
A L E E | R O U T | L O V E D
T A X M A N O F H I S W O R D
O V O I D | R O A N | E W E S
M A N T L E | I T S
      I N C H | R I A L T O
  R E D B A R O N O F B E E F
Y O Y O | B A L E | T A M E R
A B E T | L I E S | E B O N Y
W E D S | E N D S | D A N S E
```

Puzzle 1-18: Letter Scrambling
Page 21

```
B A B S | F I R M | S H I R K
I D E E | O A H U | A E R I E
N E A R | O M E N | M A S O N
G A R B E D B A D G E R
O L D S A W | I A N | R B I
        R E A D | V E N E E R
S E G O | B L A S E S A B L E
P A R M A | A G T | S P A I N
O R A N G G R O A N | A G E E
I N F I R M | N Y E T
L S T | E A T | O R I E N T
    T E N R E C C E N T E R
M A O R I | A C H E | G U R U
A G A I N | C H A N | O D D S
B E F O G | T O P E | T E S S
```

Puzzle 1-19: Crossing the Grid
Page 22

```
P T A S | M O T O R | D O L T
L O V E | E L O P E | E L I S
U N I V | S E P I A | M A M A
G I V E I T A O N C E O V E R
      N R A | F E T A L
S C A D S | I T S | V I T A L
H A L E | B A H | R E T I N A
E N G A G E M E N T R I N G S
D O O D A D | M A E | O G L E
S E L L S | C O Y | S N E E R
      Y E S O R | R E D
P R E S S C O N F E R E N C E
S A K I | A L I A S | R O O M
S T E N | L E N T O | B N A I
T A D S | E D G E D | Y E L L
```

Puzzle 1-20: Hodgepodge
Page 23

```
B E L A B O R | M O B I L E S
E R U D I T E | A B A L O N E
R E C A N T S | D O L L A R S
E W E | D E C I D E D | M A T
T H R U | R U S E S | T I G E
T O N N E | E I N | S W E E T
A N E M I C | N E C T A R S
      A E O N | D U A D
  C A N I N E S | B E D L A M
C E L L O | U H S | L L A M A
O N L Y | T R A C K | E B A N
A T E | B U O Y A N T | I N G
T A R P O N S | M E R C A D O
E U G E N I E | P L A N T A E
D R Y N E S S | S L Y N E S S
```

Puzzle 1-21: Speaking of Sports Stars
Page 24

```
V E S T | M A G I C | E L B A
E A C H | I C O S A | S O O N
T S A R | T O T A L | S C O T
  T R O Y T R O Y A G A I N
      T E E N | B O Y
C A F T A N | G N A R | A S H
A W O L | G A U S S | A H A
K A R E E M O F T H E C R O P
E K G | L E A F S | H O O P
S E E | D A T E | S H A N T Y
      T E N | E W E R
  B J O R N T O B E W I L D
S O A K | E A R E D | S O A R
P O K E | S T A R E | M A Z E
A M E N | S A L T S | A M E X
```

Puzzle 1-22: Awards Time
Page 25

```
K I R O V | S R I | P A R E
G N O M E | P U R R | A L E X
B I T E R | A L O E | G A B E
  T O N Y F R A N C I O S A
      L O T | C O B
  E D G A R A L L A N P O E
A T R E S T | E A T | E L S E
T H A N T | R A D | C R A S S
A N T I | F E R | O L I V E S
  O S C A R A N D F E L I X
      M I D | S L A
  E M M Y L O U H A R R I S
P L E A | L U N A | C E L L I
L I A R | S T I R | U N L I T
Y A N K | S T P | T E S T S
```

Puzzle 1-23: Container Collection
Page 26

```
F E A T   U M A S S   C A P P
E L L A   N O N E S   O B O E
D I E S   C R A T E R L A K E
S A C K C L O T H   A L T E R
        H E N   P L I E R S
E L E N I   A D E L E
V A T I C A N C I T Y   L I T
I R O N   P E T E R   P E N A
L A N   J A R O M I R J A G R
    B A C O N   O S H E A
S A L I N E   E V A
A L O N E   B O X I N G D A Y
B A G A T E L L E S   A R N E
O M A R   D E A R E   Z I N A
T O N Y   A U N T S   A P E R
```

Puzzle 1-24: On the Stump
Page 27

```
S L O B   R O B S   P U M P
K A P O K   E U R O   O H I O
A T I M E   S T E N   L U T E
T H E B E L T W A Y   I R E S
        P U R I M   S C A R Y
H O N G   G A T   H E Y
O N O R   I S H E R W O O D
L E B A N O N   O S B O R N E
M A S S E U S E S   N E C K
    S R I   G A B   K L E E
B U R R O   M O N K S
I S A O   M A I N S T R E A M
L E N O   U R S A   O U T R E
K N I T   L I T H   W I N E S
S O N S   L E S S   N A S A
```

Puzzle 1-25: Sound Judgment
Page 28

```
S T A T   E L O I S E   J A M
L O G E   L E G I O N   E M U
O U R M A N F L I N T   E M I
G R A P H I T E   R A Z O R
        A N Y   R O A M
L E G A T O   D E N I A B L E
I D O L   S I M O N   R I N
T W E L V E H O U R S H I F T
R I T   A K E R S   O D E R
E N H A N C E S   C H E E R Y
    D I O N   C H E
E Q U A L   A L I E N A T E
S U N   L E O P O L D A U E R
A I D   A L P I N E   B R A G
I D O   S I E G E S   S A S S
```

Puzzle 1-26: Berg-men
Page 29

```
C P A S   T A M P   A B A S H
L U L U   U R A L   Z A P P A
A M O R   N I L E   O N E A L
D A N F O G E L B E R G
S E E R S   S E V E   L U V
    D A T S   E S T A T E
O S S   T E A C H   A V E R
S T E V E N S P I E L B E R G
A R A M   S U N N I   D O E
G O R I E R   T A K E
E P S   R I C A   B E G E T
    R U B E G O L D B E R G
A S C A P   C A R E   E R I E
C H A N T   I T A R   R I A L
T E N T S   L E N S   T E D S
```

Puzzle 1-27: Metallic Mischief
Page 30

```
B I P E D   A T B A T   S A P
A S O N E   P E A R S   N B A
S O L D E R I N G F E   P O P
K N E E P A N T S   L E A V E
        S I G H   W I N N E R
I N L A I D   R H O D A
S I O U X   G S U I T   L E S
I N N S   F R I T Z   F L A K
S A G   U R I C H   F I E R Y
    J A P A N   A R G Y L E
S H O R T Y   B E L A
L A H T I   A U T O P A R T S
U R N   G E T T H E P B O U T
S P A   H A U T E   E L A T E
H O G   T U B E R   S Y R U P
```

Puzzle 1-28: Nothing Special
Page 31

```
T O L E T   A D A M   A F A R
I T A L O   B R I O   R I C E
C O M M O N C O L D   A B E S
S E E S T O   P S I   B E S T
        S U B   F A I R
O R D I N A R Y I N C O M E
S M I T E   L O V E D   P E T
H A G S   P E S O S   S T E T
E N A   O R R I N   R A I S E
S I M P L E S E N T E N C E
    A R E S   E O N
P E R U   O O P   G E R A L D
A V O N   A V E R A G E J O E
P I L E   K A T E   E N A C T
A L E S   S L E D   D O R I S
```

Puzzle 1-29: The Forest Floor
Page 32

```
D R A G   D O T     E D A M
N O V A S   O R E   S L I M E
A T E U P   N I L   P I N O N
    L O U N G E L I Z A R D
M B A   K A Y   P E T   R E S
O U T L A W   E A V E S
U N P I N   A N T E   T R U E
S N A K E I N T H E G R A S S
E Y R E   N A R Y   L U T E S
    A R O S E   S A T I R E
S S S   O N T   A I M   O S S
P L A Y L E A P F R O G
R I V A L   S E T   U N D I D
I D O L S   I R E   R A I S E
G E R E     A E R   T O T E
```

Puzzle 1-30: Apt Adjectives
Page 33

```
S E E K   S G T   S T A T U S
S T R A I N E R   W I N O N A
T O N Y T O N Y R A N D A L L
    A I R   A N T   S O O
J O C K S T R A P S   S T A N
A M A S   O U T   S L E D S
Y A K   A L A S   B O A R
  R E D R E D S K E L T O N
  S E C T   I A G O   V O X
S M A S H   H E N   M E T E
T A N K   R E S T R A I N E D
E D D   S I R   A R S
F R A N K F R A N K C A P R A
F I L I A L   T U E S D A Y S
I D E A T E   E N D   D Y E S
```

Puzzle 1-31: Window Boxes
Page 34

```
D E N E B   S A G S   M B A S
I L E T A   C L O T   C L U E
N I G H T S H A D E   K I L T
    B O W S   W O U N D S
A R I Z O N A   H A T E D
L E R O Y S   C O R O N A R Y
I C O N S   W I L D E   S E E
S I N K   C A T E S   L A B S
O T C   R A G E S   T U B A S
N E U T E R E D   P A L A T E
  R U D E R   S A L U T E S
M E T R O S   C A R L
A R A B   S H U T T E R B U G
C L I O   E I R E   S N A F U
H E N S   S P E D   T A R O T
```

Puzzle 1-32: Who Are These Guys?
Page 35

```
S H O P   B R A V A   S C O T
C A R R   R I D E S   L A K E
I D E O   A V E R T   A S I A
  J O S E C A N Y O U S E E
  P E E L   N T H
A P P E N D   R A I L   E L S
T E A R   T E N S E   V I P
H A R O L D B E T H Y N A M E
O C T   E R A S E   O D I N
S H Y   A A R E   E M M E T T
  I S M   A N T I
R I C H A R D S T A N D S
F O C I   T E A S E   A R A B
A N O N   I N T E R   T A T A
T A N G   C O A T S   E Y E D
```

Puzzle 1-33: Spherical Bodies
Page 36

```
Z I L C H   L O A F   A T M E
A D O R E   A C H E   B O I L
P L A Y I N G H A R D B A L L
S Y D   G O E S   N E E D L E
    C H A R   C A S S
W E A L T H   M O N K   B A H
A T R E E   F O R D   A R L O
H U M A N C A N N O N B A L L
O D O R   H U E Y   O H G O D
O E R   T E N T   S H O A T S
    R H E A   P A I R
I S W E A R   T I N T   B E G
S W E D I S H M E A T B A L L
M A I D   U B E R   E R N I E
S P R Y   P O N S   R O D A N
```

Puzzle 1-34: City Slickers
Page 37

```
C A R O B   A D Z     S C A R
A T O L L   D E E D   T A M E
R O M E O   A N N E   R E I N
S P A   T O N Y O R L A N D O
    I N T R O   A P T
D A N C E R   C O I N A G E S
E D G A R   P O L L S   U L E
R O A R   P A N E S   L Y L E
E R R   H O N D O   H U M I D
K E Y L A R G O   M O R A S S
    E D T   E A R E D
K A T E J A C K S O N   I C E
I G O R   G U N S   E D S E L
D E L E   E P E E   T O O L S
D E E R   S E N   S A N T A
```

Puzzle 1-35: Consonant Trigrams
Page 38

```
S L I M M E R   G E L     S A T
N I R V A N A   A V O C A D O
A N A P E S T   L E S O T H O
G E T A   U S E   E L I O T
  S E W E R   L B J R A N C H
    A T E   B Y E S
O P E R A   S A F E   X M A S
M I D D L E C   A R M Y A N T
B A S S   Y O U R   O Z O N E
      J E T S   O N A
M T V H O S T S   L O F T S
C H E E K   R A D   F E E L
G A R R E T T   P A L A N C E
E N G A R D E   E G O I S T S
E K E   S S E   D E A R E S T
```

Puzzle 1-36: Say Cheese!
Page 39

```
P A P A   T O E D   E L S E
O M A R   S U R G E   J A I L
L I N K   C R E A M   E L M O
A D J   C A P O D E I C A P I
  A D A M S   A R T
C A N E R S   F I N I S H E D
A D D E D   K I L O S   E X O
F I R M   S A F E R   B A I T
E M U   O C T E T   L A D L E
S E M I P R O S   L A T H E S
    N I A   M A C H O
M U C K E T Y M U C K   N A B
O G L E   C E A S E   A C T I
B L U R   H A R E S   S H O T
S I B S   Y S E R   S O M E
```

Puzzle 1-37: Shortenin'
Page 40

```
L Y O N   N C A A   L I B E L
A E R O   E L M S   A D O R E
M A C O N B O O K   C L O N E
S H A K E U P S   T R E M O R
    S A L   M O O
C A L   P A R T O N S H O T S
A L I E   S O H O   S A R A N
R O L E S   B R R   E R A S E
O H A R E   R E E D   E T T A
B A C O N P O W D E R   E E K
    T O Y   A U G
E M C E E D   R A D I A T O R
F E L O N   B I D E N T I M E
F R A N C   O P E N   E L A N
S E N S E   B E N D   D E N T
```

Puzzle 1-38: Birds of a Feather
Page 41

```
R A F T   M O S H   I B S E N
E R L E   O D O R   N E A L E
S E A T T L E S E A H A W K S
T A X   O T T O   M A S S E S
  A M E S   H A L T
S A L M A N   H A Z E   R A P
I D I O T   S I Z E   V I N E
D E T R O I T R E D W I N G S
E L E E   N O E L   A S S E T
S A R   T S A R   S N E E R S
  Q U I T   B A G S
I N C U R S   T E L L   C E L
T O R O N T O B L U E J A Y S
C R A T E   W A L T   A G R A
H A M E R   E R I E   M E E T
```

Puzzle 1-39: By the By
Page 42

```
U T A H   A D O S   D A B
N O R A   B O N O   E M I R S
W H I R   S T E P B Y S T E P
R E A L M   H I H O   B A H
A E N E A S   L I D   P Y R E
P L A Y B Y P L A Y   C B E R
  S E N T   S P I N E
L A O   L E A   D O W   T D S
A N N U L   D R A G
B I E R   S I D E B Y S I D E
A M B I   T A E   S E T T E R
M A Y   A M A N   D R A C O
B L O W B Y B L O W   I L E D
A S N E R   I M R E   N I N E
  E T A   C E D E   G A T S
```

Puzzle 1-40: Starting the Day Right
Page 43

```
B A C A L L   E A R   S H A
A L I C I A   S T E A D I E R
J U I C E D   S O C R A T I C
A M I E   D I A Z   A T O N E
  S P I N Y   P R U N E D
T O A S T E D   T R A M
H O S E A   I N H O T   C D S
U Z I S   E G G E D   R A I L
S E A   S N O O T   N E R V E
  E L I S   W A F F L E D
H A M M E D   M I L L I
A L I B I   C A N A   L O B E
V I N E G A R S   M I L K E D
O V E R H E A T   O N E L E G
C E O   S T S   S E D A T E
```

Puzzle 1-41: The Jacksons
Page 44

```
ELO     OMENS     TOMS
KIWI  FAGOT     SCOT
GLENDAJANETKATE
SINCE   NORA    LEA
    OCTA    ENDALL
REGGIELATOYA
OXY   ABBE    AUDIT
WIRY  REALS   BALA
STOOP   ISLA    NIL
    KEITHMICHAEL
ASTERN    ELOI
ITA  IDLE    LPGAS
MAHALIAANNETITO
AVON  ATSEA   OFNO
TEEN  NEEDY    TOT
```

Puzzle 1-42: Precious Words
Page 45

```
MARK   HOST    MOSES
OPEN   ECHO    ADOBE
RECORDHOP   DOUBT
AMETHYSTHEART
LASSO     ARM   HMO
ENS   SKATE    PEEK
    TRAIT    TERRA
EMERALDWITHENVY
MOSEY    ANNUL
MUCK   FIRST    HIS
YEA  ALL    FAUNA
  RUBYLETTERDAY
BUGLE   FREEZEDRY
ASONE   ELSA   ALOE
GETAT   DESK   SEWS
```

Puzzle 1-43: Right at Home
Page 46

```
MEWS   SCORES    ALY
ARIA   ARDENT    COO
COTTAGEINDUSTRY
HOTEL   ANTS   TODO
    SPAM   SUPERS
RAE   STP    POT
ALLA   TUBB   OSCAR
HOLDSAFULLHOUSE
STEVE   FRAU   NETS
    IVS   CRO   DOT
  ASSETS   KEPT
TRIO   UTAH   ARIEL
HENRYCABOTLODGE
ENG  ICICLE   LEGS
MAE  PONDER   LASS
```

Puzzle 1-44: Diamond Skills
Page 47

```
PELF   ALPS    CRIME
AXEL   LEAH    HOOEY
RUNATEMPERATURE
EDITH    ALONE
DEN  IWO   FAG   RPM
    BRIAR   ROYALE
  TRISTRAM    IZOD
  HITTHEJACKPOT
AIDE    DALLIERS
PRESTO    HEELS
EDS  ESS   SOT   BRA
    ATLAW   ELLIS
CATCHONESBREATH
ADORE   DRAB   ADZE
PETER   YELL   KEYS
```

Puzzle 1-45: Dog Stars
Page 48

```
LAMER   STAG    SALE
OCALA   HOUR    CLAD
SERIF   AIDA    HIND
TSK   FERLINHUSKY
  SALAD    TASTY
RAPPER   OBEYS
IRIS   STRIDE   JAB
CITES   EAT   STORY
ADZ   WASTED   RECT
  SENSE   APACHE
  COMET   ALAMO
JUNEPOINTER   CPA
ORAL   NOAH   TAKES
KILL   INSO   EXERT
EELY   OATS   DERMA
```

Puzzle 1-46: New York State of Mind
Page 49

```
MANS   ACID    THEDA
ANEW   LADE    ROTOR
EDWARDROCHESTER
  SLUE    EATER
SALERNO    SST
TUES   TROYAIKMAN
IRT   EARS    SOUSE
TOTER   TOT   EASTS
CREME   ONER    TUT
HAROLDROME   PETE
  OUS   SCARRED
  SPACE    OWER
BUFFALOBILLCODY
OPCIT   RICO   ILIE
GESTE   AVER   SLEW
```

Puzzle 1-47: Cloning Around
Page 50

```
M E A D  ■  A S S A D  ■  S A P S
A X L E  ■  R E C U R  ■  A R L O
S P I K E S P I K E  ■  L I A R
T O T E M  ■  T O S S  ■  L E N T
■  ■  C A E N  ■  S T Y L E S
D I S S E N T  ■  L E O S  ■
E L A T E D  ■  E C S T A T I C
F I D O  ■  W A D  ■  L A D E
T E E N A G E R  ■  F E L L E R
■  E W E S  ■  C O P Y C A T
C H O S E N  ■  F R E E  ■
R A N T  ■  E T R E  ■  E A V E S
A L T O  ■  S H E M P S H E M P
S E A N  ■  E A T E R  ■  A R I A
H Y P E  ■  S I S S Y  ■  B A T S
```

Puzzle 1-48: Losers
Page 51

```
R O B E  ■  A B C S  ■  W A N D S
A C E Y  ■  S E A L  ■  A G O R A
I T B E  ■  T A L E  ■  S H O U T
D E E  ■  C H U M P C H A N G E
S T R E A M  ■  T A O S  ■
■  E X T A N T  ■  R U T T A N
F A B I O  ■  E A T A T  ■  U P I
R I O T  ■  M A M E T  ■  G R I P
A D Z  ■  H E L P S  ■  B A K E S
P E O R I A  ■  A S S U M E  ■
■  O N T O  ■  P L A Y E R
N O B O D Y S F O O L  ■  T B A
A D I M E  ■  A E R O  ■  C R O C
T I L E R  ■  K E E L  ■  D O L E
S E E D S  ■  A L M S  ■  S T A R
```

Puzzle 1-49: Anatomy Lesson
Page 52

```
L L A M A  ■  S P A S  ■  B A R S
A I K E N  ■  H I L T  ■  A L E C
S M I L E  ■  A L A I  ■  C O L E
H A N D M E D O W N  ■  K E E N
■  I L E T  ■  G E T S E T
P R E F A B  ■  T Y R O  ■
R A V I  ■  A S C H  ■  A B B O T
A G E N T  ■  H O E  ■  S A L V O
M E R G E  ■  O L E G  ■  C U E S
■  E N D O  ■  A S K E R S
S P A R S E  ■  P O O H  ■
C A R L  ■  F O O T L O C K E R
A G R I  ■  O B I T  ■  W R I S T
L E A N  ■  R O S E  ■  M O N T E
D R U G  ■  D E E R  ■  E P E E S
```

Puzzle 1-50: Possessed
Page 53

```
S T O U T  ■  G O E R S  ■  M A N
I W I S H  ■  U N T I E  ■  A D O
P O L A R  ■  S T O O L  ■  H U T
■  F U L T O N S F O L L Y
A L P  ■  S E A  ■  ■  B E T E
B E E T H O V E N S F I R S T
E T T A  ■  R O A R  ■  ■
■  S U T T E R S M I L L  ■
■  N E R O  ■  I A G O
W H I S T L E R S M O T H E R
I A N S  ■  T I C  ■  R E B
G I D E O N S B I B L E  ■
G R E  ■  M I L A N  ■  O A T E S
L I N  ■  I C I N G  ■  C R E S T
E N T  ■  T O T E S  ■  K N E L L
```

Puzzle 1-51: Metalworker's Wares
Page 54

```
S P E A R  ■  D U D E  ■  S A N D
A R E N A  ■  A R I A  ■  I G O R
G O L D F I N G E R  ■  L A T E
■  T O T E  ■  N A V I E S
O B S C E N E  ■  R E S E N D S
R O T O R S  ■  B A D E R  ■
T R I P S  ■  N A T  ■  A S T R O
H E L P  ■  O N E  ■  T R A P
O S T E O  ■  M A D  ■  L E I C A
■  R U R A L  ■  D E I C E R
C R A F T E D  ■  M E A N E S T
R A D I A L  ■  P E E K  ■
A D E E  ■  I R O N M A I D E N
S I L L  ■  C A R D  ■  G R O V E
H O E D  ■  S E T S  ■  E A S E D
```

Puzzle 1-52: Here, Kitty
Page 55

```
B E A D  ■  D E L A  ■  T A R O T
O S L O  ■  E V I L  ■  O V I N E
S T A N  ■  M E S S  ■  P A C E D
C H I C K E N P O T P I E S  ■
■  N A T  ■  I L L  ■
R A I S I N  ■  A I R E  ■  C H E
A L O O F  ■  E L S E  ■  S L A W
P O T B E L L I E D S T O V E
I N A S  ■  O I S E  ■  L I N E R
D E S  ■  S T A T  ■  S I R E N S
■  P U T  ■  T O N  ■
T H E P O T T I N G S H E D
A M A T I  ■  O R A N  ■  T E A R
S E R I N  ■  M I R E  ■  O R C A
U N I T E  ■  B O A T  ■  A S H Y
```

Puzzle 1-53: Happy Birthday, America!

Page 56

```
I N G O T   I C E D   G A Z A
B O R N E   N O V A   A M O S
A L I E N   V I A L   P O R K
R O M A N C A N D L E   U R E
      L I E S   E A T C R O W
A L L   S A I L   S H E
R E A D   S O A P   I D I O M
I N D E P E N D E N C E D A Y
A D D E R   S E R E   D E F T
      M O P   D I V E   A S H
C O N S O R T   S E L A
U M A   F I R E C R A C K E R
R A M P   N I N O   P R I C E
S H E A   C L O P   S I N C E
E A S T   E L S E   E D G E D
```

Puzzle 1-54: Wag the Jaw

Page 57

```
H A G A R   A S T A   A B E D
A G A N A   M A I L   V A L E
C H I N C H I L L A   A L A S
K A T   H A N K   B E L A M I
      L I N O   R A T O N
F A L A N A   C O M A N C H E
O D O R S   F A T A L   H E N
L A C K   F A N O N   D I M E
I S H   A R T I S   C A N E R
C H I N F E S T   C A M E T O
      N O T S O   C A R E
L A V I S H   L A I R   C E O
I M A S   C H I N N Y C H I N
S I R E   U E L E   M O I R E
T E S S   T R I M   E S T E S
```

Puzzle 1-55: Notable Addresses

Page 58

```
G L E N   R E S T S   M I N D
R A V E   A T L E E   E C O N
A V I S   S H A L E   T U B A
B A L T I C A V E N U E
      R A N   N O M A N
U N S E A L   F R E E R I D E
P O I N T   A L O E   R O E
S U N S E T B O U L E V A R D
E G G   A L O T   R I G E L
T A L E N T E D   R E C E D E
S T E I N   D O C
      S E S A M E S T R E E T
K E E N   A G E N T   U C L A
E Y R E   N U R S E   M R E D
Y E A R   S E V E R   P U M A
```

Puzzle 1-56: Zoo Acts

Page 59

```
A L A S   H A R E M   M O L T
L I N E   E V A D E   A V E R
D O T E   L A T I N   N A V E
A N I M A L S   T U R T L E S
      R O T C   O A S E S
M A F I A   I N F O
I R O N B U T T E R F L Y
N A R C   T I A R A   A A R E
    T H R E E D O G N I G H T
      A S S E   A D I O S
A N G S T   L A N D
M O N K E E S   B E A T L E S
A L A E   R E L E E   R A I L
T A T E   I L I A D   E Z R A
I N S T   C A L M S   K E E P
```

Puzzle 1-57: Between Hook and Sinker

Page 60

```
B A R K   P U Z O   C A R T E
O L E O   U N I V   A L O R S
L A I R   F I N E   R A N I S
L I N E O F S C R I M M A G E
      A N I   R E O
T A P   E N T R A I N   A D S
R I A T A   E O N S   E D I T
A L L A L O N G T H E L I N E
D E E D   F O U R   S K E E T
E D S   A G R E E A S   U S S
      M B A   L E D
M A K E A B E E L I N E F O R
A G E N T   C L U E   P A V E
T E N S E   T A R N   O M E N
E S T A S   O N E S   T E N T
```

Puzzle 1-58: Pocket Change

Page 61

```
C R E S T   A R T E   A L A N
H A R P O   R E A M   S I D E
A V I A N   L A M B   K N O W
N I C K E L O D E O N   O R E
      E R A   S I T T E R
F A B   S P A T   S T A Y
A C I D   U L E E   R U P E E
T H R E E P E N N Y O P E R A
S E D A N   C O D E   E R G S
    I N D O   R O M A   S O T
C E N S O R   E D A
H A H   F I V E A N D D I M E
I T A L   O A T H   L A N E S
N I N A   L I T E   E G R E T
A N D S   E L A M   D E E R E
```

Puzzle 1-59: The Music Men
Page 62

A	L	E	C		T	H	O	L	E		S	H	E	M
V	I	D	A		H	O	M	E	R		T	O	G	A
E	M	U	S		A	L	A	M	O		R	A	G	E
R	I	C	H	A	R	D	R	O	D	G	E	R	S	
S	T	E	E	R			N	E	O	N				
		W	R	I	S	T		D	O	G	D	A	Y	
T	H	E		A	N	N	E	E		T	E	L	E	
H	O	A	G	Y	C	A	R	M	I	C	H	A	E	L
I	O	T	A		G	R	I	L	L		N	E	P	
S	P	A	R	T	A		A	L	L	O	W			
		G	E	N	T			P	A	S	T	A		
	G	E	O	R	G	E	G	E	R	S	H	W	I	N
P	I	T	Y		E	N	A	T	E		I	O	L	E
I	D	O	L		L	O	I	R	E		N	O	E	L
G	E	N	E		A	N	T	E	D		E	N	D	E

Puzzle 1-60: Lights Out!
Page 63

D	O	D	O		D	O	S	E	D		F	I	S	H
R	E	I	D		E	N	L	A	I		I	S	E	E
A	N	N	E		M	E	I	R	S		X	R	A	Y
M	O	O	N	S	E	R	E	N	A	D	E			
			S	I	R		R	A	V	E		I	T	A
A	R	S	E	N	I	C		O	N	U	S	E	S	
L	A	P			T	H	E	T	W	I	Z	O	N	E
I	C	I	E	R		E	T	H		M	I	L	A	N
G	O	R	D	O	N	F	O	O	T		D	N	S	
H	O	O	D	O	O		R	E	P	L	E	T	E	
T	N	T		S	T	E	P		M	A	E			
			S	T	E	L	L	A	B	Y	S	T	A	R
R	A	M	P		P	E	A	R	L		T	A	R	A
I	R	A	Q		A	N	I	M	O		E	M	I	T
D	I	O	R		D	I	N	E	R		R	O	D	E

Puzzle 1-61: The Hourglass
Page 64

A	T	A	R	I		S	T	A	B		S	S	T	S
N	E	G	E	V		A	I	D	A		H	A	I	L
S	A	N	D	A	L	W	O	O	D		I	N	R	E
A	L	I		N	A	T	S		L	A	N	D	E	D
		O	H	I	O		S	A	L	E	P			
L	I	S	T	O	N		S	A	N	D	R	I	N	E
E	N	A	T	E		M	O	N	D	O		P	O	A
M	A	N	O		M	E	N	D	S		G	E	L	S
A	I	D		R	I	L	E	Y		C	O	R	T	E
T	R	I	D	E	N	T	S		C	E	A	S	E	D
			N	E	V	I	S		C	A	L	L		
S	E	I	N	E	S		E	A	V	E		S	I	P
P	A	S	S		T	O	M	M	Y	S	A	N	D	S
A	R	T	E		E	R	I	E		T	R	E	E	S
S	P	A	R		R	O	L	L		A	T	E	S	T

Puzzle 1-62: Time Keepers
Page 65

L	I	L	A	C		S	W	A	P		C	L	O	T
A	G	I	R	L		T	A	D	A		H	U	M	E
R	O	M	E	O		A	T	O	P		I	L	I	A
D	R	E	N	C	H		C	R	E	W	C	U	T	S
			A	K	A		H	E	R	R				
S	P	A		W	I	N	O			I	N	C	A	S
O	R	O		A	G	E	N	T		S	P	O	R	E
F	I	R	S	T		A	T	A		T	R	A	M	P
A	N	T	I	C		T	H	R	O	W		T	O	T
S	T	A	S	H		E	T	N	A		I	R	A	
			E	V	E	R		E	T	A				
F	E	V	E	R	I	S	H		S	C	R	O	L	L
A	M	I	D		A	K	I	N		H	O	S	E	A
T	I	N	E		N	E	N	E		E	S	S	E	S
E	T	O	N		D	R	E	W		S	E	A	R	S

Puzzle 1-63: Smorgasbord
Page 66

J	O	B	S		A	B	B	A	S		O	R	E	S
A	B	U	T		T	A	I	N	T		P	O	R	T
M	I	N	E	S	T	R	O	N	E		E	U	R	O
S	E	T	P	O	I	N	T		W	O	N	T	O	N
			P	L	E	A	D		I	S	E	R	E	
L	A	B	C	O	A	T		I	D	L	E			
A	R	O	A	R		M	O	U	S	S	A	K	A	
N	E	A	R		A	S	O	N	E		A	M	I	N
G	A	Z	P	A	C	H	O			S	M	E	L	T
			O	R	E	O		C	L	I	E	N	T	S
S	A	M	O	A		W	A	L	E	S				
P	A	E	L	L	A		M	E	D	A	L	I	S	T
A	R	T	E		Z	A	B	A	G	L	I	O	N	E
D	O	O	R		O	G	I	V	E		O	N	U	S
E	N	O	S		V	O	T	E	R		N	A	G	S

Puzzle 1-64: With Apologies to Caesar
Page 67

	B	A	L	E		F	L	O	P		S	C	A	M
M	E	L	O	N		L	I	M	E		P	O	L	A
B	E	I	N	G		A	M	I	R		A	L	A	N
A	F	T	E	R	I	G	O	T	T	O	R	O	M	E
			L	A	D			A	S	T	R	O	S	
V	E	N	I	V	I	D	I	V	I	S	A			
A	R	M	E	E		A	R	E	N	A		A	T	L
A	G	E	R		S	T	E	N	S		B	R	E	A
L	O	X		S	T	U	N	T		W	E	I	R	D
	I	C	A	M	E	I	S	A	W	A	N	D		
C	A	N	N	E	S			E	L	A				
I	B	O	U	G	H	T	M	E	A	P	I	Z	Z	A
T	A	L	I		I	R	O	N		O	L	I	O	S
E	T	A	T		N	E	R	D		L	E	O	N	E
D	E	N	S		G	E	E	S		E	D	N	A	

Puzzle 1-65: So Long!
Page 68

```
S N U G ■ A C E R ■ ■ I S L A M
N O N O ■ R E P O ■ ■ S H A L E
A L T O ■ G R I T ■ ■ S A M O S
G O O D B Y E C O L U M B U S ■
■ ■ ■ S E L A ■ ■ E E E ■ ■ ■ ■
S A D ■ T E L S T A R ■ B E T ■
C L E A T ■ ■ A E S ■ B E L A ■
A F A R E W E L L T O A R M S ■
M I L E ■ E S E ■ ■ K N E E S ■
P E T ■ C A S S A V A ■ T R E ■
■ ■ L A V ■ ■ P O P E ■ ■ ■ ■ ■
A R R I V E D E R C I R O M A ■
M A I N E ■ A S I A ■ A N O N ■
O F F E R ■ M A L L ■ S L O T ■
S T E R N ■ P U S S ■ E Y R E ■
```

Puzzle 2-1: The Sundance Kid Grows Up
Page 70

```
E D N A ■ S C A T ■ B R A S ■ E T T A
R E I N S T A T E ■ R E C E S S I O N
A L L T H E P R E S I D E N T S M E N
L E S S E R ■ I N T O ■ S O O ■ E S E
■ ■ ■ I N A ■ S A C K ■ R U M ■ ■ ■
S N E A K E R S ■ T H E N A T U R A L
A R A N ■ R E A M ■ E L O ■ S T A R E
G A U G E ■ S U E S ■ P T A ■ E D I E
■ ■ L A S ■ C L O D ■ E L M ■ I S R
R O B E R T R E D F O R D M O V I E S
E P I ■ L E I ■ S A G O ■ S P A ■ ■
A R T A ■ T V S ■ S I G H ■ S L A S H
C A T C H ■ E L S ■ T E A R ■ E L I A
T H E H O T R O C K ■ T H E S T I N G
■ ■ ■ E V E ■ B R I G ■ A L P ■ ■ ■
I S M ■ E N D ■ A V O N ■ A R E O L E
T H E G R E A T W A L D O P E P P E R
C E L E S T I A L ■ F A R S E E I N G
H A T E ■ S S T S ■ S K E E ■ E A T S
```

Puzzle 2-2: Put Up Your Dukes
Page 72

```
M A T T ■ S N A G ■ C A A N ■ S P U D
E V E R ■ H E R R ■ O N T O ■ T I N A
T E L E V I S I O N S T A R P A T T Y
■ V A N S ■ C O M E ■ O T T O S
E L L I S ■ D E S I ■ M A L I
D O O N E S B U R Y C H A R A C T E R
A L S O ■ A R E S ■ A M U R ■ A L A
M A E ■ S U E S ■ S C R A M ■ A S T I
■ T U N A ■ S O U P ■ A L T O S
N I C K N A M E O F J O H N W A Y N E
E T H O S ■ I N T O ■ Y E N S
M A A S ■ P U D G Y ■ B E E S ■ R A Y
A L I ■ C A R E ■ B O N D ■ S O L E
N O R T H C A R O L I N A S C H O O L
■ R E E L ■ R A G E ■ L E T U P
A T S E A ■ R A N T ■ A R A B
G R E A T B R I T A I N R O Y A L T Y
R O A D ■ A U T O ■ M A L T ■ N O N E
A N T S ■ Y E A R ■ E G O S ■ G U T S
```

Puzzle 2-3: Ancient History
Page 74

```
M A L T ■ B L U R ■ N A P A ■ A H A B
A S E A ■ E A S E ■ A M I D ■ G A L A
S H A M ■ E T N A ■ T O T O ■ O D O R
C O D E O F H A M M U R A B I ■ R E B
O R E ■ I C E ■ E A R ■ E T U I
T E R E S A ■ T R E A T S ■ E R A S E
■ P E K O E ■ L O T S ■ I N C A
D E S I ■ E R N I E ■ M E N U ■ S I T
A T O L L ■ T E R S E ■ M A C A W
G A L O O T ■ T O T A L ■ P L E A T S
■ O G L E D ■ N E V E R ■ A G L E T
R E M ■ A R E A ■ S E V E R ■ E L L A
A V O N ■ M A R S ■ E D E M A
P E N N Y ■ R E T I R E ■ S E N S O R
■ S E E D ■ A D A ■ G E M ■ A P E
G A S ■ S W O R D O F D A M O C L E S
O L E O ■ A B E L ■ T O M B ■ H I R E
E G A D ■ R O B E ■ E D E L ■ I V A N
S A L E ■ F E A R ■ R O S E ■ P A S T
```

Puzzle 2-4: Legendary Ladies
Page 76

```
P L U S   P A P A   E T T A   A M O S
R U S T   O R A L   N E A T   F A R E
A L E E   N A I L   S E L L   F R E E
M U R P H Y B R O W N   C A R R Y O N
      S E T     W E A R   S L O W
O T T   E A S T   T R I M   S N O W S
D R E   L I T E R   E G A D   T R E E
O U S T   L A N E S   A R E A   T R E
R E H A B   N O B I S   A R C H E R
    M I L D R E D P I E R C E
D I N E R O   L E A R N   O N S E T
E T A   D I L L   S T A T S   T E A R
L E N S   S O A P   S T E A L   E R A
E M C E E   B R A T   E R L E   P L Y
    Y A Y A   K N E W   T V A
E N D L E S S   D A I S Y M I L L E R
T A R A   H A L O   D E S I   L O D E
O P E N   E V E R   O M E N   O V E N
N E W T   S E T A   W I R E   T E N T
```

Puzzle 2-5: Hidden Cities
Page 78

```
W O R S T   S P A D   H E R R   L E T T
A L I C E   T A M E   A L E E   E N U R E
L O S A N G E L E S   R I N D   A C T I N
T R E T   A L O N E   B A T O N R O U G E
    T A L E   R H O S   U N D
C A M E L S   M A T E R   E D A   E G G S
A F I R E   B A R E R   M E N   D R E W
S O N S   S A N F R A N C I S C O   A N E
T O N   D E R N S   O I L I E R   N I P
S T E A M E R S   S E T T E   C A D E T
  A R I S E   A W A R E   O P H I R
K A P U T   A L A T E   C L A I M A N T
A G O   R A I S I N   F I E N D   P U R
B A L   I N D I A N A P O L I S   R I D E
O M I T   C O D   B R A I N   W E D G E
B A S E   I L E   M O O L A   L A S S E S
    T H E   D E U M   F I F I
W A S H I N G T O N   I D E E S   D I A L
A L T E R   R O O D   S A C R A M E N T O
S A Y R E   A N N E   E Z R A   I N T E R
  N E S S   D E E D   S E U L   S T O N E
```

Puzzle 2-6: Corporal Punishment
Page 80

```
F A R R   G E T A T   S A I L S   S A S H
E R I E   I N A N E   U N T I E   I S T O
S L A P S T I C K S   P O U N D C A K E S
T O L E T   D E L L A   S P E A R M I N T
      A R C   T E A S E   A T A   N O S
    A T T I R E   T R E E L E S S
S E A   P U N C H C A R D S   S E P A L
H O P S   S T E E L   S A T U P   M O L E
E L D E S T   O R E S   E T A   A K I N
D I A N E   M A I   B E E L I N E
S A N T A   S W A T T E A M S   S T A G E
    C E R T A I N   I L K   M I R E S
A D I N   A L P   N O E L   R E C O N S
N U N C   S T E P S   P R A D O   S U R A
E D G E S   R A P S E S S I O N   N E Y
    S T A R S H I P   S N O O D S
B E A   A L E   T I T A N   E M U
A L B E R T A N S   N O B I S   A T E S T
S M A C K E R O O S   S O C K D R A W E R
S E T H   R U S S O   I N A I R   T E R I
O R E O   S P Y O N   R E D D Y   E R A S
```

Puzzle 2-7: Top of the Deck
Page 82

```
L E V E R   E L I S H A   P A T   S A O
A M I N E   R E P E A T   E V E   A R N E
K I N G S G O F O R T H   K I N G L E A R
E R E   W I D T H   E P O S   R A N I N
    R E N E   G E N R E   R A D A R S
Y O K E L S   C H O O S E   T A P S
A R I E L   H A B A   D E A N E   K A F
L I N D   T H E K I N G A N D I   T I N A
T O G   F R I S E   O T I S   S O N I C
A N O   O A R S   H E R O D   G A R G L E
    F A R C E   G O N E R   P A N I C
R E J E C T   R A N T S   M R E D   R O B
A C A R E   P O N D   G A I L Y   E I R
S U Z Y   K I N G O F K I N G S   P O L A
P A Z   S E T A L   L E A N   S A L E S
    S T A Y   A R I A N S   L I N E R S
D E M E A N   S N I P S   S A G E
U R I E L   G A D S   A L A I N   Y I P
K I N G K O N G   K I N G O F C O M E D Y
E N T E   B A A   E L A I N E   R A T E L
    S Y R   I T S   D E N N I S   A R I S E
```

Puzzle 2-8: Museum Tour
Page 84

C	O	L	A		C	O	S	T	A			C	A	R		A	L	E	U	T
O	B	E	Y		A	R	N	E	L		F	A	R	O		F	A	U	N	A
L	E	O	N	A	R	D	O	D	A	V	I	N	C	I		L	U	G	E	S
I	A	N		S	T	E	W		M	E	T	O	O		C	A	R	E	S	S
C	H	E	A	T	E	R		T	E	X	A	N		N	O	M	E	N		
		L	I	L		L	O	D	E	S		L	O	R	E	L	E	I	S	
T	R	A	I	N		S	E	P	A	R	A	T	I	O	N			D	D	E
R	O	L	E		S	I	N	O			O	A	R	S		B	E	L	A	
E	V	E		C	R	A	F	T	S	M	A	N			S	A	L	E	M	
T	E	X	T	U	R	E	S		A	T	A	L	E		R	O	T	A	R	Y
		A	S	P	E	N		A	T	A	L	L		M	A	R	O	C		
A	G	N	A	T	E		T	R	A	C	T		R	E	F	E	R	R	E	D
P	E	D	R	O		A	E	R	I	A	L	I	S	T		O	R	E		
A	N	E	S		M	I	R	E			A	L	A	S		R	I	G	A	
I	R	R		A	V	A	L	A	N	C	H	E	S		L	U	X	O	R	
L	E	C	A	R	R	E	S		D	I	A	R	Y		D	Y	S			
		A	R	E	A	S		P	O	T	T	S		I	A	S	K	Y	O	U
A	T	L	A	S	T		D	E	L	T	A		A	M	M	O		A	L	T
C	A	D	R	E		F	R	A	F	I	L	I	P	P	O	L	I	P	P	I
T	R	E	A	T		C	A	R	O		P	R	E	E	N		O	P	E	L
S	O	R	T	S		C	B	S			A	E	R	I	E		N	Y	S	E

Puzzle 2-9: Relocating Nearby
Page 86

A	L	O	N	G		O	B	O	E		S	E	A	T	O		P	U	T	S
S	E	I	N	E		F	O	R	M		I	N	D	I	A		E	L	A	N
H	E	L	E	N	O	F	W	O	O	D	S	T	O	C	K		O	T	R	O
			E	M	I	L		O	A	R	S		A	R	R	O	W			
	C	H	O	S	E	N		M	A	D	L	Y		L	A	R	I	A	T	S
L	E	A	V	I	N	G	R	E	N	O		P	I	N	T	A				
I	D	L	E	S		I	N	S		E	R	A	S		H	A	V	E		
P	E	E	R		S	E	N	S	E	D		V	I	N	O		O	V	E	N
	T	O	P	E	K	A	L	I	N	E	M	A	N			P	E	L	T	
S	S	R		W	A	R	S		S	O	R	E		B	E	R	L	E		
L	I	E		E	N	O		M	A	R	T	Y		A	R	E		S	U	R
O	M	I	T	S		F	A	R	O		A	R	O	N		E	M	S		
G	I	N	A		U	T	I	C	A	B	I	L	L	C	O	D	Y			
A	L	E	C		T	U	S	H		E	G	O	I	S	M		O	S	S	O
N	E	R	O		U	N	T	O		O	L	D			P	U	T	I	N	
		M	A	R	I	S		O	R	L	A	N	D	O	V	I	C	E		
A	T	T	A	I	N	S		T	R	U	S	S		O	A	T	E	R	S	
D	E	I	S	T		P	E	A	S		A	N	I	L						
Z	E	A	L		S	P	I	R	I	T	O	F	C	O	L	U	M	B	I	A
E	T	R	E		I	T	E	M	S		T	O	T	E		C	O	A	T	I
S	H	A	W		P	A	R	S	E		T	E	S	S		K	O	R	A	N

Puzzle 2-10: Wanderlust
Page 88

```
M O N A C O ▮ P E N P A L ▮ O G L E D
E V A D E R ▮ C L E E S E ▮ C R E D O
R E V O L T ▮ T A K E T O T H E A I R
E N E ▮ L E I ▮ S T L O ▮ H E A R T Y
▮ ▮ M A G N E T O S ▮ P A R S ▮ ▮
G O F O R A S P I N ▮ H O N ▮ E T A L
A R U M ▮ T I C ▮ R A K E D ▮ A M A
F A R ▮ A L E C ▮ M A Z E ▮ E M B E R
F L Y T R A P ▮ C O V E R G R O U N D
▮ O C T ▮ B E V E L ▮ N I P ▮ ▮
H I T T H E T R A I L ▮ M A D E I R A
E R O S E ▮ R O S E ▮ P A T E ▮ R A N
N O G ▮ D R A K E ▮ H A L ▮ H I C K
S N A P ▮ A C E ▮ S A I L T H E S E A
▮ ▮ L E V Y ▮ B O R D E A U X ▮ ▮
E S C A P E ▮ C R U D ▮ T I M ▮ E W E
S T A Y O N C O U R S E ▮ L A D L E R
T A P E D ▮ A M I C E S ▮ O N E I L L
A B O D E ▮ T E N E T S ▮ R E B A T E
```

Puzzle 2-11: Puzzle People
Page 90

```
R E E L S ▮ S H A H ▮ I R A S ▮ T M A N
E R R O L ▮ K A L E ▮ B E L T ▮ S H I N E
C R O C O D I L E D U N D E E ▮ T A N T E
T O D A T E ▮ E C O N ▮ U N P L A N N E D
O R E L ▮ T O Y ▮ N I E C E ▮ I R T ▮
▮ H E R ▮ I S E E ▮ L O T ▮ E M E
B A T M A S T E R S O N ▮ K E N ▮ F L A N
E R R A N T ▮ D A M N ▮ F I T ▮ F E I N T
S P E N D ▮ F E N ▮ O U T ▮ S I Z Z L E
S A K I ▮ T A N ▮ I S T S ▮ O I L ▮ A Y R
▮ C H R I S T O P H E R W R E N ▮
A S P ▮ A I L ▮ Y O Y O ▮ U L E ▮ I M A M
D I S A R M ▮ P R O ▮ S I S ▮ A N I T A
E N A C T ▮ P I E ▮ R A I N ▮ A N E M I C
P A L E ▮ T O N ▮ N E W T G I N G R I C H
T I M ▮ S I R ▮ M E S A ▮ O D E ▮
▮ E E L ▮ E A T E R ▮ T S E ▮ S A L T
R E L E N T I N G ▮ D D A Y ▮ A S H I E R
E V E R S ▮ C A P T A I N K A N G A R O O
B A S I E ▮ E R I E ▮ N Y E T ▮ T R E N T
S N E E ▮ S E E N ▮ G A S P ▮ S I D E S
```

Puzzle 2-12: Musical Letter Drop
Page 92

```
. S O P O R . C A R A F E . . . T S E T S E
S P R U C E . O B E R O N . E I T H E R
P E E R A N D T H E W O L F . S C H E M A
E L A S . O U T O F . T A U N T . A B E T
E L D E R . B A R E . L I M O . E N A S
. . S O B I G . R A O . . P A D . R T E
U M A . B E N E S . T O U T Q U I N T E T
B U F F E T . P U L S A R . S T E E R S
O N T O . R A G A S . E R O . I E R S
A G E E . A B O N E R . C A R O L E .
T O R . L Y I N G D U T C H M A N . D E S
. N O I S E D . B A L E E N . A B B Y
. C O R N . O R B . L I E N S . I R O N
C L O N E D . L E A D E N . O U T I N G
D A N E M A C A B R E . T R A M P . E Y E
E M O . A D O . O B I . A L S O P .
. O F A N . I T E M . C E D E . N E R O L
A R A S . E N A T E . A L I C E . R A C E
S I F T E R . N U T C R A C K E R S I T E
S N A R E D . D E P U T E . L O O S E R
I G N O R E . E R A S E S . S E N A T .
```

Puzzle 2-13: Nothing Heavy
Page 94

```
M A T A . A P R O N . P A R . D A L I S
I T I S . C L O S E . R E I N . E L I S E
L I G H T H O U S E B E A M S . N I G E R
O L E . R I D E . D E S K S . N I C H E S
S T R A I N S . C H R I S . F O R E T
. G A G . S O A R S . P I R O S H K I
D E L E D . D A L M A T I A N S . E A T
A R I D . A E R O . A R N E . C A R S
B I G . G R A N D D A M S . L O D E N
S C H E D E E N . U R I B E . M O R E N O
. T R U N K . G R A M S . F A R E D .
C O H O S T . S H O N E . C O L D S N A P
A N O S E . C O C K E D H A T . E M O
R A R E . I L E S . R E M S . T S A R
E I S . C E N T R A L B A Y . M A S S E
T R E A T I S E . A B E E T . D A D .
. H I R E S . R U B I N . S O F A B E D
S N A R E R . G O G O L . L O C I . A V A
A A R O N . L I G H T A S A F E A T H E R
S T R U T . A N E T . N O M A N . A I R E
H O Y T S . B A R . I N E R T . B A T S
```

Puzzle 2-14: Big Brags
Page 96

```
L O G I C ■ T A F T ■ P R O B E ■ E L M S
A D O R E ■ E V E R ■ R E L A X ■ L A I T
N O B E L P R I Z E ■ I S E R E ■ A N N E
E R E ■ L E N D ■ S A M E ■ C A N A D A
■ T H I N E ■ P L A T I N U M D I S K
L O W E S T ■ R A I L ■ C I T E S ■
A L E R T ■ G R I S T ■ H E L E N ■ M A D
T I E ■ C L U E S ■ F U M E D ■ T A P E
H O N O R R O L L ■ L A M A ■ D U M A S
■ G E E S E ■ P A T O N T H E B A C K
■ O M A H A S ■ S H I E R ■ R E V I S E
A C A D E M Y A W A R D ■ S O L O N ■
S A L E M ■ M E S S ■ L O V I N G C U P
P L A N ■ A L B E E ■ T E L E X ■ O N E
S A Y ■ C L O U T ■ P E S O S ■ T O N T O
■ C O L A S ■ S O R T ■ P A R S O N
M E D A L O F H O N O R ■ C A R E T ■
O M E L E T ■ B A L I ■ C H I P ■ A L I
W I L D ■ T A M E R ■ B L U E R I B B O N
E L L E ■ E R A S E ■ L A T E ■ T A L O N
R E A R ■ D A R E D ■ E W E R ■ S T E P S
```

Puzzle 2-15: Fruity Flavors
Page 98

```
S I G N S ■ G L O B ■ B I T E ■ G U I S E
T R A I T ■ R U H R ■ O D E A ■ A N G E L
E M I L Y ■ E L I A ■ B E E S ■ E L L E S
W A T E R M E L O N ■ C A N T A L O U P E
■ E A T S ■ D I A L S ■ B I C ■
B O N I N G ■ A N A T ■ D U C K P I N
O H A R E ■ S A L E M ■ C U R S ■ S O R E
L A V A ■ S T R A W B E R R I E S ■ M A S
O R E ■ D E I C E ■ L E A P ■ E V E N T
S A L T I N E S ■ N A V A L ■ A E G I S
■ O U S T S ■ B A T I K ■ M I T E R ■
S T R E P ■ D E B T S ■ C O V E R A G E
C E A S E ■ A E R O ■ B A S E D ■ N O B
A N N ■ L O G A N B E R R I E S ■ M A R E
L O G S ■ R E N E ■ M E A N Y ■ P A T E R
P R E L U D E ■ P I C S ■ F R E E S T
■ O N E ■ E L A T E ■ A L D O ■
T A N G E R I N E S ■ P I N E A P P L E S
O M E G A ■ S T A S ■ T O G O ■ P O I N T
G I V E S ■ E R S E ■ O W E N ■ E R N I E
S E E D Y ■ R E E D ■ R A R E ■ D E E D S
```

Puzzle 2-16: Animal Atlas
Page 100

```
B A B E . E A S E D . E S T O P . G A L A
A N O X . O L L I E . C E A S E . O N E R
G N U O R L E A N S . H A M S T E R D A M
. S T R A I N . P O O L E . U M I A K S
. C I T E . B O R I S . N I L .
R A K I S H . E R I A N . T W I R L E R S
A N O S E . B U L L G A R I A . A W O L
N E A T . N O O N . D E N S E . E V A
C Y L . F A I N T S . H E A D . V A L E T
H E A T E D L Y . A B O L T . S I M A R S
. L O D E S . E L O P E . T E N O N .
S T U P O R . E R A S E . B R I C K B A T
A R M O R . A V I D . S E R E N E . A G E
L A P . A S P I C . L A T E . P T A H
E C U S . W I C H E E T A H . W R O T E
M E R C H A N T . C R O N E . S H E R E E
. R U Y . P S E U D . A L E S .
S U P E R B . A R T I S . M O R J N I
A P E A L A C H I A . L A M B P E D U S A
S T E M . C H I N S . E D I L E . I T E M
H O P S . K I T T Y . D O T E D . A S E A
```

Puzzle 2-17: Home Stretch
Page 102

```
B A R R . A M B O . T H A D . A B E L E
A L O E . D E E P . S A O N E . R E L I T
L A S T W O R D S . P H O T O F I N I S H
D I S R O B E S . B O O K S . R A T T L E
. I R E S . M A K E S . M I D . E E L
A S H E S . E R A S E . S I G N S .
W A I V E D . I C I N G O N T H E C A K E
A U R A . A T O L L . E P A C T . U R A L
S T A L E M A T E . E R I C H . S L I M Y
H E M . R I P S . T R U N K . M A P L E
. C R E E . P E N N E . B A R T .
. M O R O N . B R A I D . L A R A . E F T
R A R E R . T R O P E . D E A T H B L O W
E G A D . C H I N O . L E A S H . L I R E
F I N I S H I N G T O U C H . A V I A T E
. T E E N Y . P R A Y S . I N S E T
P A S . C E E . C R E E L . H A R D .
A B A S E S . B R A N D . H A B A N E R O
C O U P D E G R A C E . F I N A L E X A M
E D D I E . O A T E R . E L K S . S I Z E
R E I N S . D Y E D . N O S E . S T E N
```

Puzzle 2-18: Heave, Ho!
Page 104

```
T E M P S   I L K A   L O T S A   R A S P
I L I A C   S A U R   A C R E S   O H N O
P I T C H F O R K S   C H U C K S T E A K
P O T T E R   C L E V E R   T S Q U A R E
I T S   M E T H A N E   E C O   U N D E R
      B E E R   I R A   I R E A D
C A F E   P E G B O A R D S   A B A T E S
H I L T   O V E R   S I T A R   S H O E
E D I T   R I T U A L   M E L E E   R N A
R E P O S T   I R I S   R E D C R O S S
    S R O   W I N G S P A N S   T A W
I R I S H M A N   O P E C   H O T R O D
G A D   O U T D O   S E E T H E   T U B A
O R E S   S T E V E   T H A I   A G I N
R E S E T S   P A S S B O O K S   I S E E
    T R Y S T   P O L   E T A L
T A S T E   C H A   D E P O S I T   A A H
U N C L E A R   L E S S E N   N E S T L E
F I R E D R I L L S   S L I N G S H O T S
T S A R   E P E E S   E E O C   T U N E S
S E M S   S T E N O   R E N O   S T E R E
```

Puzzle 2-19: Tee Off
Page 106

```
L E A   C U R A T E   C H A S E   H A T E
O W L   A N I M A L   L A S E R   A G I N
R E E   C H A I N O F E V E N S   R E N T
D R S C H O L L S   U R E A   E R N I E
    O R E L S E   G R I T   D I V I D E R
S A F E T Y   C R O C O D I L E E A R S
A C H E S   B R I E R   O V E R T
A M O K   G R A T E   F E W E S T   P A D
R E F   S E A M E N G I N E S   S U L L A
    F O U N T S   E X E R T S   S A I L
R O M A N O   B O N E S   T W E N T Y
O L A F   A S S I S I   E R R A R E
M E N S A   E N G L I S H S E E R   O P T
E O N   T U X E D O   A A N D W   A F R O
    O E S T E   E A R E D   H I T O N
C R U S A D E R R A B B I   C A T H A Y
H I N T S A T   A L B S   T R A N C E
A D D L E   A I D E   S H A N G H A I S
I D E E   M I S S E D T H E B O A   P A T
S E A R   O C H E R   E A S I E R   E G O
E N D S   D E E D S   A M E N D S   S O P
```

Puzzle 2-20: First Names
Page 108

B	A	L	M		C	I	T	E	S		L	O	F	T	S		S	A	N	D
A	N	O	A		E	N	R	O	L		A	N	I	O	N		A	M	O	I
E	N	I	D		D	U	A	N	E		Z	O	R	B	A		M	O	P	E
R	O	S	E	M	A	R	Y		E	L	I		M	A	R	G	A	R	E	T
		L	O	R	N		S	P	I	E	L		T	E	E	N				
A	D	M	I	T	S		C	L	E	A	R	E	D		S	E	T	T	E	R
C	R	A	N	E		W	H	I	R	R		N	O	T		S	H	A	L	E
T	O	N	E		S	H	I	P			S	O	N	A	R		A	R	T	S
U	N	E		S	T	O	M	P		R	E	S	O	L	E	S		S	O	O
P	E	S	T	E	R		P	E	C	A	N		R	O	S	A	L	I	N	D
			A	N	A	S		R	A	D	O	N		N	O	L	O			
C	L	A	U	D	I	N	E		P	A	R	I	S		R	E	T	I	R	E
H	A	D		S	N	I	G	G	E	R		P	O	T	T	S		N	O	D
A	D	A	M		S	P	A	R	S			P	R	E	S		J	U	T	E
R	E	N	A	L		E	D	O		C	H	E	A	T		P	E	R	O	N
S	N	O	R	E	D		S	P	A	C	E	R	S		D	I	N	E	R	S
			J	A	R	S		E	L	I	A	S		M	I	N	N			
V	E	R	O	N	I	C	A		L	I	D		V	I	R	G	I	N	I	A
A	L	A	R		F	A	L	S	E		S	L	I	M	E		F	E	N	D
M	I	N	I		T	R	A	I	N		O	A	S	E	S		E	R	N	E
P	A	T	E		S	E	E	D	S		R	O	A	S	T		R	O	S	S

Puzzle 3-1
Page 112

COMPUTERS ARE DEFINITELY SMARTER THAN PEOPLE. WHEN HAVE YOU EVER HEARD OF SIX COMPUTERS GETTING TOGETHER TO FORM A COMMITTEE?

Puzzle 3-2
Page 112

VANNA WHITE IS LIKE MY POSTMAN. SHE TAKES LIFE ONE LETTER AT A TIME.

Puzzle 3-3
Page 112

FOR THE FIRST-TIME COAL-WALKER, THE WHOLE RITUAL WAS A FEET OF COURAGE.

Puzzle 3-4
Page 113

THE TOWN REVENUE COLLECTOR SOMETIMES FOUND HIS JOB OVERLY TAXING.

Puzzle 3-5
Page 113

THE FLIPPANT MOON-WALKER JUST COULDN'T SENSE THE GRAVITY OF THE SITUATION.

Puzzle 3-6
Page 113

NORMALCY IS WHEN YOU RUN OUT OF MONEY; INSOLVENCY IS WHEN YOU RUN OUT OF EX-CUSES; BANKRUPTCY IS WHEN YOU RUN OUT OF TOWN.

Puzzle 3-7: 15 x 15 Squares
Page 114

Puzzle 3-9: 17 x 17 Squares
Page 116

Puzzle 3-8: 19 x 19 Squares
Page 115

Puzzle 3-10: 15 x 15 Squares

Page 117

Puzzle 3-11: 15 x 15 Squares

Page 118

Puzzle 3-12: Poetry
Page 119

T	E	R	E	N	C	E	■	T	H	I	S	■	I	S	■	S	T	U	P
I	D	■	S	T	U	F	F	■	Y	O	U	■	E	A	T	■	Y	O	U
R	■	V	I	C	T	U	A	L	S	■	F	A	S	T	■	E	N	O	U
G	H	■	T	H	E	R	E	■	C	A	N	T	■	B	E	■	M	U	C
H	■	A	M	I	S	S	■	T	I	S	■	C	L	E	A	R	■	T	O
■	S	E	E	■	T	H	E	■	R	A	T	E	■	Y	O	U	■	D	R
I	N	K	■	Y	O	U	R	■	B	E	E	R	■	B	U	T	■	O	H
■	G	O	O	D	■	L	O	R	D	■	T	H	E	■	V	E	R	S	E
■	Y	O	U	■	M	A	K	E	■	I	T	■	G	I	V	E	S	■	A
■	C	H	A	P	■	T	H	E	■	B	E	L	L	Y	A	C	H	E	■

A	**AUTUMN LEAVES**	J	**LIVIDITY**
B	**EUCALYPTUS**	K	**AYE AYE**
C	**HIGH CHURCH**	L	**SCOTTY**
D	**OUT OF BOUNDS**	M	**TEETER TOTTER**
E	**USHERETTE**	N	**PHOEBE**
F	**STAFFORDSHIRE**	O	**OARS**
G	**MUCKRAKER**	P	**EIGHTY**
H	**AVARICIOUS**	Q	**MACHETE**
I	**NOBLESSE OBLIGE**	R	**SHUNTED**

Puzzle 3-13: New World
Page 120

Q	U	I	C	K	■	W	E	L	L	■	G	O
■	H	I	D	E	■	I	N	■	T	H	I	S
■	C	A	V	E	■	L	U	C	K	I	L	Y
■	M	A	N	S	■	E	M	E	R	G	I	N
G	■	I	N	T	E	L	L	I	G	E	N	C
E	■	I	S	■	M	O	R	E	■	T	H	A
N	■	A	■	M	A	T	C	H	■	F	O	R
■	T	H	E	S	E	■	D	I	M	W	I	T
T	E	D	■	D	I	N	O	S	A	U	R	S

A	**DRAUGHT**	J	**CHICKEN**
B	**ANTHILL**	K	**ATTACH**
C	**WHEELIES**	L	**REQUIEM**
D	**ENSUED**	M	**TREWS**
E	**STICK**	N	**OSMICS**
F	**OLD TIME**	O	**OLIVIA**
G	**MINGY**	P	**NIGGLE**
H	**NOMAD**		
I	**INFER**		

Puzzle 3-14: A Letter
Page 121

```
D E A R   P E N   P A L   O N C E   A G A I N
  I   T A K E   P E N   I N   H A N D   Y O U
  D R O P P E D   I T   R A T S   N O W   Y O
U   H A V E   T O   S A Y   O N C E   A G A I
N   I   T A K E   P E N   I N   H A N D   B U
T   I   D R O P P E D   I T   S O   O N C E
M O R E   I   T A K E   P E N   I N   H A N D
  I S N T   T H E R E   S O M E T H I N G   E
L S E   Y O U   C O U L D   B E   D O I N G
```

A **ANIMOSITIES**
B **CAPTIVATE**
C **HARDSHIP**
D **ANNOYANCE**
E **RANGED**
F **LINKED**
G **INGENUITY**
H **ENDURANCE**
I **BOTHERATION**
J **ROPE SOCKET**

K **OPPONENT**
L **WEEDY**
M **NAGGED**
N **ENDUES**
O **POOH POOHED**
P **INHUMANE**
Q **SPOOKY**
R **TRIBULATION**
S **LAPIDATE**
T **EDINA**

Puzzle 3-15: Question for Willard Scott
Page 122

```
W H A T   D O   T H E Y   M E A N   O N   T
H E   T V   W E A T H E R   F O R E C A S T
  W H E N   T H E Y   S A Y   W E   A R E
G O I N G   T O   H A V E   T H U N D E R S
H O W E R   A C T I V I T Y   T H E Y   M E
A N   W E   A R E   N O T   G O I N G   T O
  H A V E   A N   A C T U A L   T H U N D E
R S H O W E R   P E R   S E   B U T   T H U
N D E R S H O W E R   A C T I V I T Y   W H
I C H   L O O K S   V E R Y   S I M I L A R
  T O   T H E   U N T R A I N E D   E Y E
```

A **BEHIND THE SCENES**
B **ATTACHE**
C **RIGHT HAND MAN**
D **REHASH**
E **YESTERDAY**
F **CHEVY**
G **LEFTOVER**
H **AVENGE**
I **WAVING**
J **YOU CANT TAKE IT WITH YOU**
K **OTHERWISE**

L **UNDERWRITE**
M **ROTTEN**
N **WATCH**
O **AMNESTY**
P **YOUTH HOSTEL**
Q **THROW AWAY**
R **OVERWHELM**
S **TRIVIA**
T **HOOSIER**
U **ENDURE**
V **THOREAU**
W **ON THE WAGON**
X **PET**

Puzzle 3-16: Policing the Barn

Page 123

I	N		H	A	N	S		O	L	D		M	I	L	L
H	I	S		T	H	R	E	E		B	L	A	C	K	C
A	T	S		W	A	T	C	H		T	H	E		B	I	N	S
	F	O	R		T	H	I	E	V	I	N	G		R	A	T	S
	W	H	I	S	K	E	R		A	N	D		C	L	A	W
T	H	E	Y		C	R	O	U	C	H		I	N		T	H	E
	N	I	G	H	T		T	H	E	I	R		F	I	V	E
E	Y	E	S		S	M	O	U	L	D	E	R	I	N	G		G
R	E	E	N		A	N	D		B	R	I	G	H	T		J	E
K	K	E	L		A	N	D		J	E	S	S	U	P		A	N
D		O	N	E		E	Y	E	D		J	I	L	L

A	**WHITEFISH**	L	**ALL IN**
B	**ANNIVERSARY**	M	**R**UNNING STITCH
C	**LIBERALS**	N	**ERTE**
D	**T**HATCHED	O	**FINCH**
E	**EDDY**	P	**INJURED**
F	**R**OBINSON	Q	**VEHEMENT**
G	**D**UGONGS	R	**EWELL**
H	**EJECTS**	S	**ELKHART**
I	**LICKERISH**	T	**YAKKED**
J	**ALPHABETIC**	U	**EDITH**
K	**M**AH JONGG	V	**SHOWS**

Appendix B
Working Non-Crossword Puzzles

1n this appendix, I show you how to work the puzzles you find in Part III, namely the cryptogram, diagramless, and acrostic.

Cracking the Cryptogram Code

Cryptograms are all about letter replacement. Letters in cryptograms have been switched around, creating a funky-looking message that you need to decipher.

In a cryptogram, every letter stands for a different one (and only one) throughout the message. For example, "B" may represent "T" through the cryptogram, and "T" may mean "C." Although the pattern of the sentence looks familiar, the "words" read as if they are in some kind of secret code. Under each of the letters in the code, you see a space. As you decipher each letter in the code, you write it in the space. After you fill in each of the spaces, you have decoded the cryptogram, and you see a message in the spaces under the cryptogram letters.

The "code" changes from puzzle to puzzle, as though the alphabet flies up in the air, with the letters landing in different places, for each puzzle. Unfortunately, cracking the code on one puzzle doesn't give you a Rosetta Stone that you can apply to all other cryptograms.

Cryptogram words are exact replicas of the actual words they disguise. For example, if you see a three-letter word as part of a cryptogram, you know that a three-letter word appears in the quote or phrase hidden within the puzzle.

Typically, a cryptogram message is a quotation (complete with punctuation). The author's name may appear at the end of the cryptogram.

Note that some cryptograms offer a hint by revealing the identity of one of the disguised letters. You may want to ignore the help, or you may welcome a helping hand until you get the hang of it.

To work the cryptogram, follow these steps:

1. **Jot down the alphabet on scrap paper.**

   You need to do a little prep work first. You use this list to keep tabs on the letters you have already matched up and, consequently, which letters are still "unused."

2. **Scan the cryptogram for one-letter words, which are typically A or I.**

   Of course, you won't know which of the letters is the right one until you work a little more into the puzzle, but if you have a good feeling about one letter over the other, go ahead and pencil it in.

3. **After you crack the code on a letter, pencil in all occurrences of that letter in the puzzle. For example, where you find L to replace A, identify all the A's as L's through the cryptogram.**

   And I do mean pencil! You may need to experiment many times before you actually match up a letter. Don't attempt to work a cryptogram with a pen unless you really enjoy the smell of corrector fluid.

4. **Scan the cryptogram for two-letter words, then three-letter words, and so on, matching letters up as you go.**

   With each grouping of words, the message should come more and more into focus.

Table B-1 lists the most common words that appear in cryptograms; the words in each length category are listed in frequency of appearance.

Table B-1	Cryptogram Repeaters
Number of Letters	*Repeaters*
1	A and I
2	IT, IN, IS, IF, AT, ON, TO, OF, AS, and AN
3	THE, AND, FOR, ARE, and BUT
4	THAT, THIS, THAN, and THEN

You also need to be on the lookout for the following patterns as you work your way through the cryptogram:

✔ **Apostrophes:** Where an apostrophe appears near the end of a word followed by a single letter, your choice on that last letter is limited to S or T (or sometimes D). When it follows a single letter, that letter must be I to give you I'D, I'LL, or I'VE. Where an apostrophe is followed by two letters, your choice opens to 'LL, 'RE, and 'VE.

✔ **Double letters:** Check for EE, OO, FF, LL, SS, TT, and MM, in that order.

✔ **Final letters:** Check for E, T, S, D, N, and R, in this order, at the end of words.

✔ **Initial letters:** Check for T, A, O, M, H, and W at the beginning of words.

✔ **Suffixes:** Check for ING and LY in longer words.

The cryptogram's alphabet may not contain all 26 letters of the standard alphabet, depending on which letters show up in the message. A cryptographer may try to confuse you by deliberately eliminating some letters from the message altogether.

The key to cryptogram decoding, according to Laura Z. Hobson, author of the classic novel *Gentleman's Agreement* as well as scores of cryptograms, is to bear in mind that the most commonly used letter in English is E. Experienced crypt solvers often begin the decoding process by looking for E first. The most popular consonant is T. After you determine which letters represent E and T, you can move on to the next group of commonly used letters. Expert consensus ranks O and S in that category. M follows, according to Hobson. Other runners-up are A, I, and N.

Attempting the Diagramless

In a diagramless puzzle, you get Across and Down clues, but no grid to fill with the answers to the clues. Your job is to sketch out a grid (according to the dimensions shown at the top of the puzzle) by using the answers to the clues.

One of the neat aspects of conventional crosswords is that you don't need any special equipment to play the game. As long as you have a writing utensil, you can play.

When you tackle the diagramless puzzle, however, you need some additional equipment. Although some people solve the diagramless in their heads, most acrossionados like to see the grid on paper. Of course, you can use the back of an envelope in a pinch (I have). But in order to be sure that you're on the right square, you may need a supply of graph paper and a clean eraser.

Try to keep two sheets of graph paper handy while solving a diagramless puzzle. With the extra sheet, you have the opportunity to experiment as you try to uncover a general pattern.

Some sources supply a blank grid for you on the page in the correct dimensions, so that all you have to do is carefully plot the pattern. But if you don't have a black-and-white grid pattern to look at, the first step in attempting the diagramless is to refer to the dimensions indicated at the top of the puzzle. The dimensions look like a math formula, as in "15 x 15." For a 15 x 15 puzzle, draw a frame that measures 15 squares across and down on your graph paper to help you focus on the emerging pattern. If the dimensions are something like 15 x 17, then the first number is the Across dimension, and the second number is the Down dimension.

After you have either located or prepared your grid, you need to look for another piece of critical information. The puzzle will tell you where the first Across entry begins. (Without this piece of info, the puzzle would be impossible to solve.) Go ahead and write the number 1 in the appropriate square.

Your next step is to determine the length of the first Across entry. Unlike a crossword, you want to approach the diagramless from 1 Across for best results. Without a grid, you don't have that visual reference to how many letters are in each word and where the entries belong. Instead, you have two ways to determine how many letters appear in the 1 Across entry:

- ✔ Look at the number of the second Across clue. If it's 6, for example, then you can surmise that the entry for 1 Across contains five letters.
- ✔ Check that Down clues 1 through 5 don't appear in the Across column.

If the second Across clue is 6 Across, you know that the first word consists of five letters. The five Down clues, from 1 through 5, that don't have an Across function confirm your assumption.

Fill in a black square to the left of and above each number that appears in both Across and Down columns.

What distinguishes 1 Across from every other Across clue is that the solver can be certain that each letter of its entry serves as the first letter of a Down entry. In this case, you can blacken the sixth square after filling in the Across entry. Insert the numbers 1 through 5 in the appropriate squares and try to solve as many of the first five Down clues as you can. Before long, you create a block of answers that sets the puzzle on its path.

Don't worry about the clues: Diagramless clues are simpler than those of the average crossword because the constructor doesn't want to compound the handicap.

Because diagramless puzzles don't usually follow the square shape of a crossword, you can't make assumptions about where answers fall in the grid until you have made some progress. But you do have some information on your side:

- ✔ **You know that the grid is usually symmetrical.** In most cases, the pattern on top is a mirror image of the bottom. After you have plotted the pattern for the top half, you can transfer it to the bottom, and the other way around, too. Less often, the symmetry is left to right.

- ✔ **You know that the second Across answer follows 1 Across somehow.** In the standard crossword (and in most diagramless puzzles), the second Across entry appears directly to the right of the first entry in the grid in the same line. But the diagramless makes an exception: The second Across entry may appear one line down and to the left of 1 Across. As entries emerge, you can determine where the second Across entry belongs in the grid.

What if the second Across clue doesn't appear in the Down column? If the 6 Across entry isn't included in the Down column, for example, your solving takes a different direction, because now you know that the second Across answer appears directly *below* 1 Across. Chances are that the answer to 6 Across may begin to emerge after you fill in some of the first five Down entries. If the second Across number also appears in the Down column along with two more Down clues, then it most likely appears to the right of 1 Across, following the typical crossword format. Following the example, 6 appears in both Across and Down, while 7 and 8 are only clued Down. The third Across clue, then, is 9.

Even before you proceed with the second Across answer, I recommend jotting down any answers that pop out at you next to the lists of clues. Scanning all the way through the Across and Down clues and writing down as many entries as you can beside the clues is helpful. Islands of answers may emerge this way. Sometimes you can solve separate parts of the puzzle and unite them later. Only confirmed acrossionados try to discern the pattern before working the clues. The fun of the diagramless lies in coordinating the two as you solve.

Every entry that appears in both the Across and Down columns in a diagramless has a black square to its left and above it. Every entry that appears only in the Down clues has a black square above it and below its final letter.

After you see a black-and-white pattern start to emerge at the top part of your graph, you can safely turn your grid upside down and sketch in the mirror image below. In fact, if you find the entries easier to solve at the bottom, you may want to approach the diagramless from the bottom.

Solving an Acrostic

A truly great puzzle is not only fun, but also enlightening. Rather than a random collection of words, the acrostic grid contains an excerpt from a written work. Entries in the grid only read across, not down, moving from top row to bottom, reading left to right.

The acrostic grid is accompanied by a word list. After you solve the words in the word list, the initial letters of the answer words spell out the author and title of the work that is quoted in the grid.

Technically, the double aspect of the acrostic describes the way the two basic elements of the puzzle interact. You work with the same two variables of the crossword — the grid and clues — but in a new way. You use a two-part solving process for an acrostic:

1. **First, you have to solve the clues in the word list.**

   The clues are not hard at all. In fact, in the case of a missing word, the acrostic constructor may cite the source. Instead of numbers, you find the word list (about two dozen words) sorted by letters from A through Z.

2. **Next, you transfer the letters you have so far from the word list into their assigned squares in the grid.**

   Every letter serves in the grid as well as in an answer on the word list. As you fill in the word list, you note a number beneath each letter that indicates its placement in the grid. After you fill in the squares, a quotation of about 25 words emerges as you read the grid from left to right.

Black squares in the acrostic grid serve as spaces between words. Every white square contains a number and letter, which corresponds to a letter in one of the words in the word list.

The acrostic clues don't contain any tricks: They are completely straightforward. If you look up the answers in the dictionary, you find yourself staring right at the clues. In looking at a typical acrostic, for example, you find that the constructor pulls no punches. When a clue reads "Unsteady" followed by six dashes, the answer is a commonly used synonym like WOBBLY. When the answer in a word list consists of more than one word, the constructor indicates that fact in parentheses, as in "Insectivore, also called potamogale (5, 5)" for OTTER SHREW.

Acrostic clues may require some interpretation. When you have a clue such as "Thumb" followed by nine dashes, do you stare at your fingers, or do you take it for a verb, as in HITCHHIKE? Words from acrostic clues are in the dictionary, but you may have to move beyond the first definition you find.

Words in the quotation may run on into two rows. The beginning of a word may appear on one line at the far right, and the final letters appear in the next line below to the far left. That split includes words of one syllable, as in TH on the top line and ERE on the next line, below and to the left, to read as THERE. Only a black square indicates the end of the word, not the outside frame of the grid, as per the standard crossword.

The empty grid can give you some helpful hints about the way the sentence unfolds:

- **Single-letter words:** When you see a white square between two black squares, the two obvious choices in the English language are A and I. (On the rare occasion, you may come across an initial, as in "J. D." Salinger.) If multiple single-letter words appear in the grid, odds are that the excerpt is in the first person, and you can safely insert I in various parts of each place.

- **Three-letter words:** Most often, you're looking at THE or AND.

FOR DUMMIES
BOOK REGISTRATION

Register This Book and Win!

We want to hear from you!

Visit **dummies.com** to register this book and tell us how you liked it!

- Get entered in our monthly prize giveaway.

- Give us feedback about this book — tell us what you like best, what you like least, or maybe what you'd like to ask the author and us to change!

- Let us know any other *For Dummies* topics that interest you.

Your feedback helps us determine what books to publish, tells us what coverage to add as we revise our books, and lets us know whether we're meeting your needs as a *For Dummies* reader. You're our most valuable resource, and what you have to say is important to us!

Not on the Web yet? It's easy to get started with *Dummies 101: The Internet For Windows 98* or *The Internet For Dummies* at local retailers everywhere.

Or let us know what you think by sending us a letter at the following address:

For Dummies Book Registration
Dummies Press
10475 Crosspoint Blvd.
Indianapolis, IN 46256

…FOR DUMMIES™

BESTSELLING BOOK SERIES